SACRAMENTO PUBLIC LIBRARY Y

D1108917

FIRE POWER

CREATED BY **ROBERT KIRKMAN**
AND **CHRIS SAMNEE**

SACRAMENTO PUBLIC LIBRARY

ROBERT KIRKMAN
Creator, Writer

CHRIS SAMNEE
Creator, Artist

FIRE POWER VOLUME 4: SCORCHED EARTH
MARCH 2022 FIRST PRINTING
ISBN: 978-1-5343-2103-8

Published by Image Comics, Inc. Office of
publication: PO BOX 14457, Portland, OR
97293. Copyright © 2022 Robert Kirkman,
LLC and Chris Samnee. Originally published
in single magazine format as FIRE POWER™
#13-18. FIRE POWER™ (including all
prominent characters featured herein),
its logo and all character likenesses are
trademarks of Robert Kirkman, LLC and
Chris Samnee, unless otherwise noted.
Image Comics® and its logos are registered
trademarks and copyrights of Image
Comics, Inc. All rights reserved. No part
of this publication may be reproduced or
transmitted in any form or by any means
(except for short excerpts for review
purposes) without the express written
permission of Image Comics, Inc. All
names, characters, events and locales in
this publication are entirely fictional. Any
resemblance to actual persons (living or
dead), events or places, without satiric
intent, is coincidental. Printed in Canada.

SKYBOUND.

FOR SKYBOUND ENTERTAINMENT

ROBERT KIRKMAN Chairman
DAVID ALPERT CEO
SEAN MACKIEWICZ SVP, Editor-in-Chief
SHAWN KIRKHAM SVP, Business Development
BRIAN HUNTINGTON VP, Online Content
ANDRES JUAREZ Art Director
ARUNE SINGH Director of Brand, Editorial
SHANNON MEEHAN Public Relations Manager
ALEX ANTONE Senior Editor
JON MOISAN Editor
AMANDA LaFRANCO Editor
JILLIAN CRAB Graphic Designer
DAN PETERSEN Sr. Director, Operations & Events

Foreign Rights & Licensing Inquiries:
contact@skybound.com
SKYBOUND.COM

FOR IMAGE COMICS, INC.

TODD MCFARLANE President
JIM VALENTINO Vice President
MARC SILVESTRI Chief Executive Officer
ERIK LARSEN Chief Financial Officer
ROBERT KIRKMAN Chief Operating Officer
ERIC STEPHENSON Publisher / Chief Creative Officer
NICOLE LAPALME Controller
LEANNA CAUNTER Accounting Analyst
SUE KORPELA Accounting & HR Manager
MARLA EIZIK Talent Liaison
JEFF BOISON Director of Sales & Publishing Planning
DIRK WOOD Director of International Sales & Licensing
ALEX COX Director of Direct Market & Speciality Sales
CHLOE RAMOS Book Market & Library Sales Manager
EMILIO BAUTISTA Digital Sales Coordinator
JON SCHLAFFMAN Specialty Sales Coordinator
KAT SALAZAR Director of PR & Marketing
DREW FITZGERALD Marketing Content Associate
HEATHER DOORNINK Production Director
DREW GILL Art Director
HILARY DILORETO Print Manager
TRICIA RAMOS Traffic Manager
MELISSA GIFFORD Content Manager
ERIKA SCHNATZ Senior Production Artist
RYAN BREWER Production Artist
DEANNA PHELPS Production Artist

IMAGECOMICS.COM

MATT WILSON
Colorist

RUS WOOTON
Letterer

AMANDA LAFRANCO
Editor

ANDRES JUAREZ
Logo, Collection Design

JILLIAN CRAB
Production

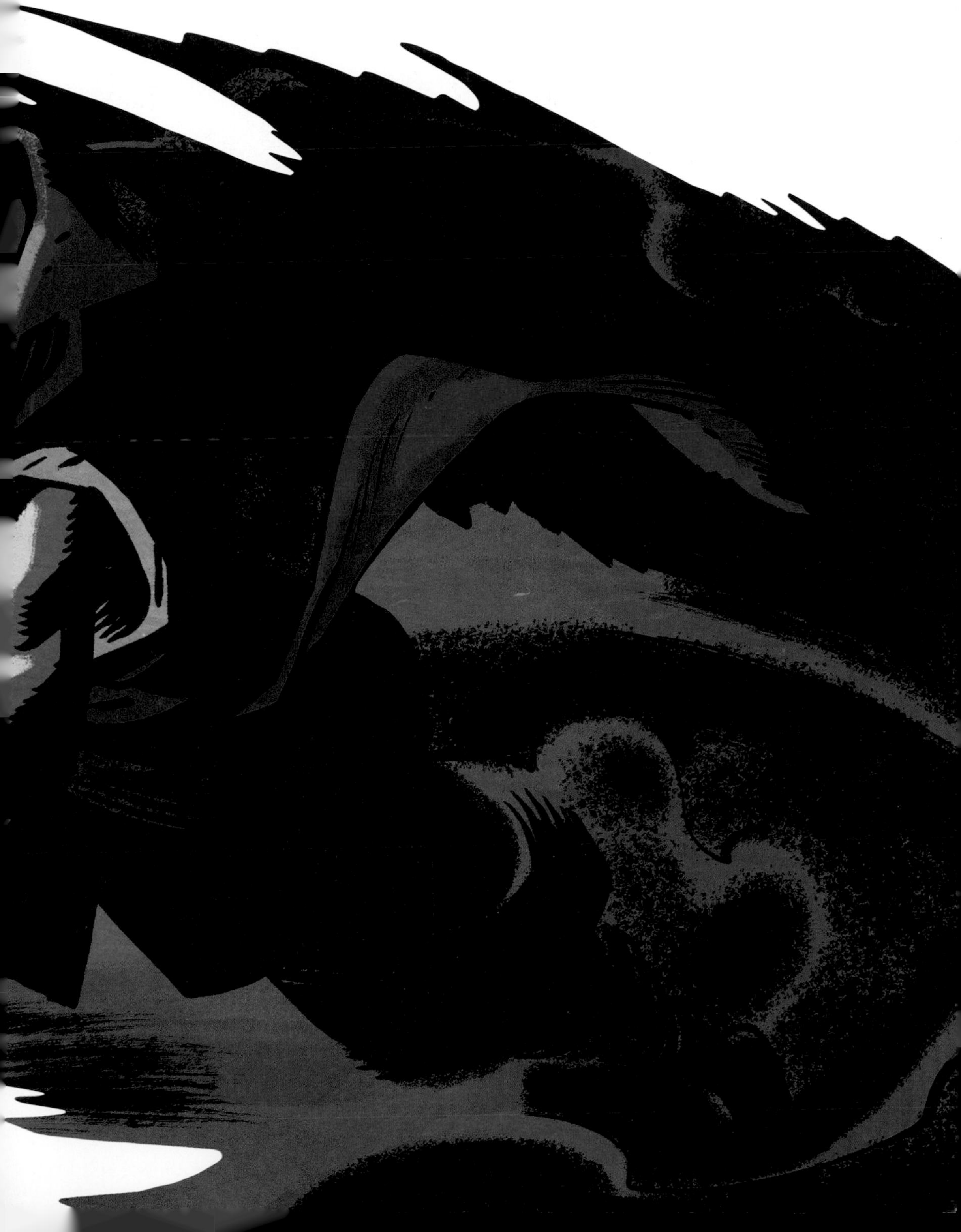

CHAPTER FOUR

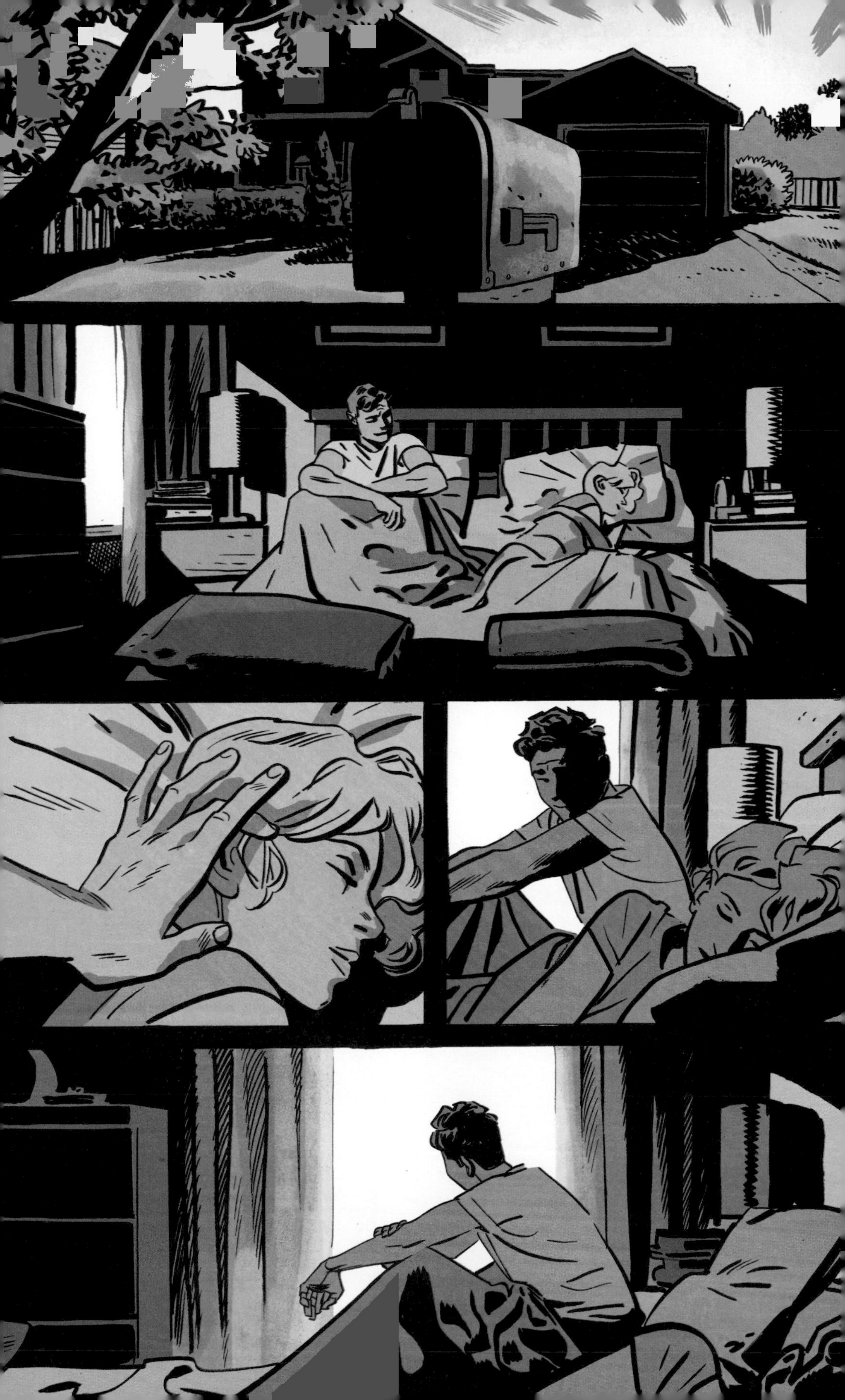

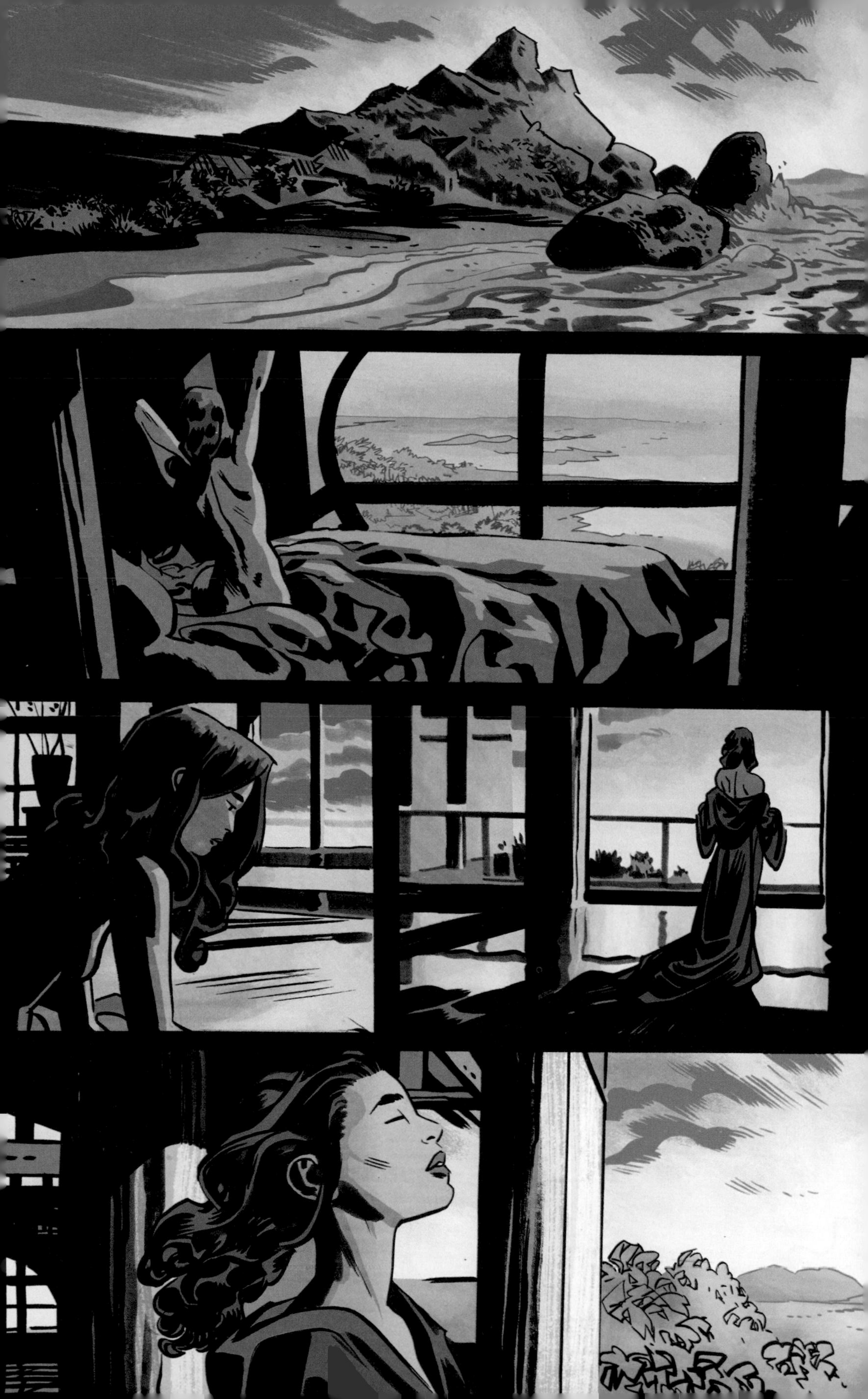

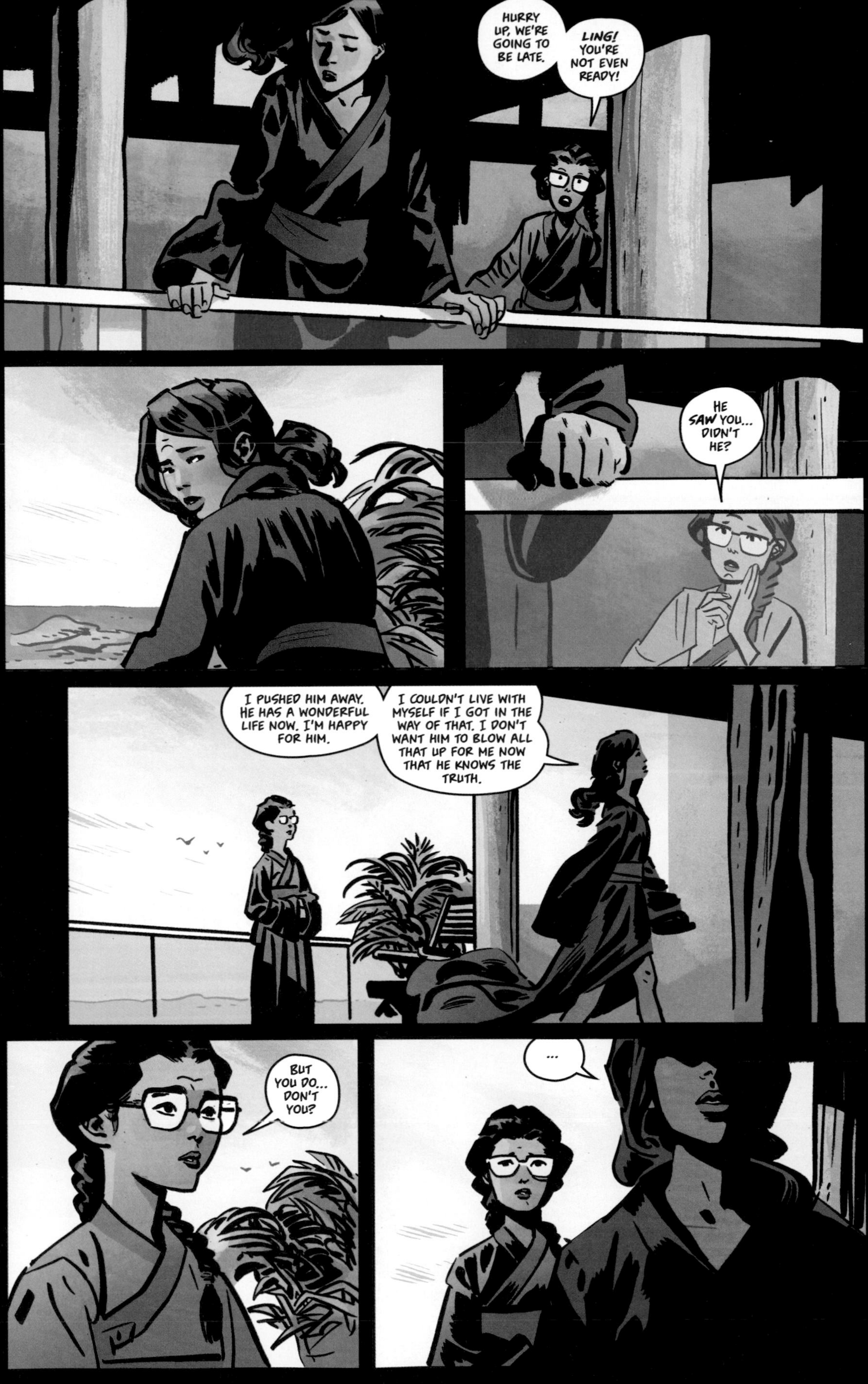
HURRY UP, WE'RE GOING TO BE LATE.
LING! YOU'RE NOT EVEN READY!
HE SAW YOU... DIDN'T HE?
I PUSHED HIM AWAY. HE HAS A WONDERFUL LIFE NOW. I'M HAPPY FOR HIM.
I COULDN'T LIVE WITH MYSELF IF I GOT IN THE WAY OF THAT. I DON'T WANT HIM TO BLOW ALL THAT UP FOR ME NOW THAT HE KNOWS THE TRUTH.
BUT YOU DO... DON'T YOU?
...

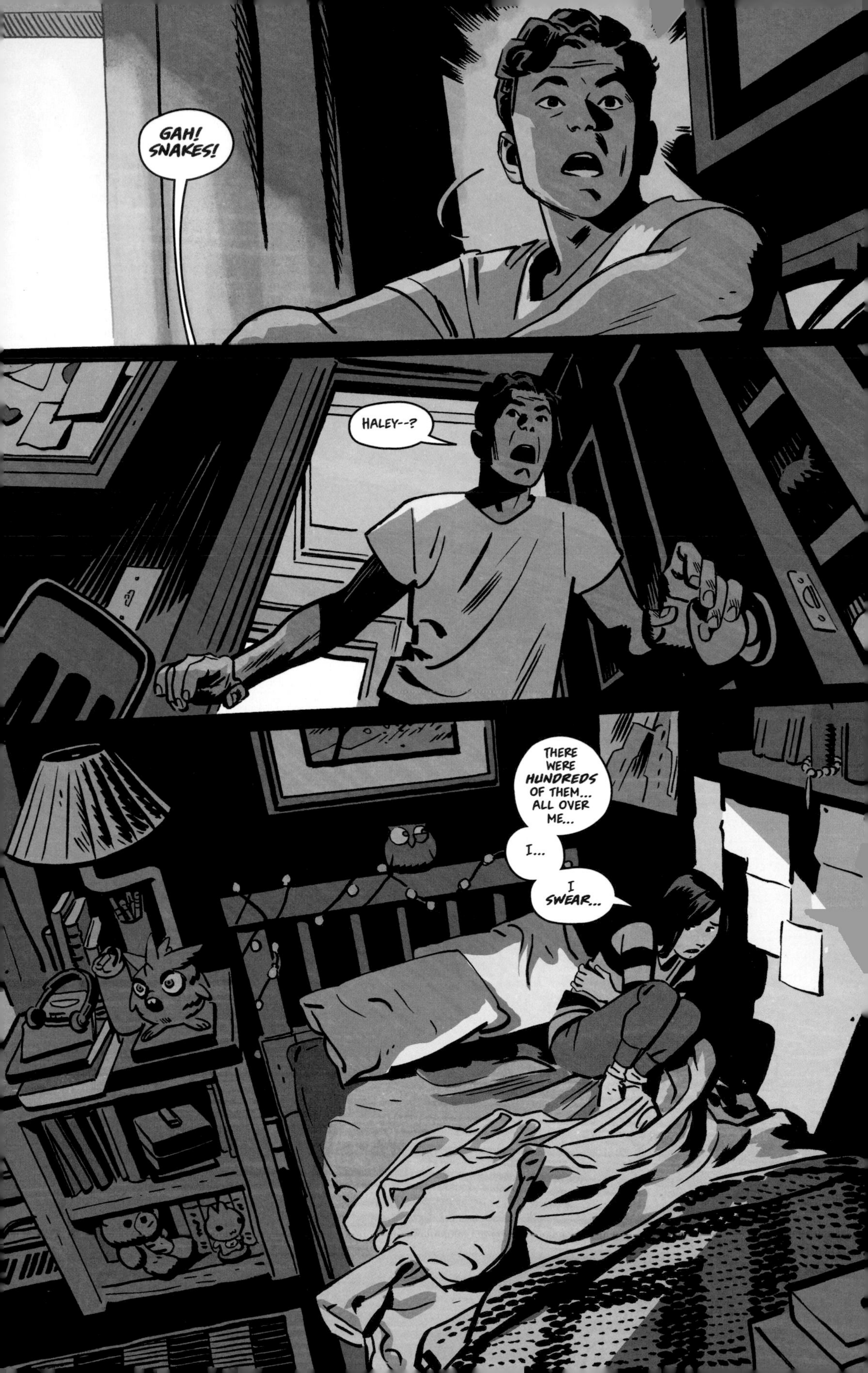
GAH! SNAKES!
HALEY--?
THERE WERE HUNDREDS OF THEM... ALL OVER ME...
I...
I SWEAR...

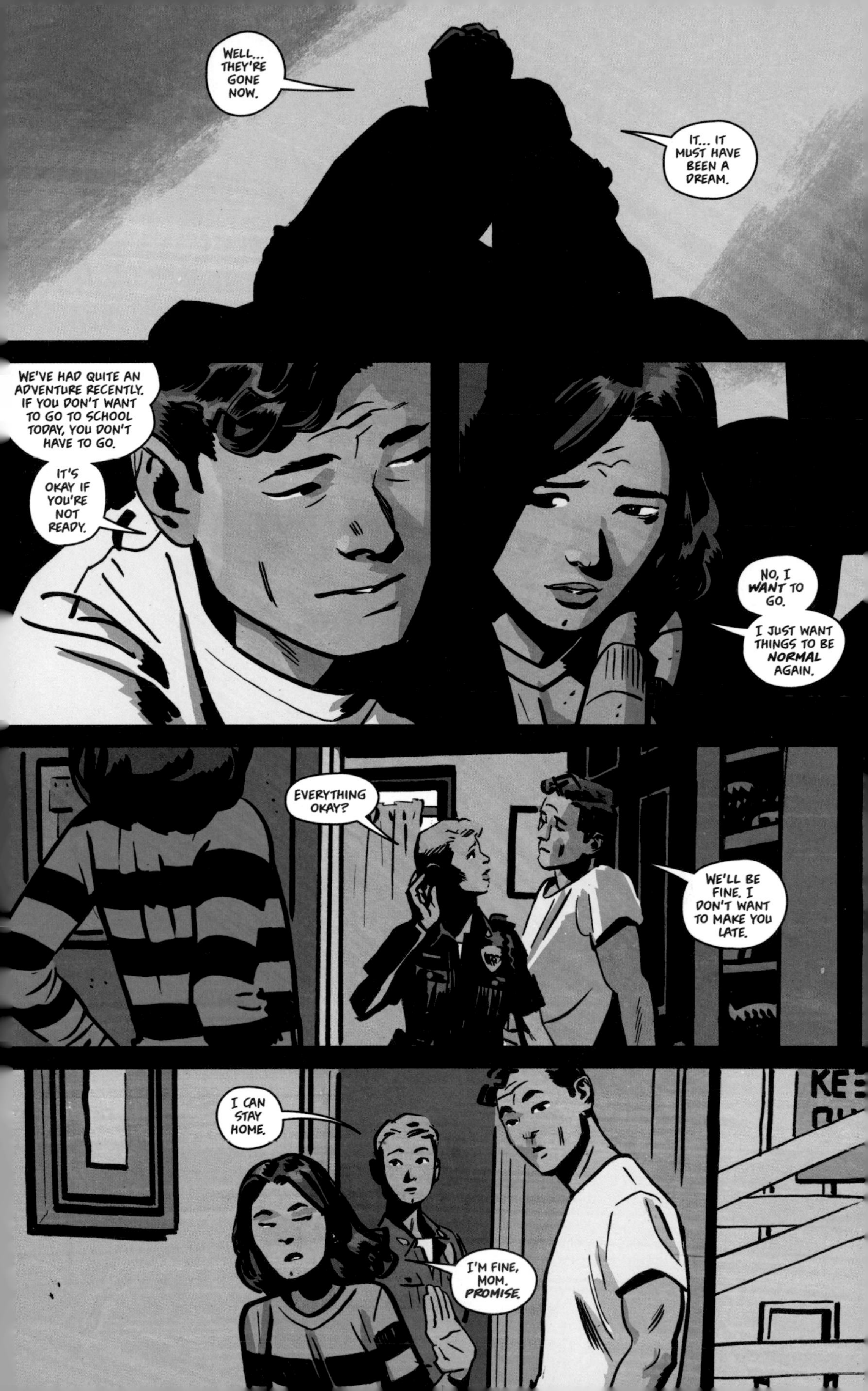
WELL... THEY'RE GONE NOW.
IT... IT MUST HAVE BEEN A DREAM.
WE'VE HAD QUITE AN ADVENTURE RECENTLY. IF YOU DON'T WANT TO GO TO SCHOOL TODAY, YOU DON'T HAVE TO GO.
IT'S OKAY IF YOU'RE NOT READY.
NO, I *WANT* TO GO.
I JUST WANT THINGS TO BE **NORMAL** AGAIN.
EVERYTHING OKAY?
WE'LL BE FINE. I DON'T WANT TO MAKE YOU LATE.
I CAN STAY HOME.
I'M FINE, MOM. ***PROMISE.***

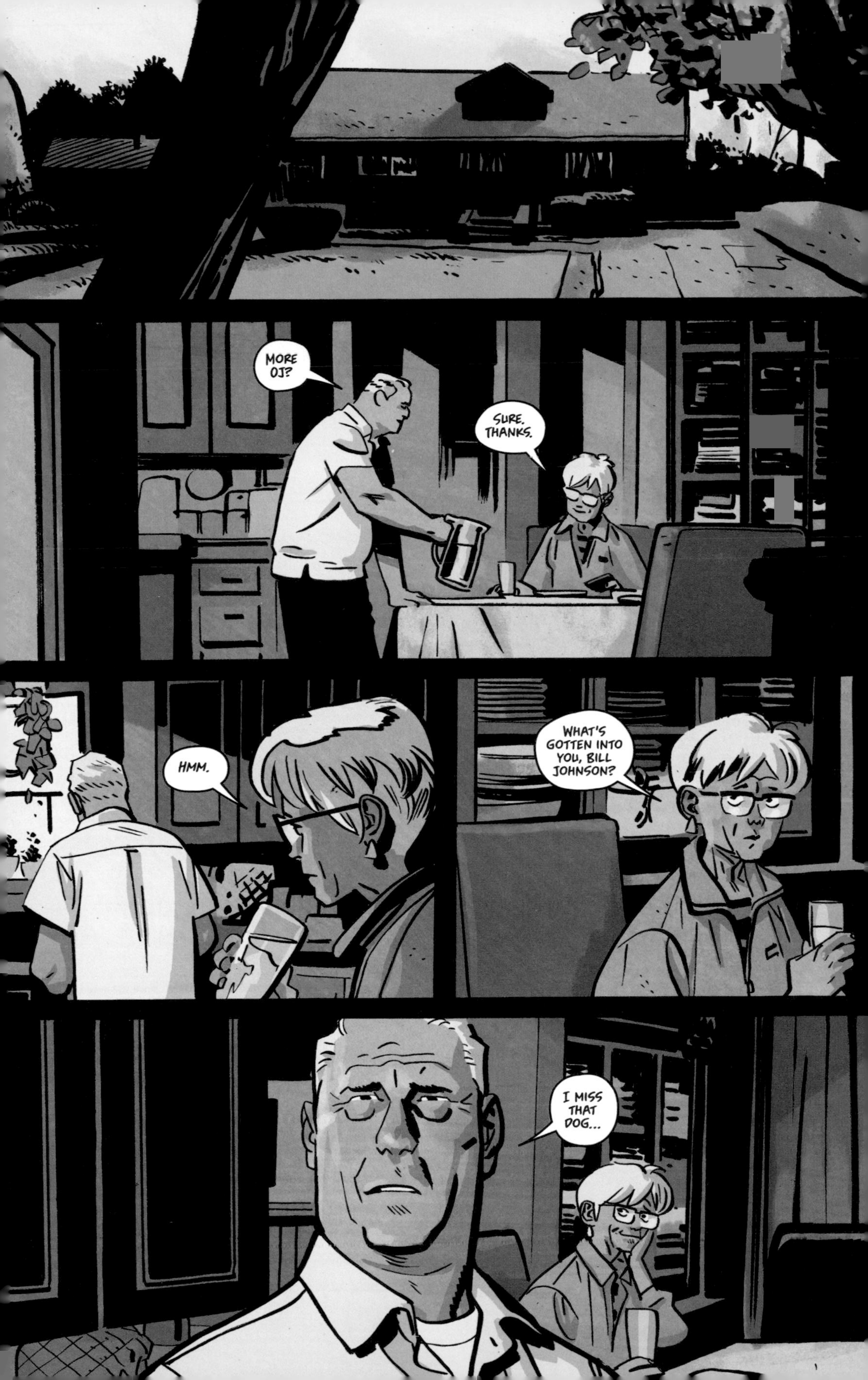

MORE OJ?
SURE. THANKS.
HMM.
WHAT'S GOTTEN INTO YOU, BILL JOHNSON?
I MISS THAT DOG...

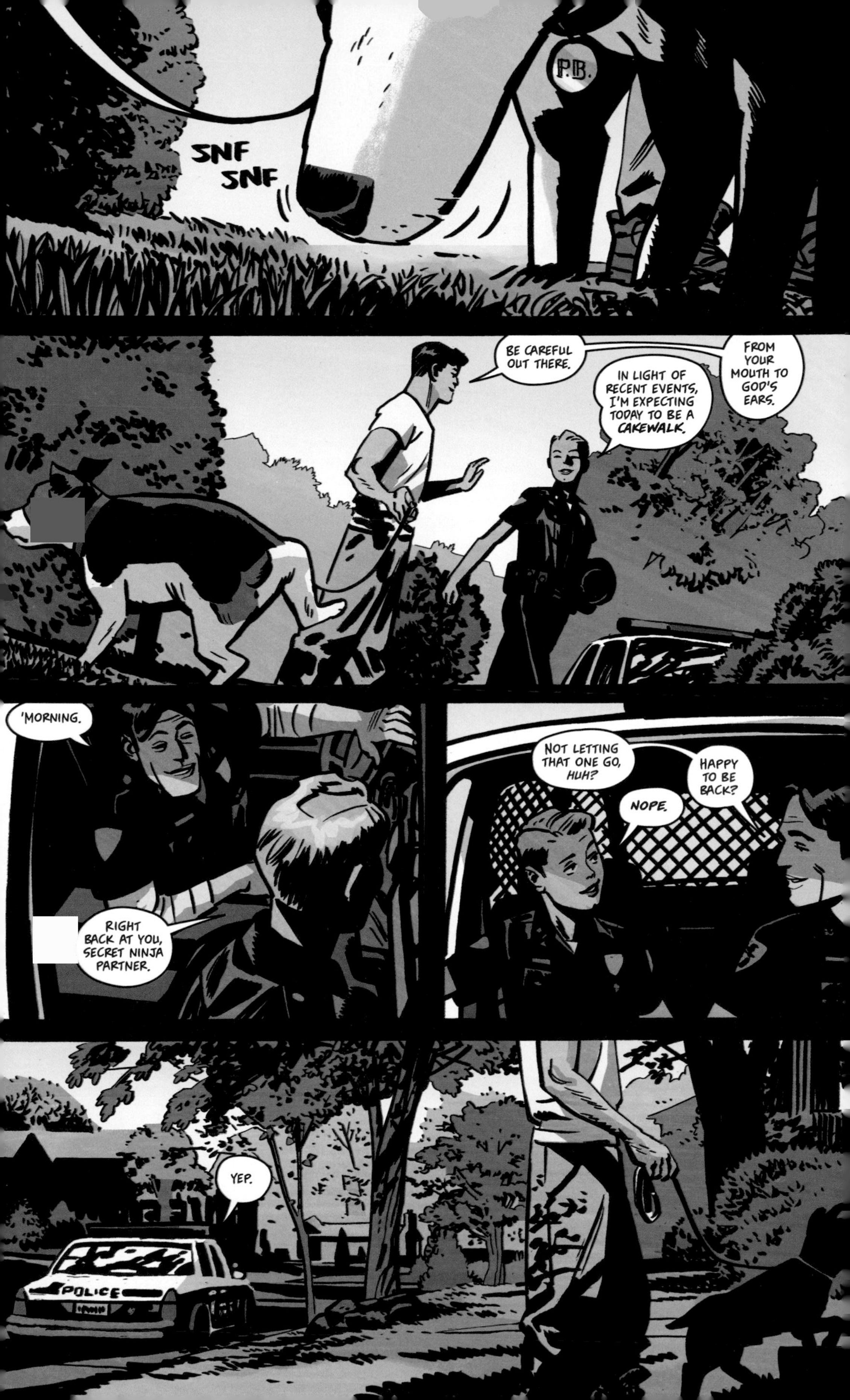
P.B.
SNF
SNF
BE CAREFUL OUT THERE.
IN LIGHT OF RECENT EVENTS, I'M EXPECTING TODAY TO BE A CAKEWALK.
FROM YOUR MOUTH TO GOD'S EARS.
'MORNING.
RIGHT BACK AT YOU, SECRET NINJA PARTNER.
NOT LETTING THAT ONE GO, HUH?
HAPPY TO BE BACK?
NOPE.
YEP.
POLICE

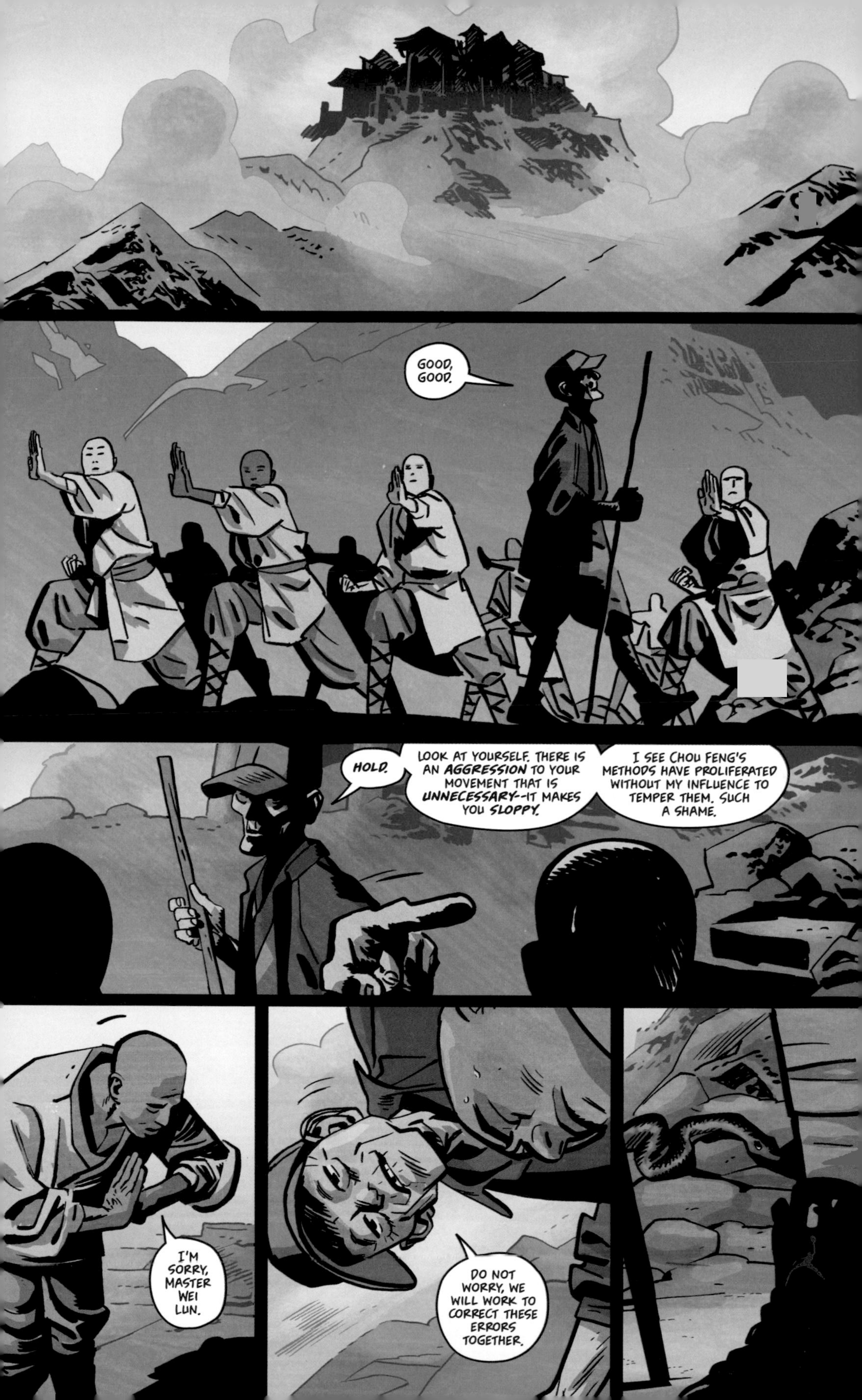
GOOD, GOOD.
HOLD.
LOOK AT YOURSELF. THERE IS AN AGGRESSION TO YOUR MOVEMENT THAT IS UNNECESSARY--IT MAKES YOU SLOPPY.
I SEE CHOU FENG'S METHODS HAVE PROLIFERATED WITHOUT MY INFLUENCE TO TEMPER THEM. SUCH A SHAME.
I'M SORRY, MASTER WEI LUN.
DO NOT WORRY, WE WILL WORK TO CORRECT THESE ERRORS TOGETHER.

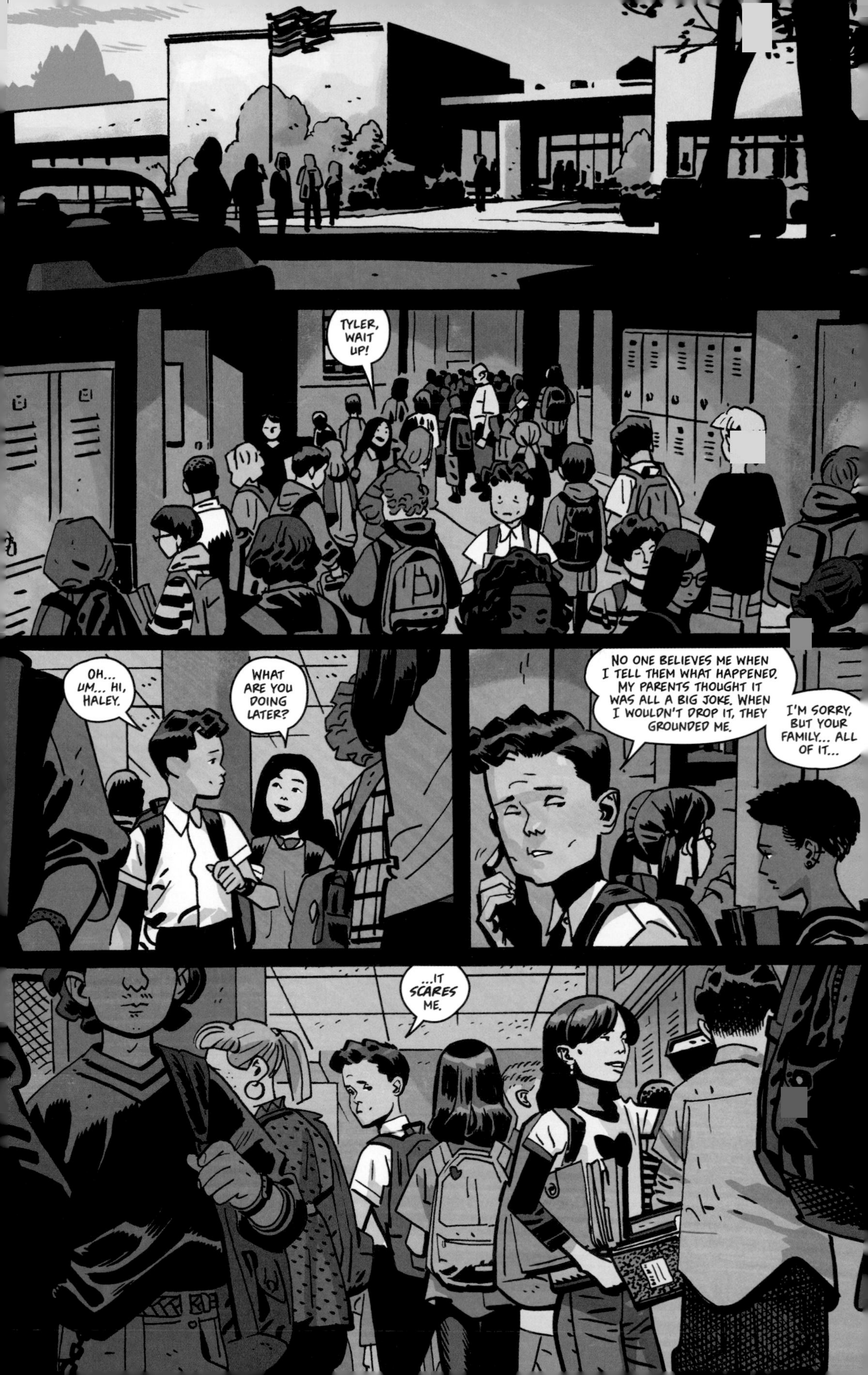
TYLER, WAIT UP!
OH... UM... HI, HALEY.
WHAT ARE YOU DOING LATER?
NO ONE BELIEVES ME WHEN I TELL THEM WHAT HAPPENED. MY PARENTS THOUGHT IT WAS ALL A BIG JOKE. WHEN I WOULDN'T DROP IT, THEY GROUNDED ME.
I'M SORRY, BUT YOUR FAMILY... ALL OF IT...
...IT SCARES ME.

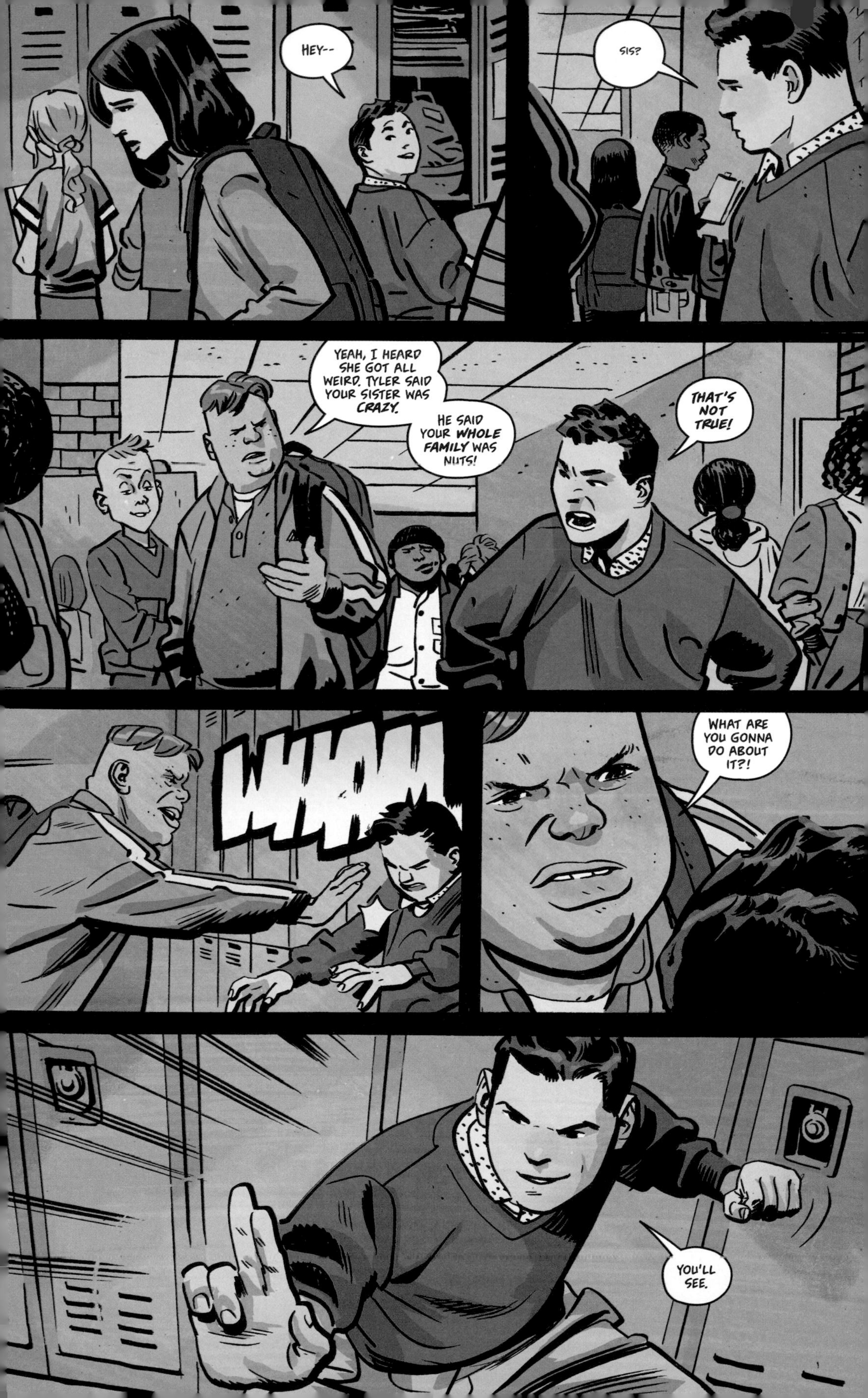
HEY--
SIS?
YEAH, I HEARD SHE GOT ALL WEIRD. TYLER SAID YOUR SISTER WAS CRAZY.
HE SAID YOUR WHOLE FAMILY WAS NUTS!
THAT'S NOT TRUE!
WHAM
WHAT ARE YOU GONNA DO ABOUT IT?!
YOU'LL SEE.

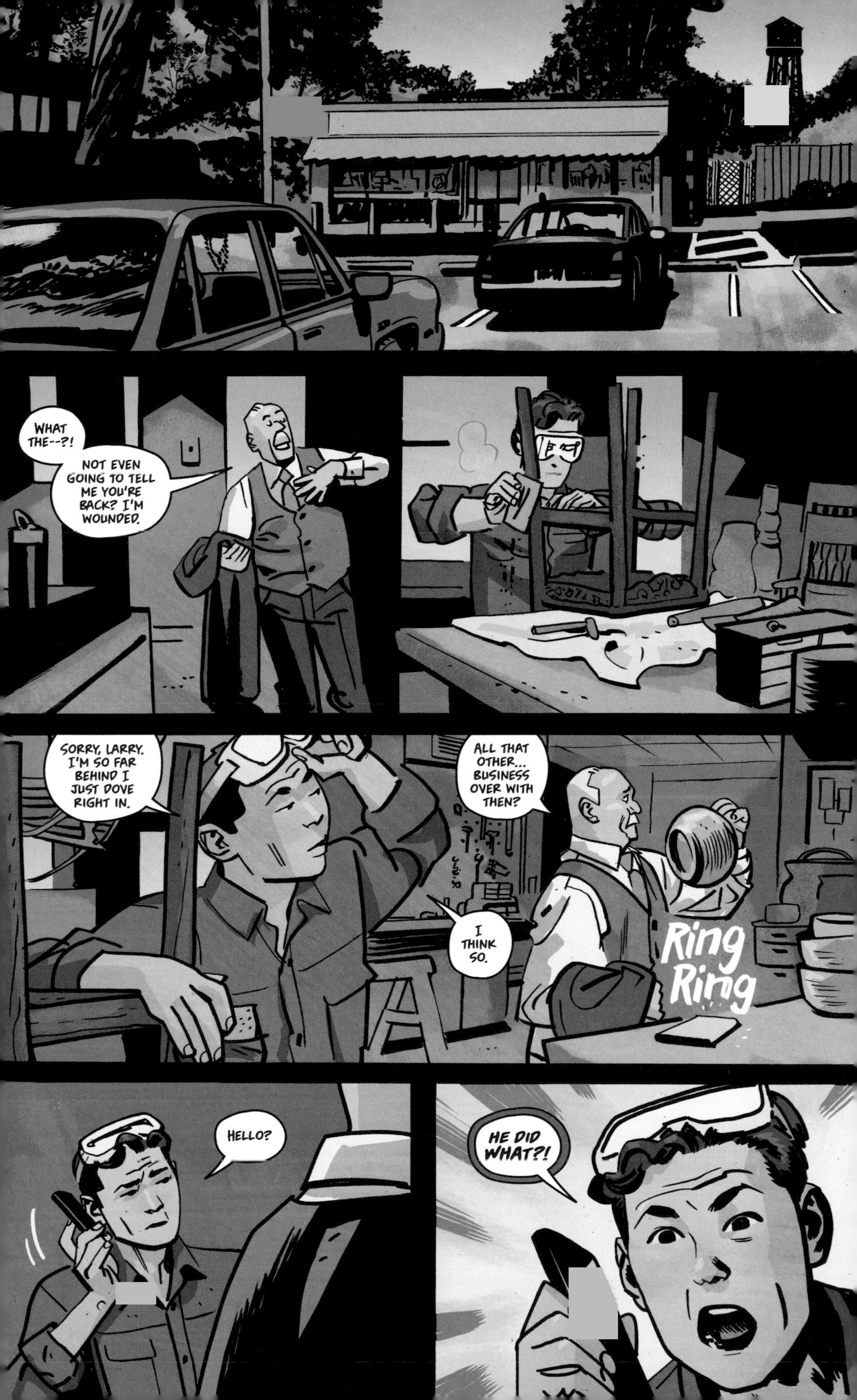
WHAT THE--?!
NOT EVEN GOING TO TELL ME YOU'RE BACK? I'M WOUNDED.
SORRY, LARRY. I'M SO FAR BEHIND I JUST DOVE RIGHT IN.
ALL THAT OTHER... BUSINESS OVER WITH THEN?
I THINK SO.
Ring Ring
HELLO?
HE DID WHAT?!

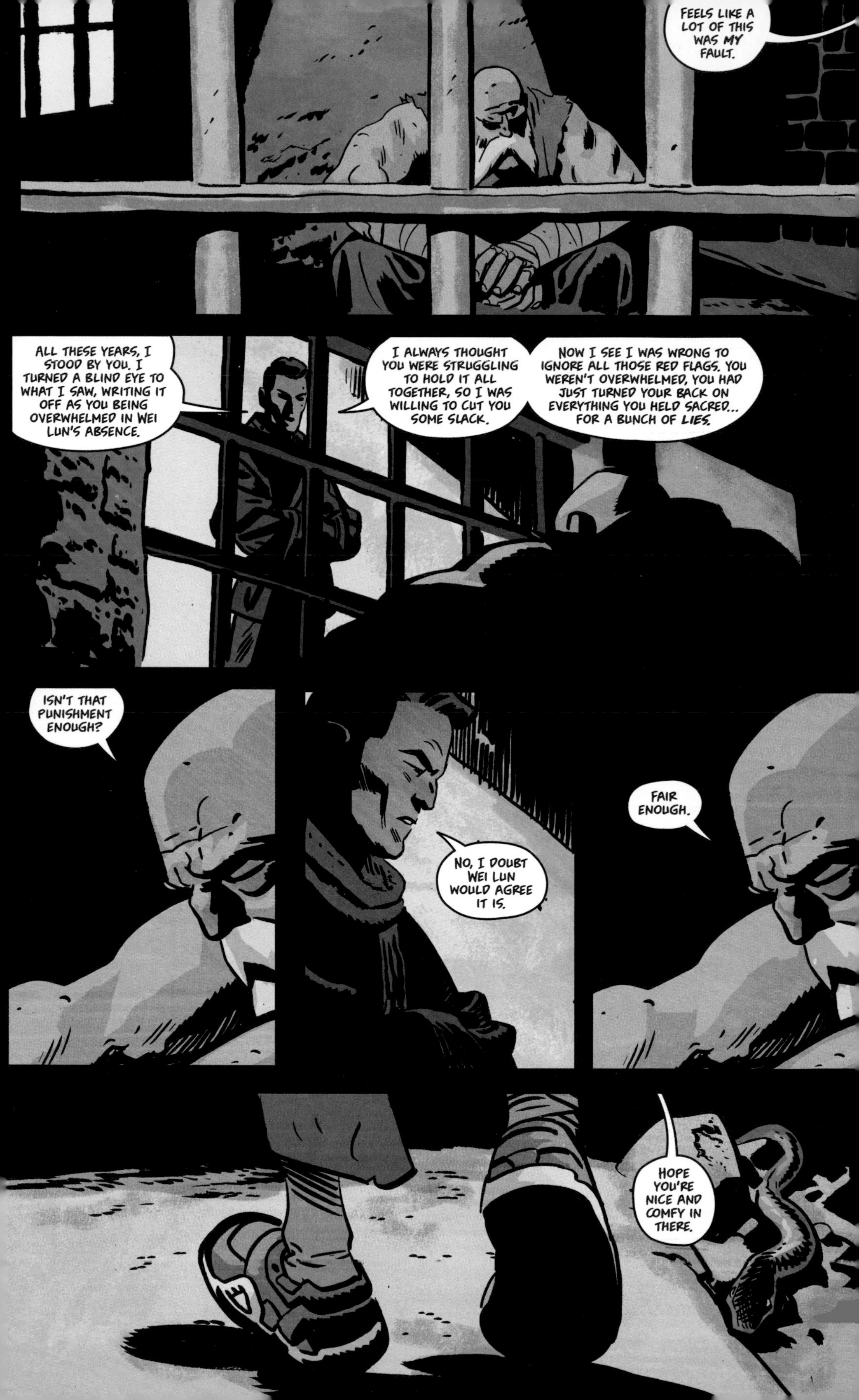
FEELS LIKE A LOT OF THIS WAS MY FAULT.
ALL THESE YEARS, I STOOD BY YOU. I TURNED A BLIND EYE TO WHAT I SAW, WRITING IT OFF AS YOU BEING OVERWHELMED IN WEI LUN'S ABSENCE.
I ALWAYS THOUGHT YOU WERE STRUGGLING TO HOLD IT ALL TOGETHER, SO I WAS WILLING TO CUT YOU SOME SLACK.
NOW I SEE I WAS WRONG TO IGNORE ALL THOSE RED FLAGS. YOU WEREN'T OVERWHELMED, YOU HAD JUST TURNED YOUR BACK ON EVERYTHING YOU HELD SACRED... FOR A BUNCH OF LIES.
ISN'T THAT PUNISHMENT ENOUGH?
NO, I DOUBT WEI LUN WOULD AGREE IT IS.
FAIR ENOUGH.
HOPE YOU'RE NICE AND COMFY IN THERE.

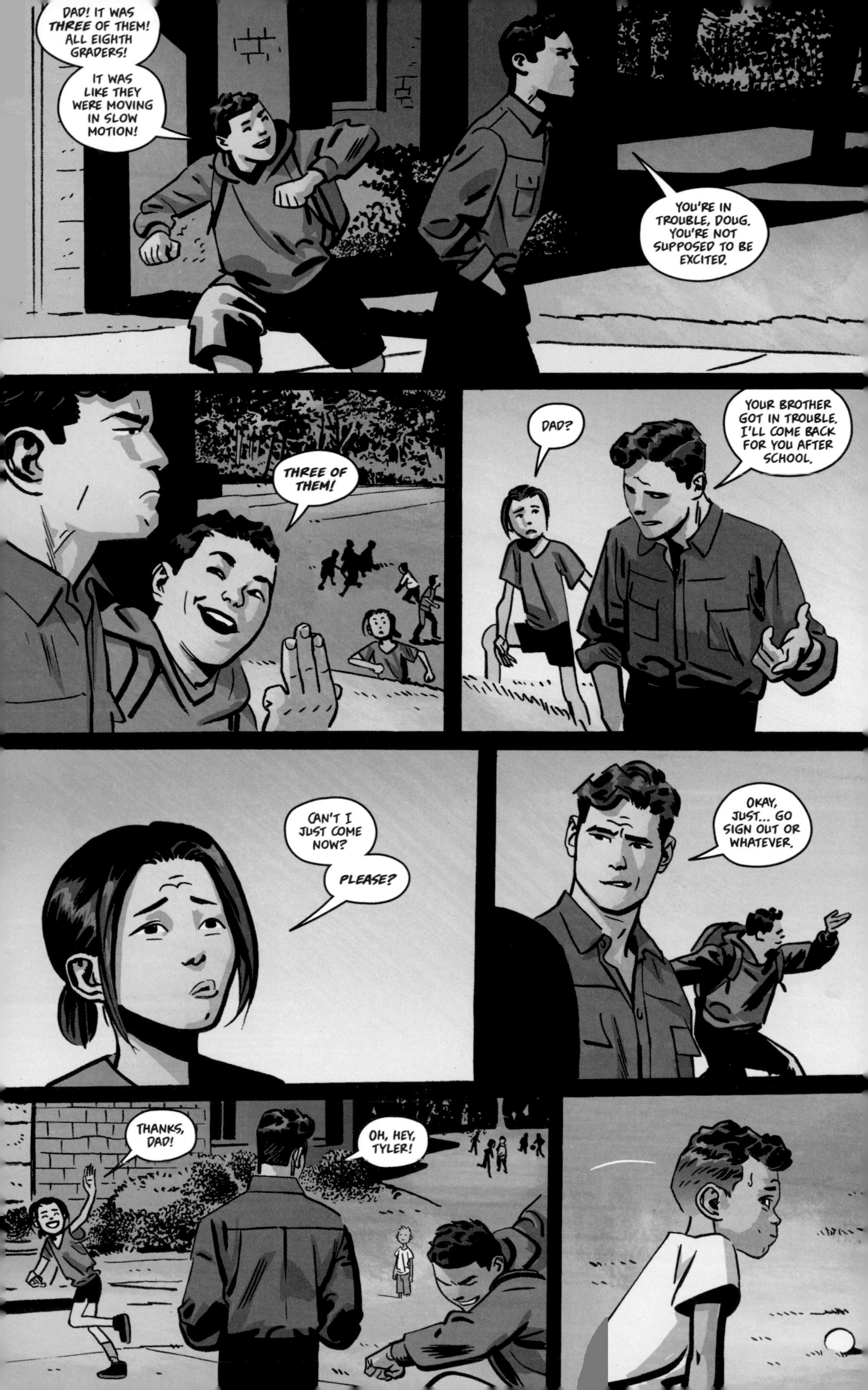
DAD! IT WAS THREE OF THEM! ALL EIGHTH GRADERS!
IT WAS LIKE THEY WERE MOVING IN SLOW MOTION!
YOU'RE IN TROUBLE, DOUG. YOU'RE NOT SUPPOSED TO BE EXCITED.
THREE OF THEM!
DAD?
YOUR BROTHER GOT IN TROUBLE. I'LL COME BACK FOR YOU AFTER SCHOOL.
CAN'T I JUST COME NOW?
PLEASE?
OKAY, JUST... GO SIGN OUT OR WHATEVER.
THANKS, DAD!
OH, HEY, TYLER!

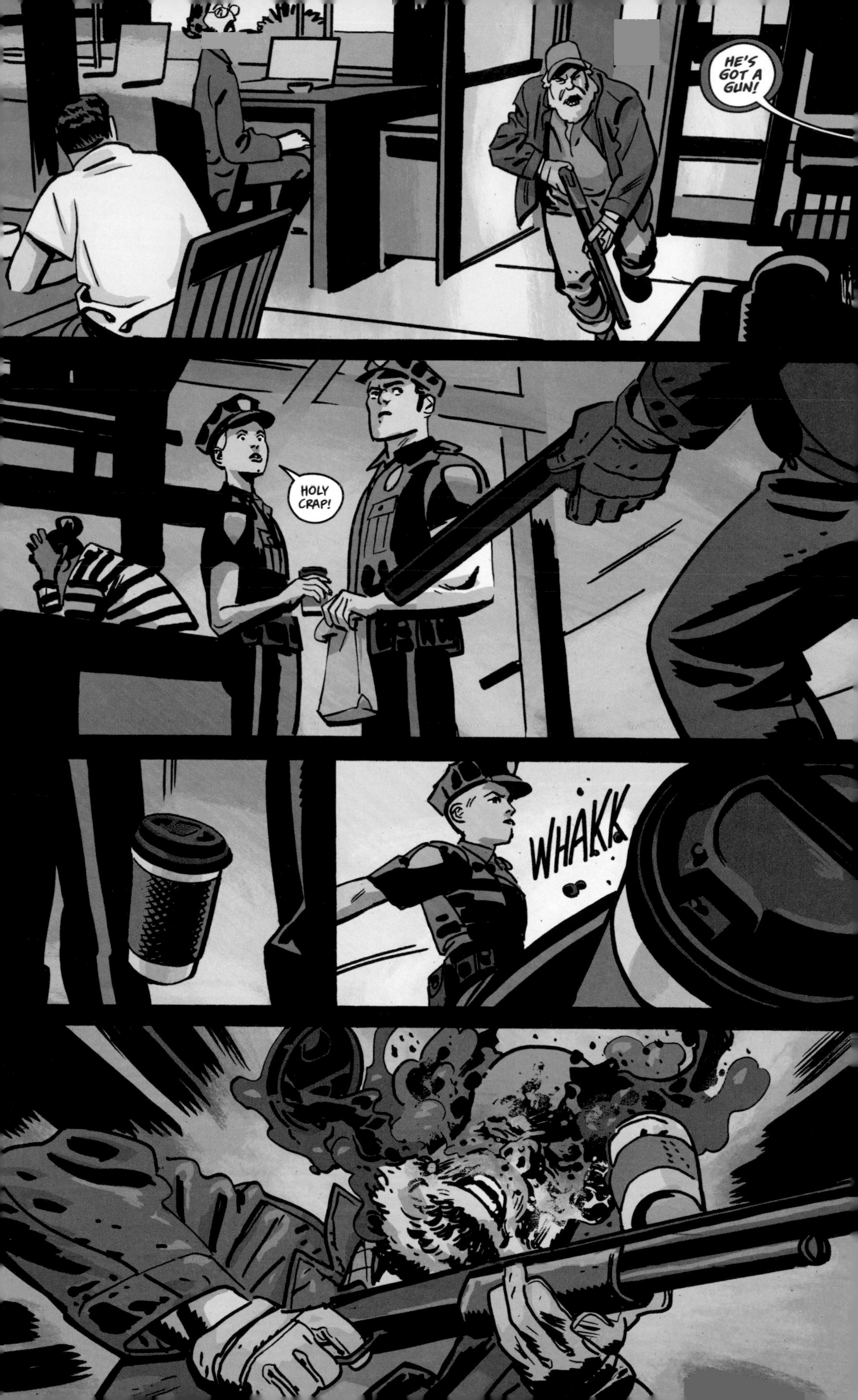
HE'S GOT A GUN!
HOLY CRAP!
WHAKK

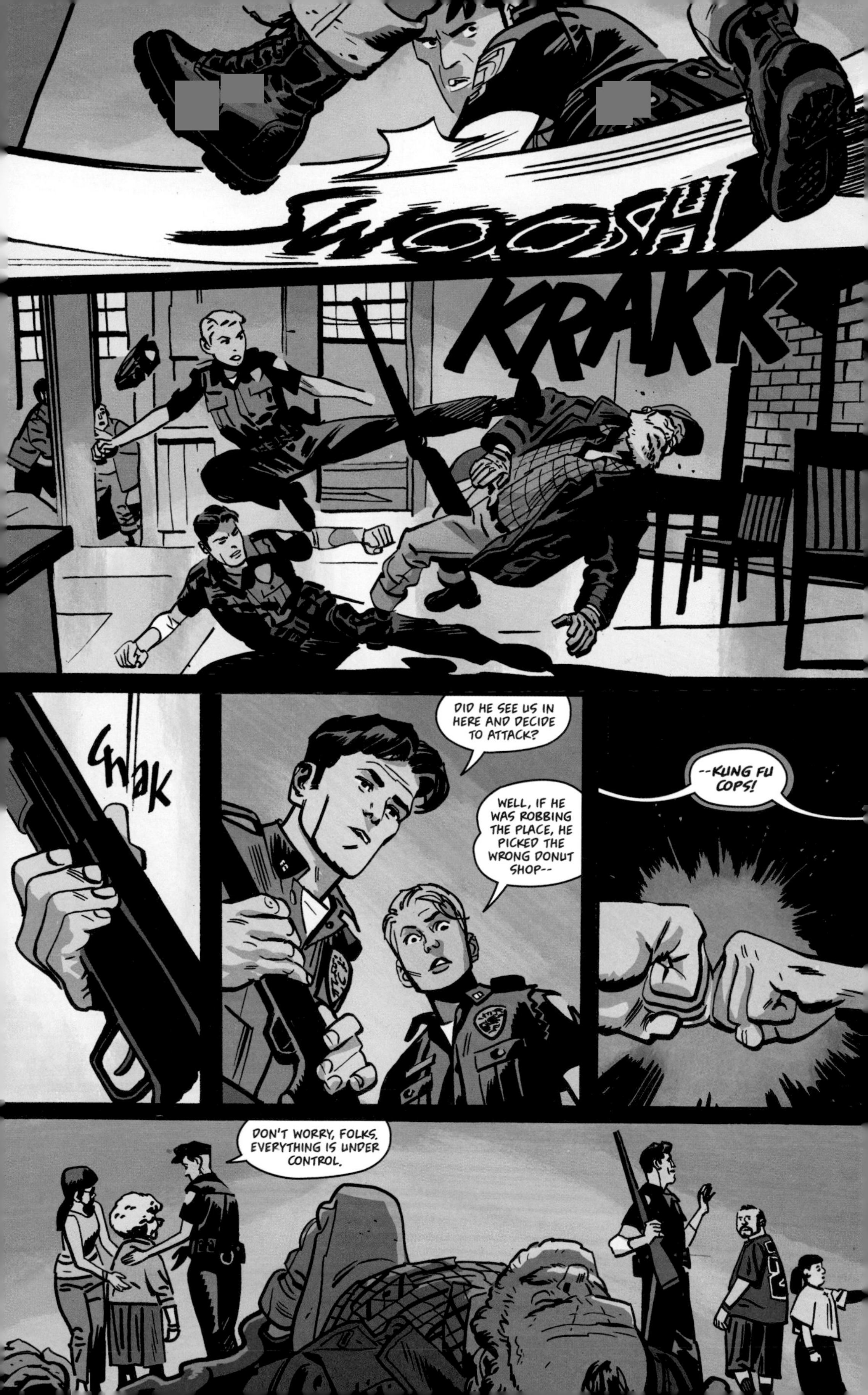
SWOOSH
KRAKK
CHAK
DID HE SEE US IN HERE AND DECIDE TO ATTACK?
WELL, IF HE WAS ROBBING THE PLACE, HE PICKED THE WRONG DONUT SHOP--
--KUNG FU COPS!
DON'T WORRY, FOLKS. EVERYTHING IS UNDER CONTROL.

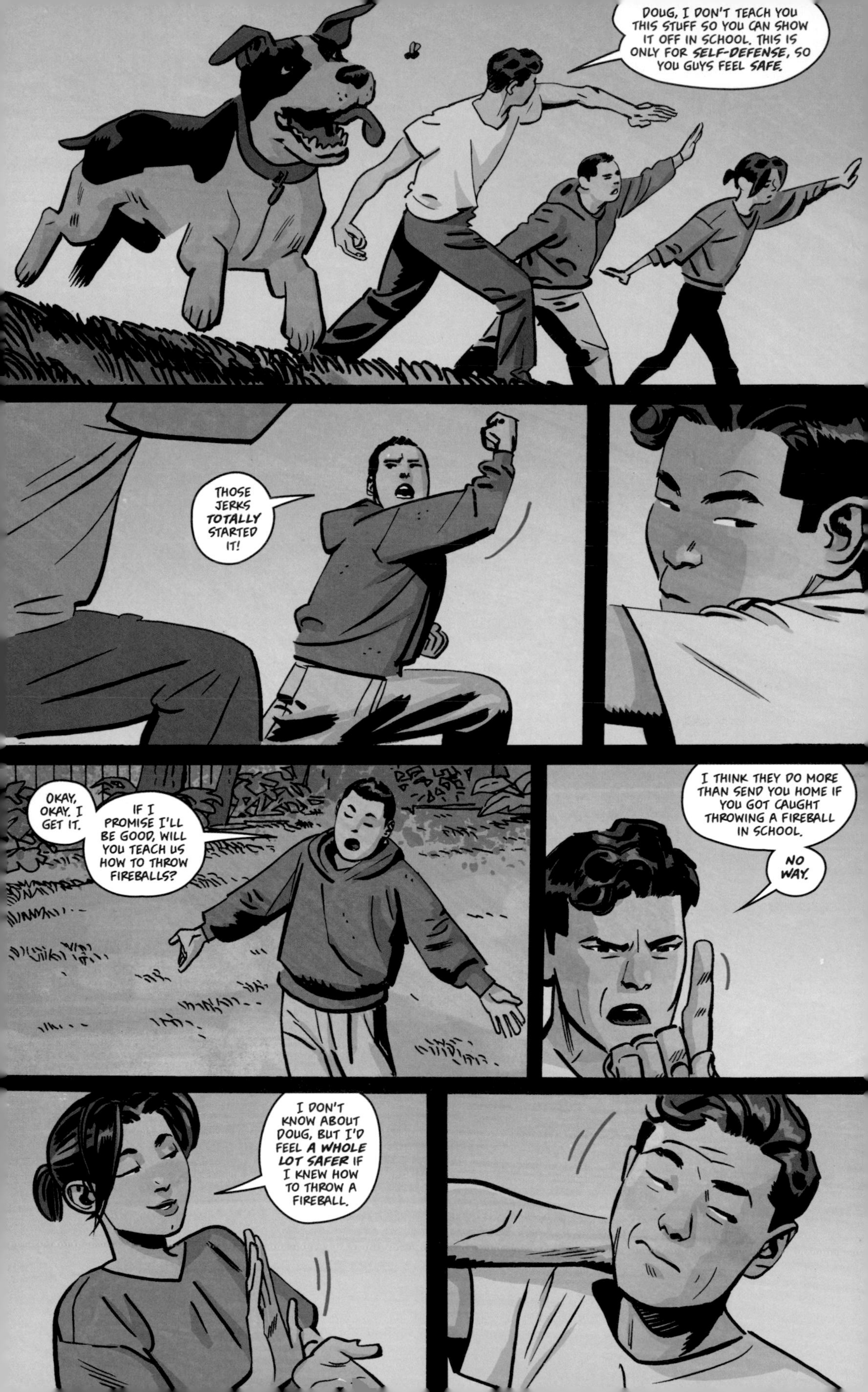
DOUG, I DON'T TEACH YOU THIS STUFF SO YOU CAN SHOW IT OFF IN SCHOOL. THIS IS ONLY FOR SELF-DEFENSE, SO YOU GUYS FEEL SAFE.
THOSE JERKS TOTALLY STARTED IT!
OKAY, OKAY. I GET IT.
IF I PROMISE I'LL BE GOOD, WILL YOU TEACH US HOW TO THROW FIREBALLS?
I THINK THEY DO MORE THAN SEND YOU HOME IF YOU GOT CAUGHT THROWING A FIREBALL IN SCHOOL.
NO WAY.
I DON'T KNOW ABOUT DOUG, BUT I'D FEEL A WHOLE LOT SAFER IF I KNEW HOW TO THROW A FIREBALL.

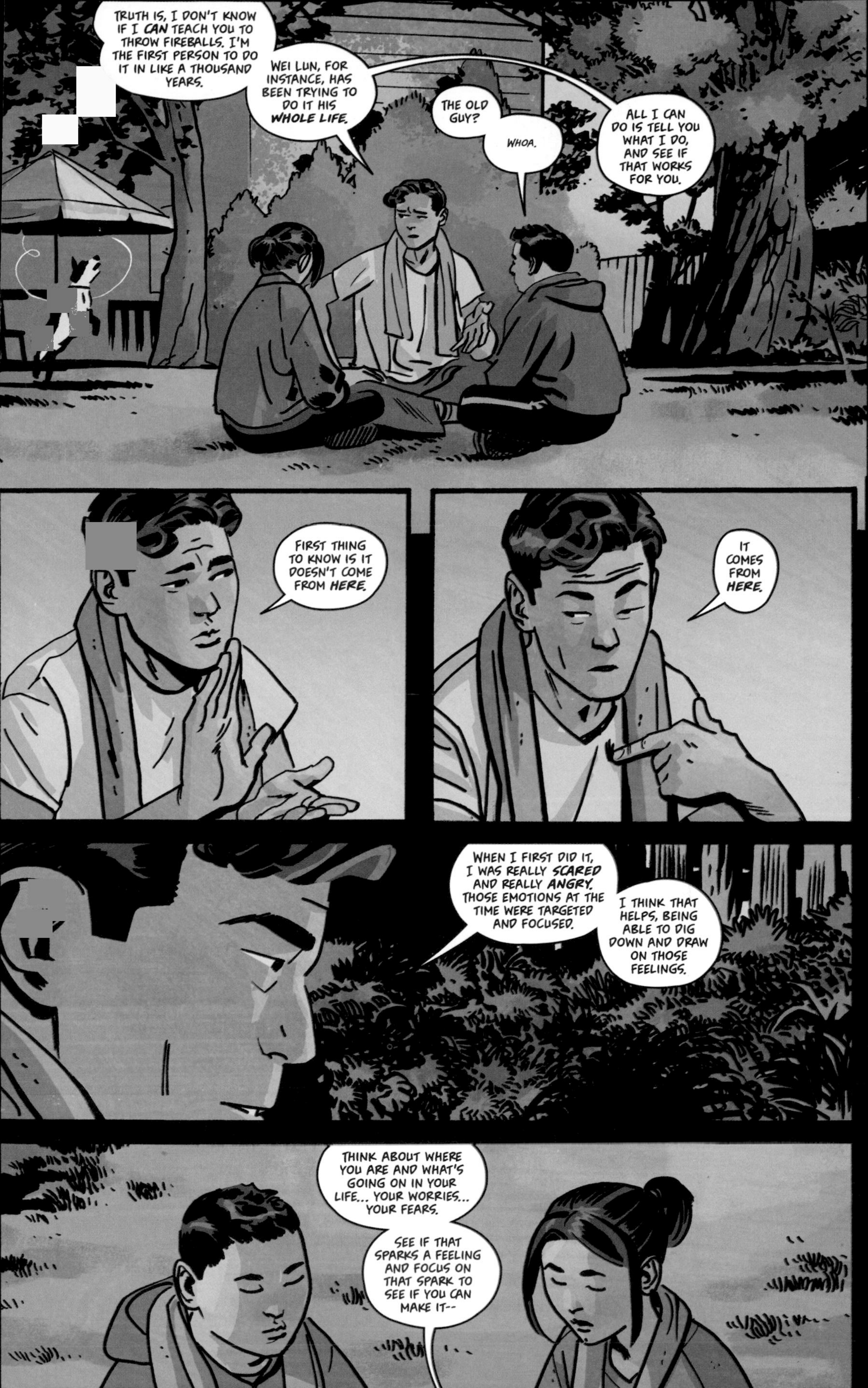
TRUTH IS, I DON'T KNOW IF I CAN TEACH YOU TO THROW FIREBALLS. I'M THE FIRST PERSON TO DO IT IN LIKE A THOUSAND YEARS.
WEI LUN, FOR INSTANCE, HAS BEEN TRYING TO DO IT HIS WHOLE LIFE.
THE OLD GUY?
WHOA.
ALL I CAN DO IS TELL YOU WHAT I DO, AND SEE IF THAT WORKS FOR YOU.
FIRST THING TO KNOW IS IT DOESN'T COME FROM HERE.
IT COMES FROM HERE.
WHEN I FIRST DID IT, I WAS REALLY SCARED AND REALLY ANGRY. THOSE EMOTIONS AT THE TIME WERE TARGETED AND FOCUSED.
I THINK THAT HELPS, BEING ABLE TO DIG DOWN AND DRAW ON THOSE FEELINGS.
THINK ABOUT WHERE YOU ARE AND WHAT'S GOING ON IN YOUR LIFE... YOUR WORRIES... YOUR FEARS.
SEE IF THAT SPARKS A FEELING AND FOCUS ON THAT SPARK TO SEE IF YOU CAN MAKE IT--

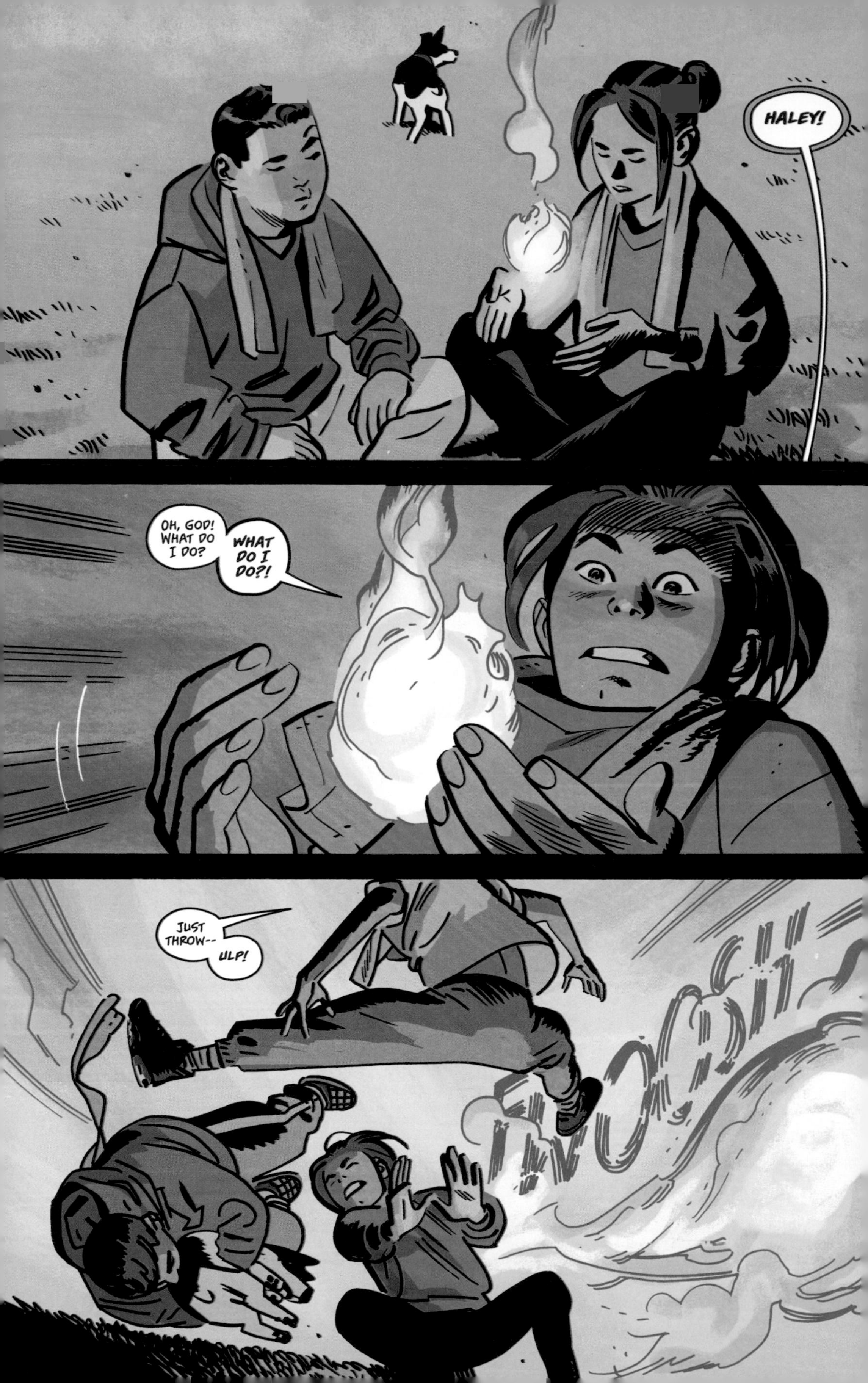
HALEY!
OH, GOD! WHAT DO I DO?
WHAT DO I DO?!
JUST THROW--
ULP!
FWOOSH!!

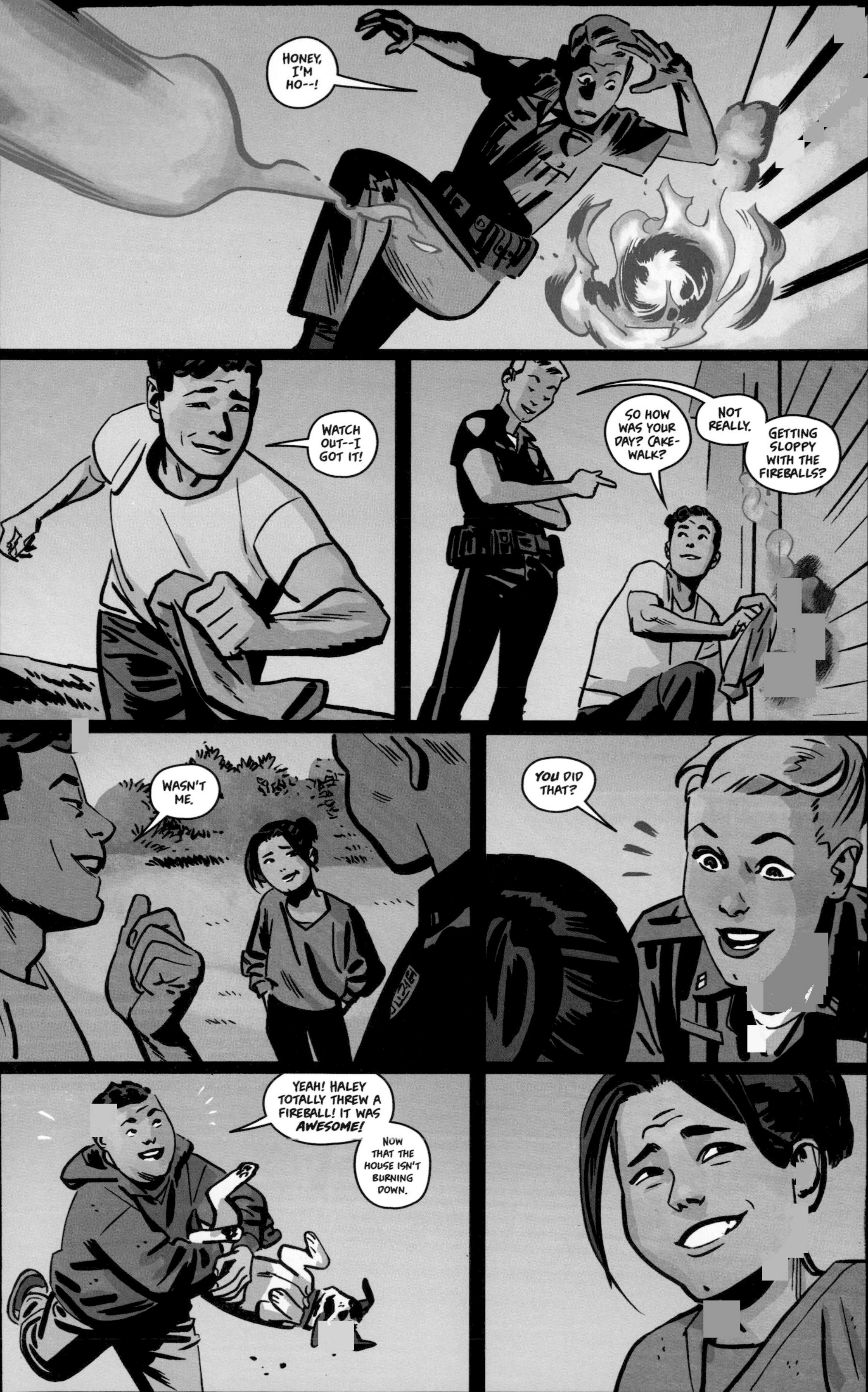
HONEY, I'M HO--!
WATCH OUT--I GOT IT!
SO HOW WAS YOUR DAY? CAKE-WALK?
NOT REALLY.
GETTING SLOPPY WITH THE FIREBALLS?
WASN'T ME.
YOU DID THAT?
YEAH! HALEY TOTALLY THREW A FIREBALL! IT WAS AWESOME!
NOW THAT THE HOUSE ISN'T BURNING DOWN.

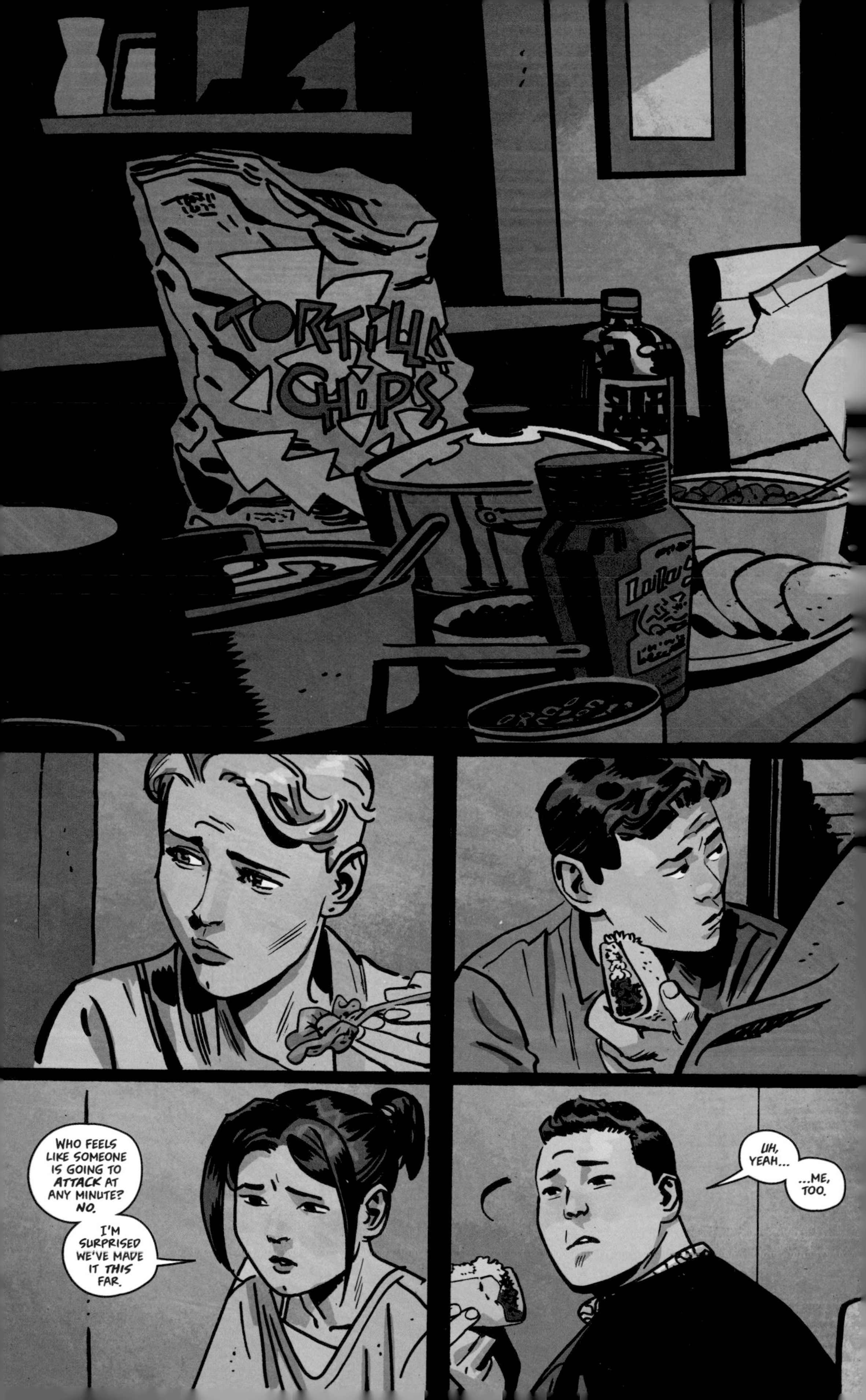
TORTILLA CHIPS
WHO FEELS LIKE SOMEONE IS GOING TO ATTACK AT ANY MINUTE? NO.
I'M SURPRISED WE'VE MADE IT THIS FAR.
UH, YEAH...
...ME, TOO.

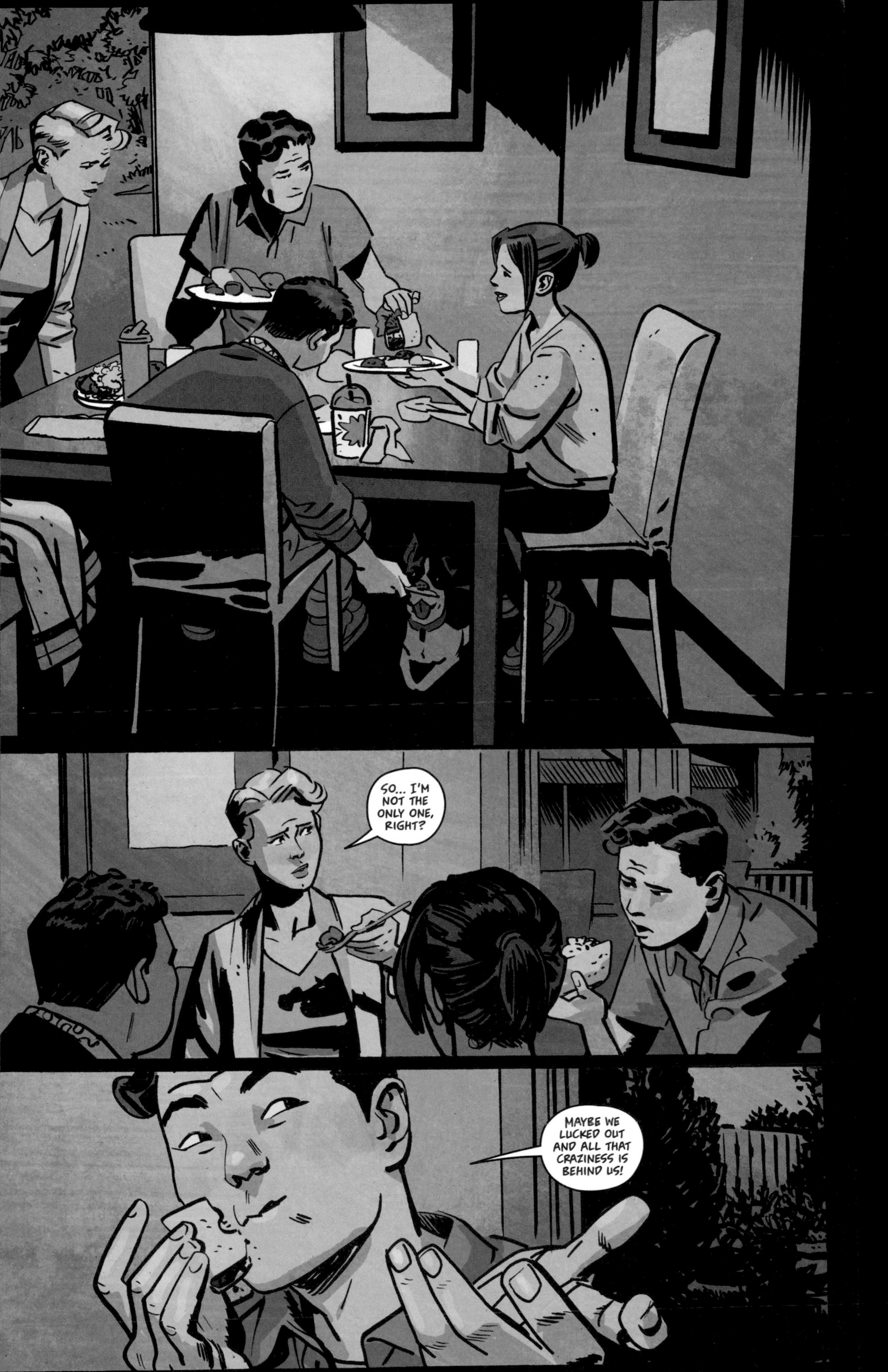
SO... I'M NOT THE ONLY ONE, RIGHT?
MAYBE WE LUCKED OUT AND ALL THAT CRAZINESS IS BEHIND US!

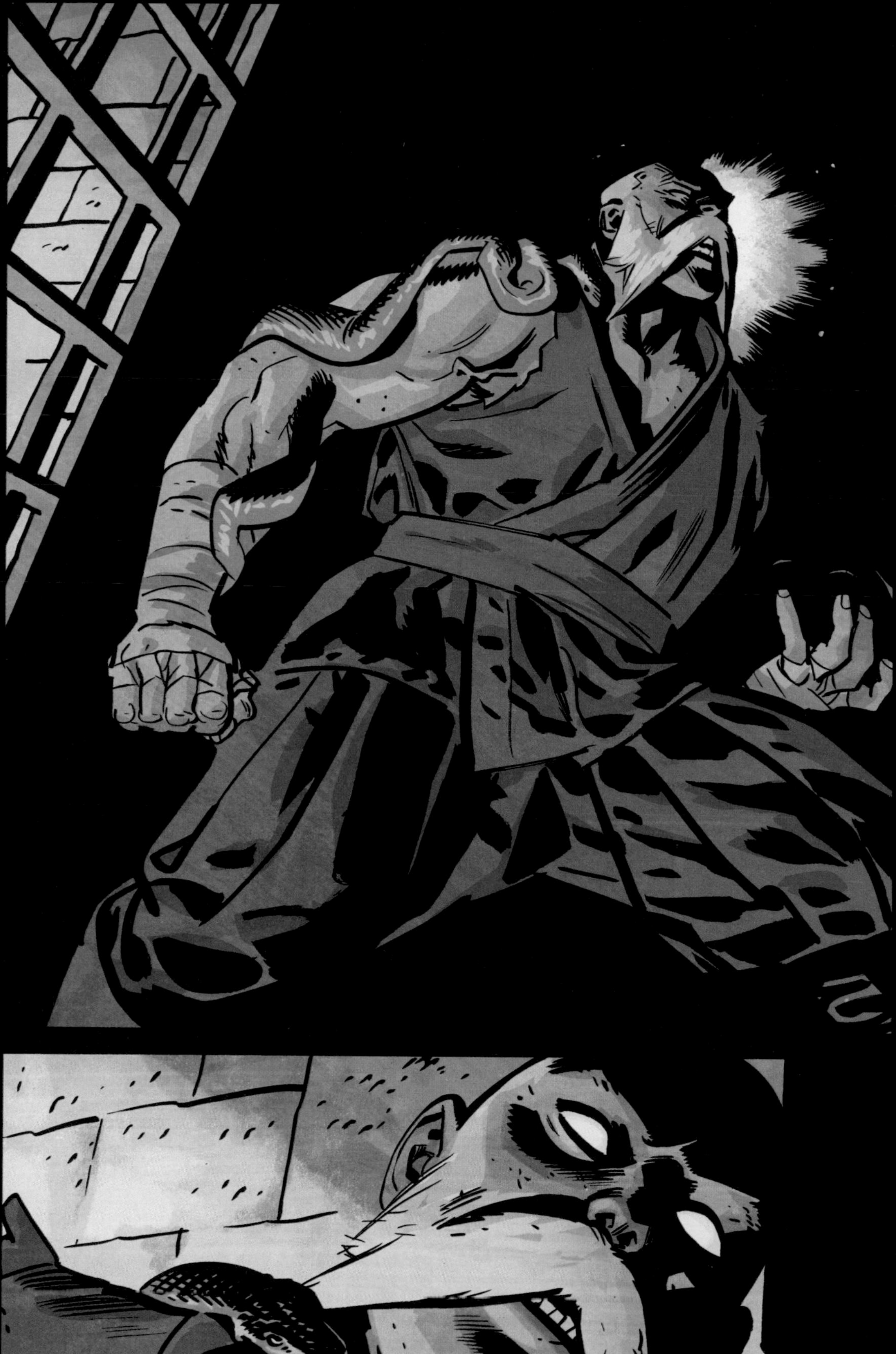

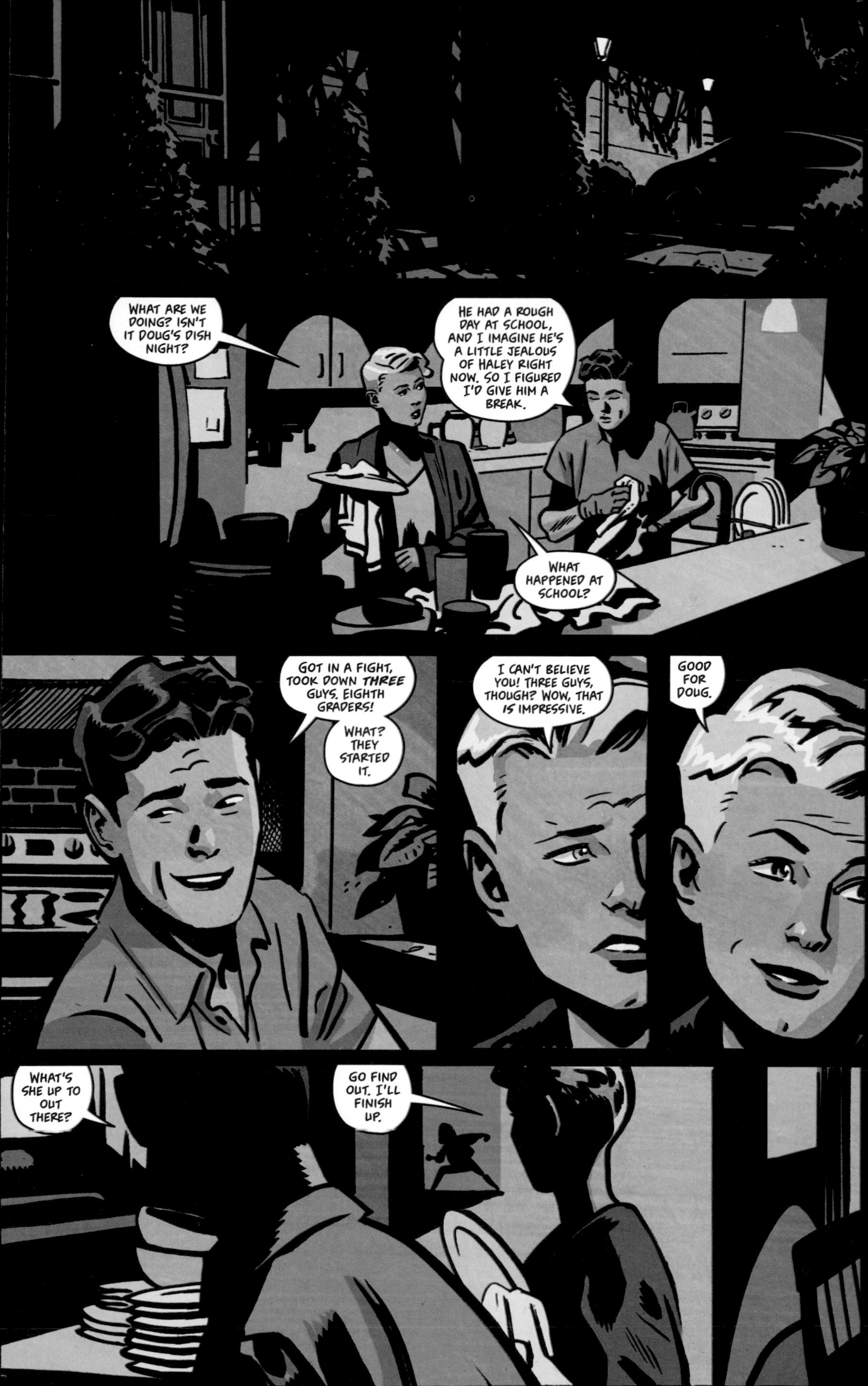
WHAT ARE WE DOING? ISN'T IT DOUG'S DISH NIGHT?
HE HAD A ROUGH DAY AT SCHOOL, AND I IMAGINE HE'S A LITTLE JEALOUS OF HALEY RIGHT NOW. SO I FIGURED I'D GIVE HIM A BREAK.
WHAT HAPPENED AT SCHOOL?
GOT IN A FIGHT, TOOK DOWN THREE GUYS. EIGHTH GRADERS!
WHAT? THEY STARTED IT.
I CAN'T BELIEVE YOU! THREE GUYS, THOUGH? WOW, THAT IS IMPRESSIVE.
GOOD FOR DOUG.
WHAT'S SHE UP TO OUT THERE?
GO FIND OUT. I'LL FINISH UP.

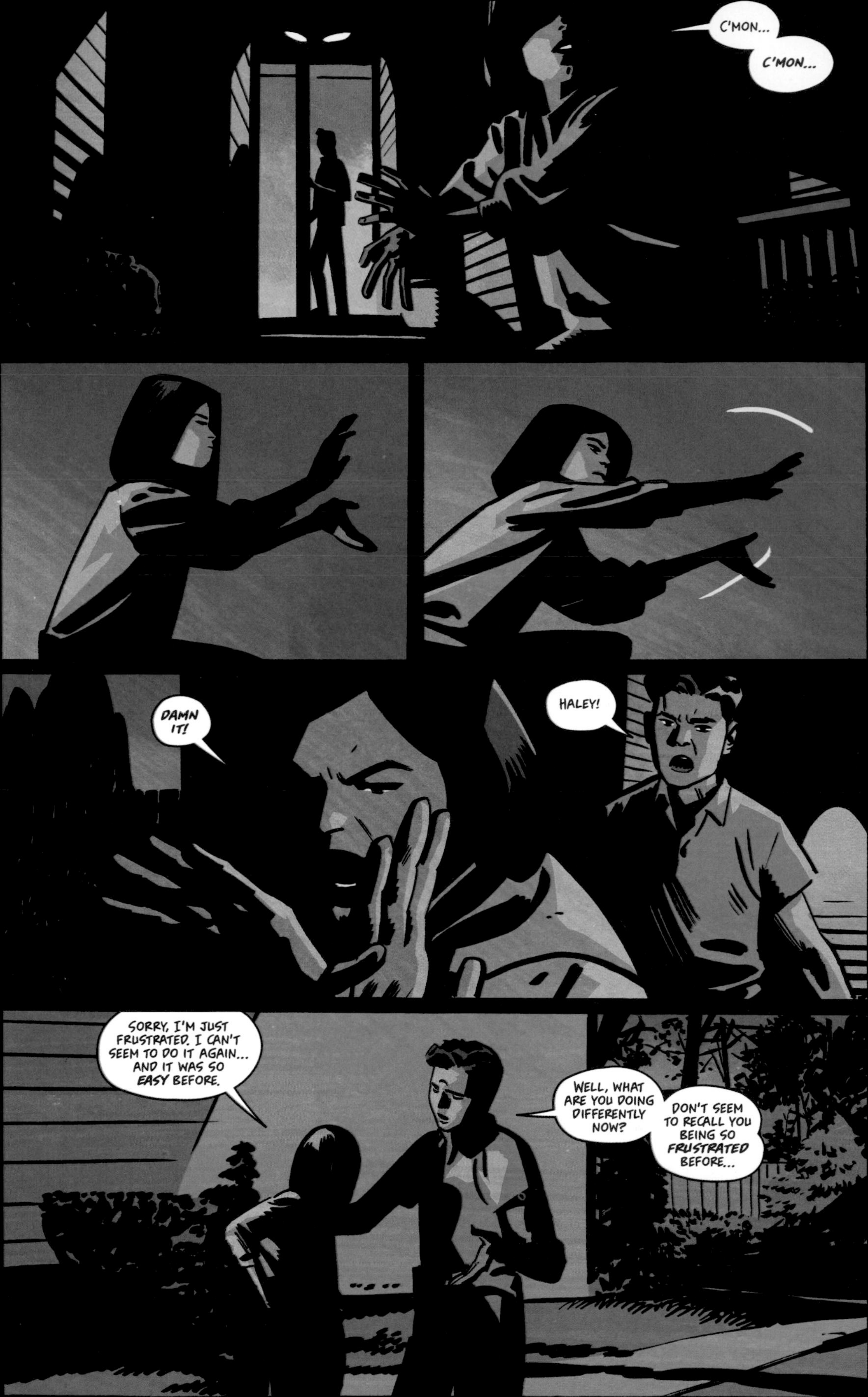
C'MON...
C'MON...
DAMN IT!
HALEY!
SORRY, I'M JUST FRUSTRATED. I CAN'T SEEM TO DO IT AGAIN... AND IT WAS SO EASY BEFORE.
WELL, WHAT ARE YOU DOING DIFFERENTLY NOW?
DON'T SEEM TO RECALL YOU BEING SO FRUSTRATED BEFORE...

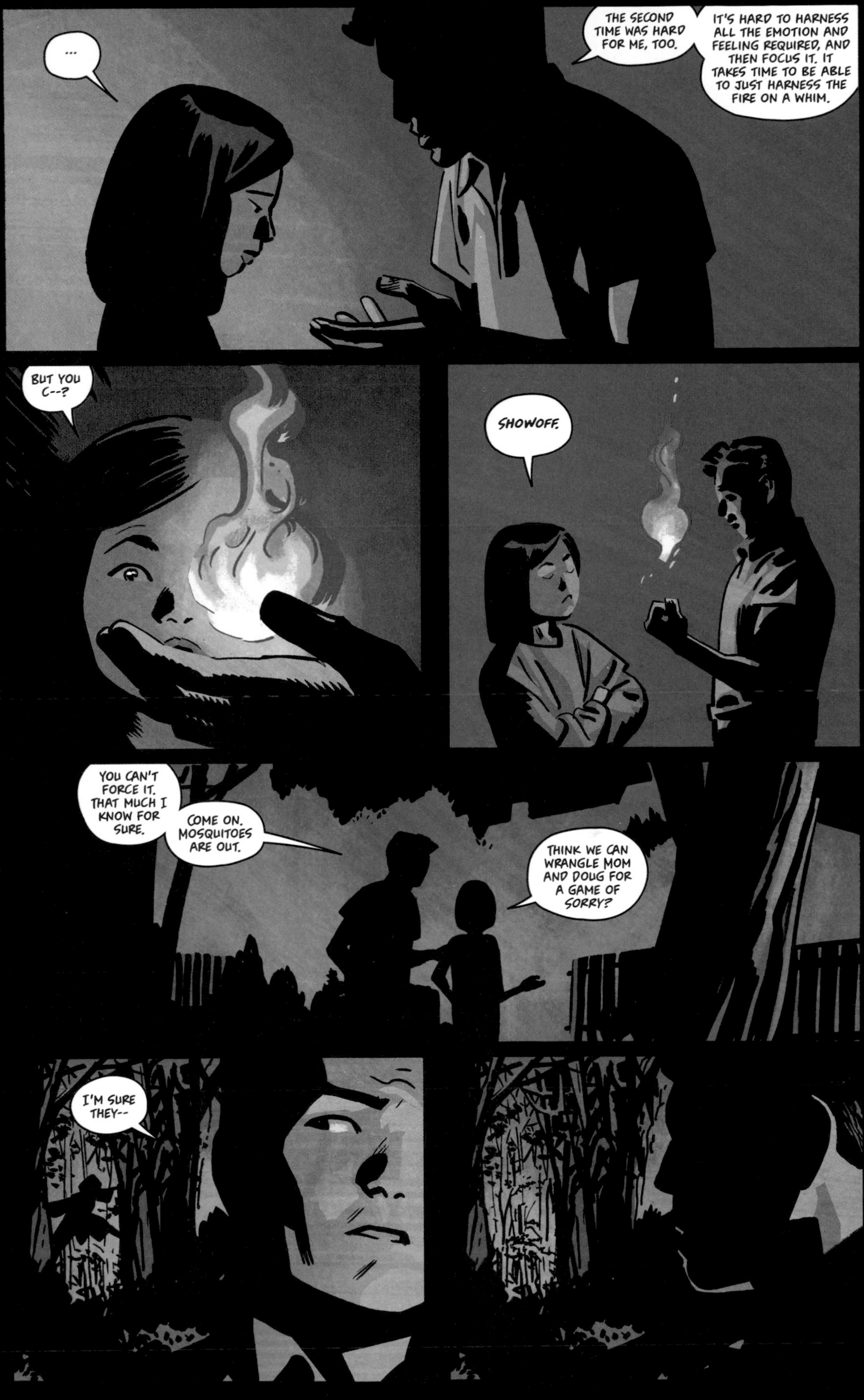
...
THE SECOND TIME WAS HARD FOR ME, TOO.
IT'S HARD TO HARNESS ALL THE EMOTION AND FEELING REQUIRED, AND THEN FOCUS IT. IT TAKES TIME TO BE ABLE TO JUST HARNESS THE FIRE ON A WHIM.
BUT YOU C--?
SHOWOFF.
YOU CAN'T FORCE IT. THAT MUCH I KNOW FOR SURE.
COME ON. MOSQUITOES ARE OUT.
THINK WE CAN WRANGLE MOM AND DOUG FOR A GAME OF SORRY?
I'M SURE THEY--

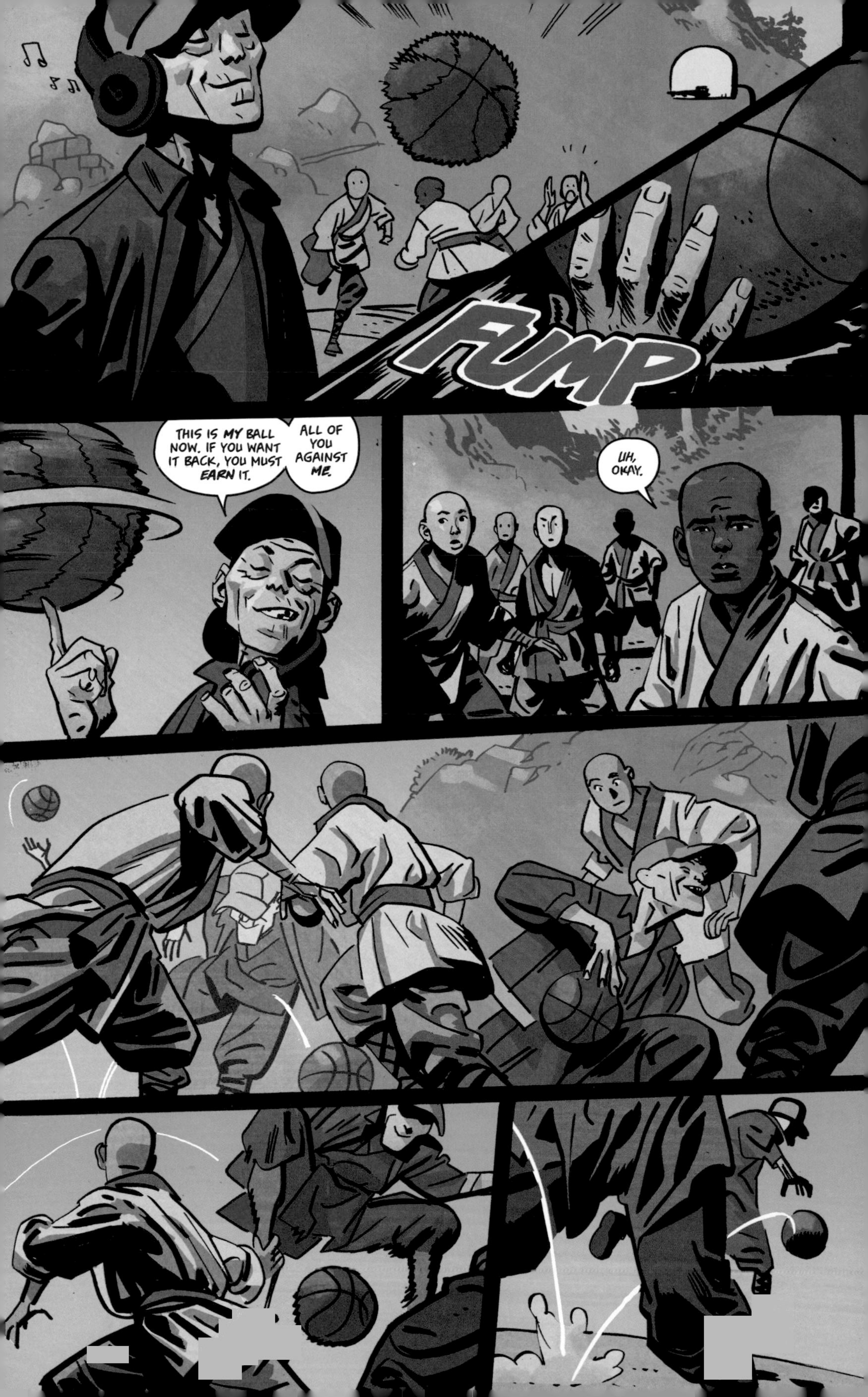
FUMP
THIS IS MY BALL NOW. IF YOU WANT IT BACK, YOU MUST EARN IT.
ALL OF YOU AGAINST ME.
UH, OKAY.

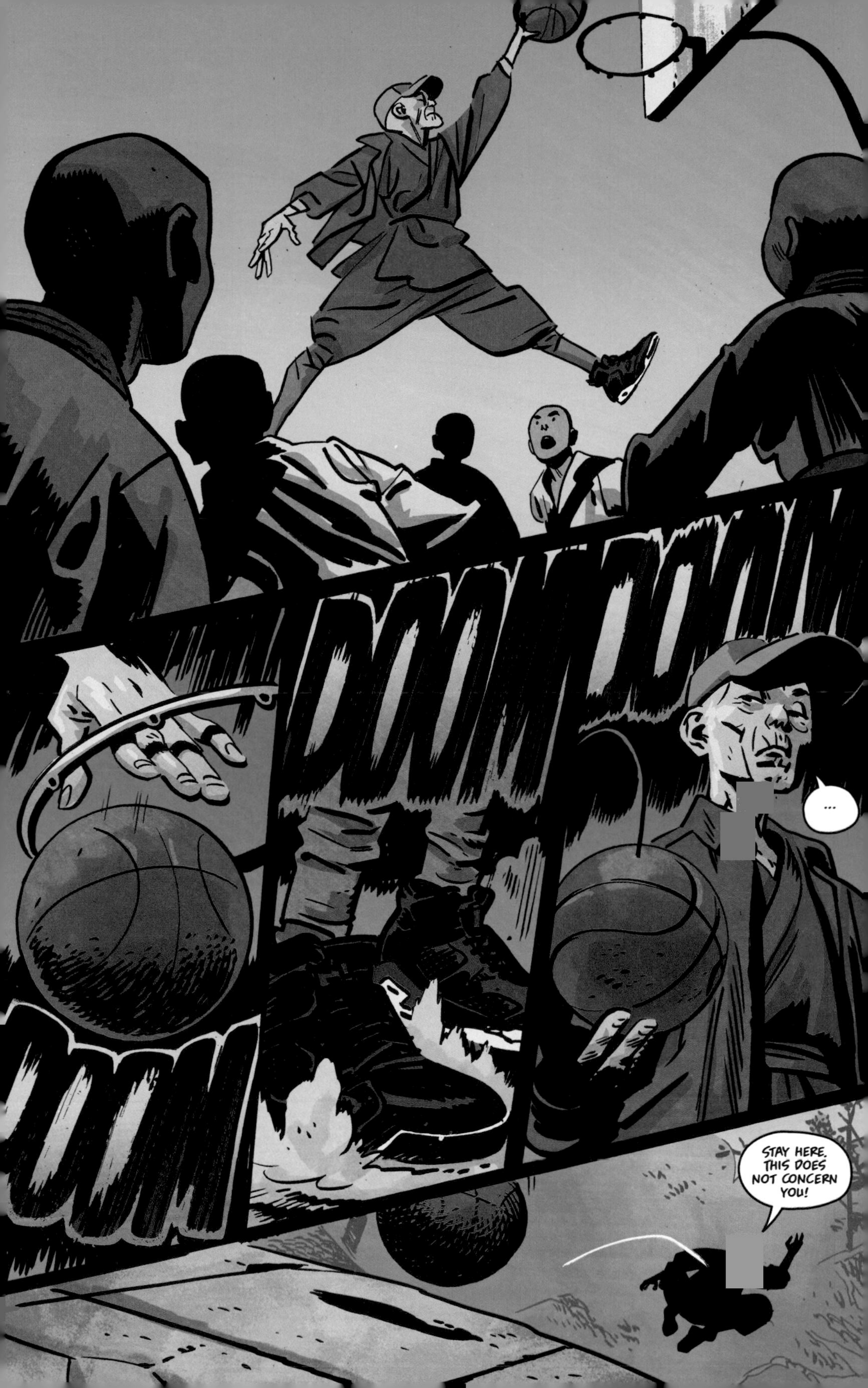
...
STAY HERE. THIS DOES NOT CONCERN YOU!

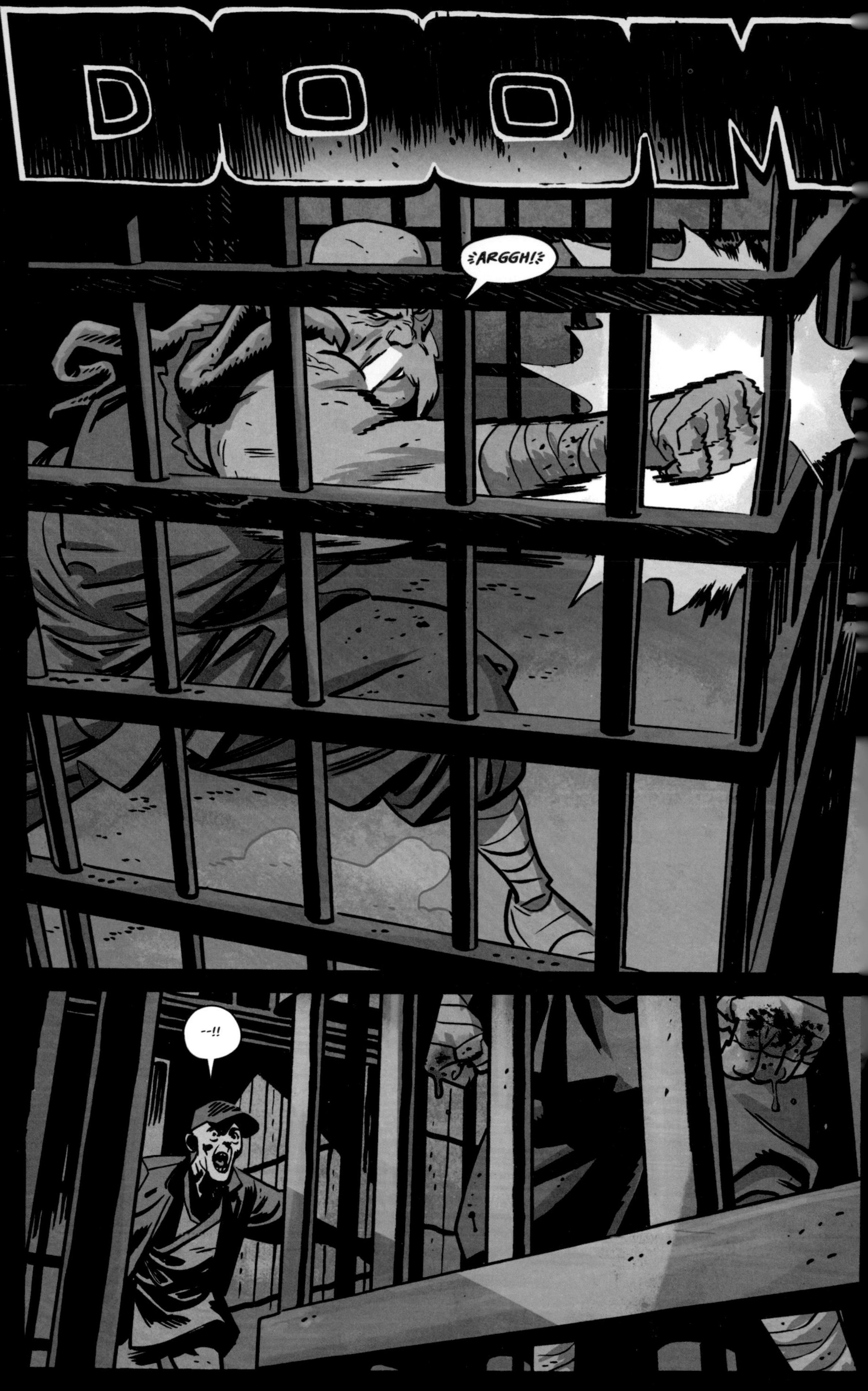
DOOOM
ARGGH!
--!!

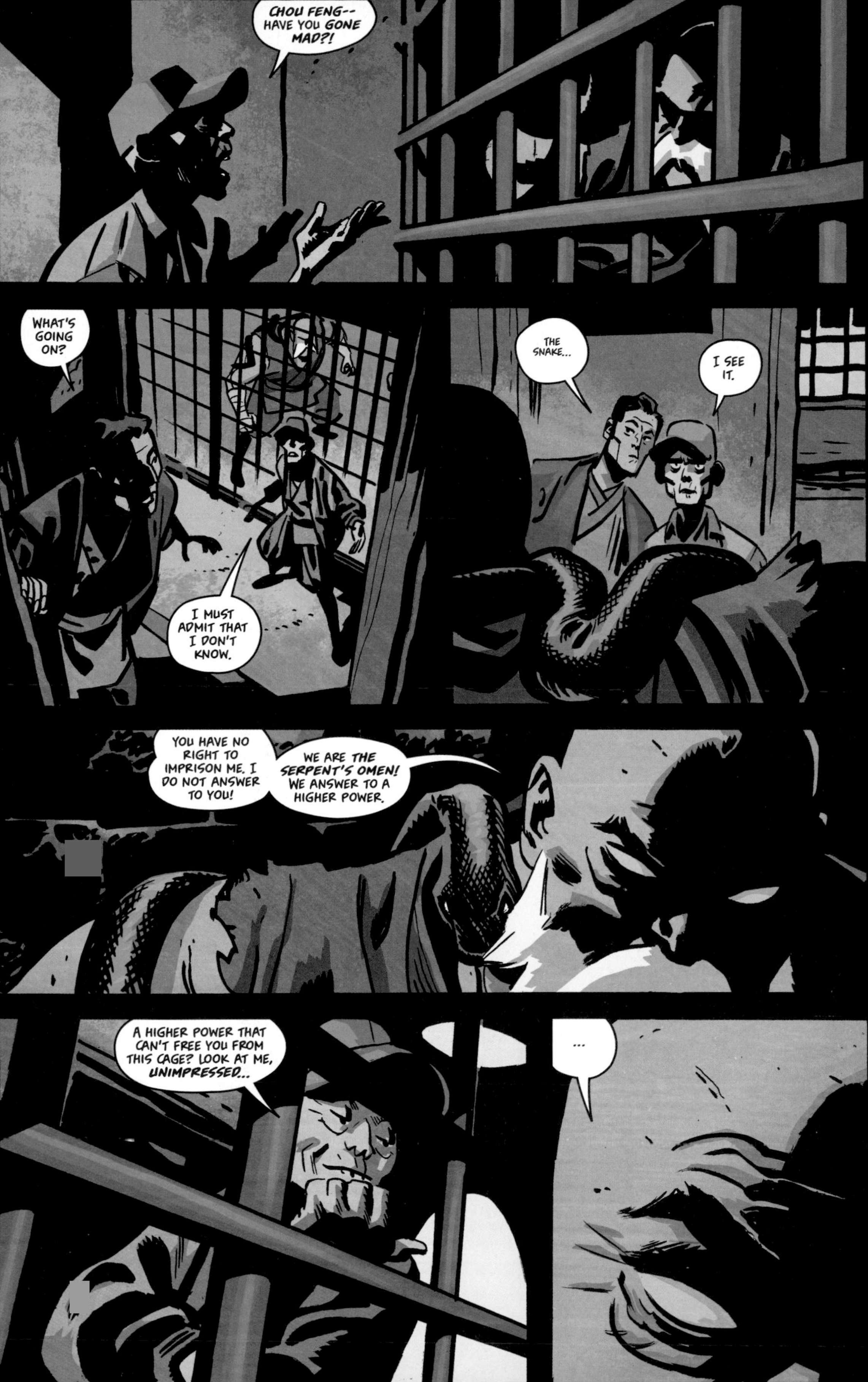
CHOU FENG-- HAVE YOU GONE MAD?!
WHAT'S GOING ON?
I MUST ADMIT THAT I DON'T KNOW.
THE SNAKE...
I SEE IT.
YOU HAVE NO RIGHT TO IMPRISON ME. I DO NOT ANSWER TO YOU!
WE ARE THE SERPENT'S OMEN! WE ANSWER TO A HIGHER POWER.
A HIGHER POWER THAT CAN'T FREE YOU FROM THIS CAGE? LOOK AT ME, UNIMPRESSED...
...

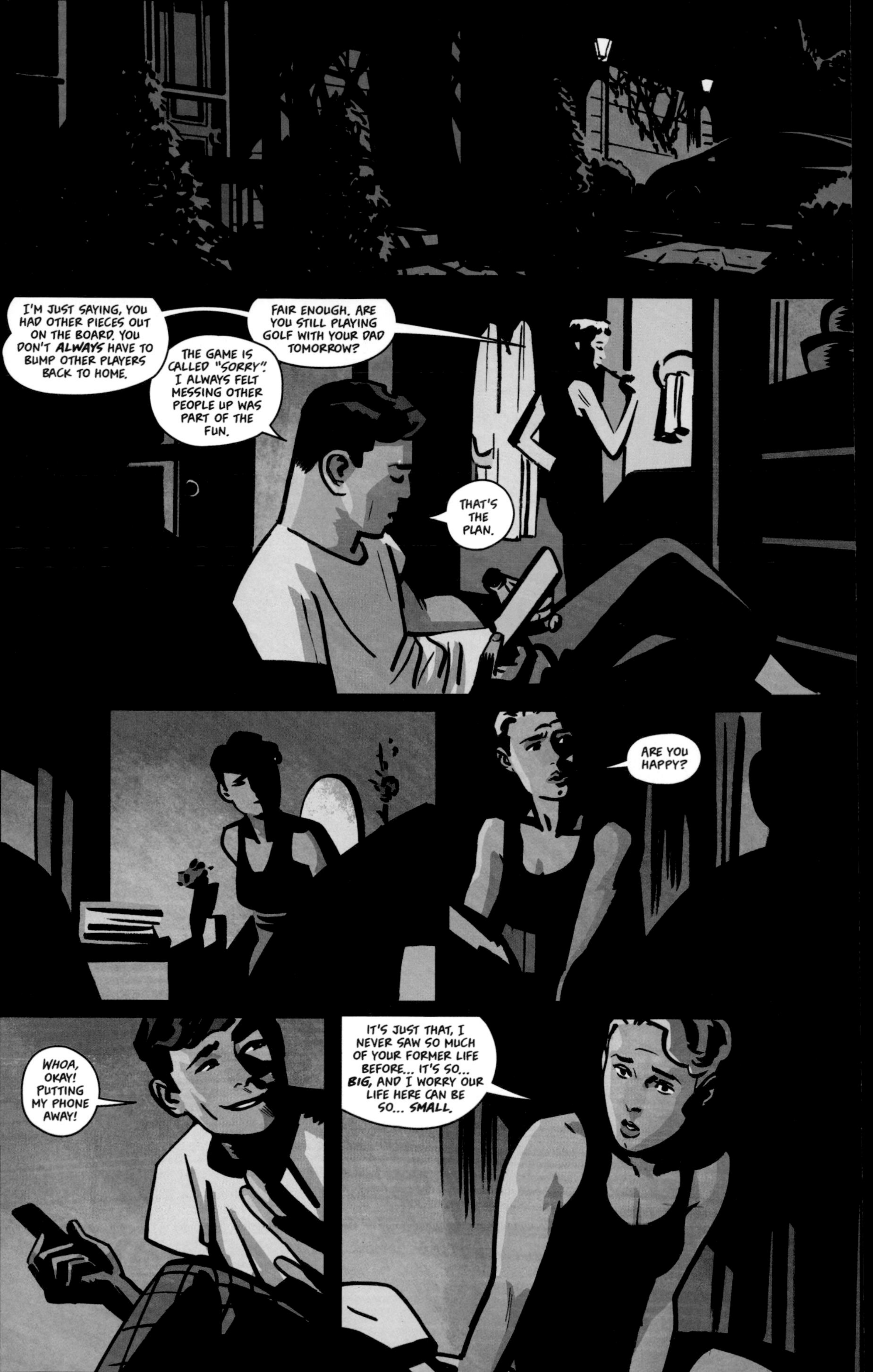
I'M JUST SAYING, YOU HAD OTHER PIECES OUT ON THE BOARD. YOU DON'T ALWAYS HAVE TO BUMP OTHER PLAYERS BACK TO HOME.
THE GAME IS CALLED "SORRY". I ALWAYS FELT MESSING OTHER PEOPLE UP WAS PART OF THE FUN.
FAIR ENOUGH. ARE YOU STILL PLAYING GOLF WITH YOUR DAD TOMORROW?
THAT'S THE PLAN.
ARE YOU HAPPY?
WHOA, OKAY! PUTTING MY PHONE AWAY!
IT'S JUST THAT, I NEVER SAW SO MUCH OF YOUR FORMER LIFE BEFORE... IT'S SO... BIG, AND I WORRY OUR LIFE HERE CAN BE SO... SMALL.

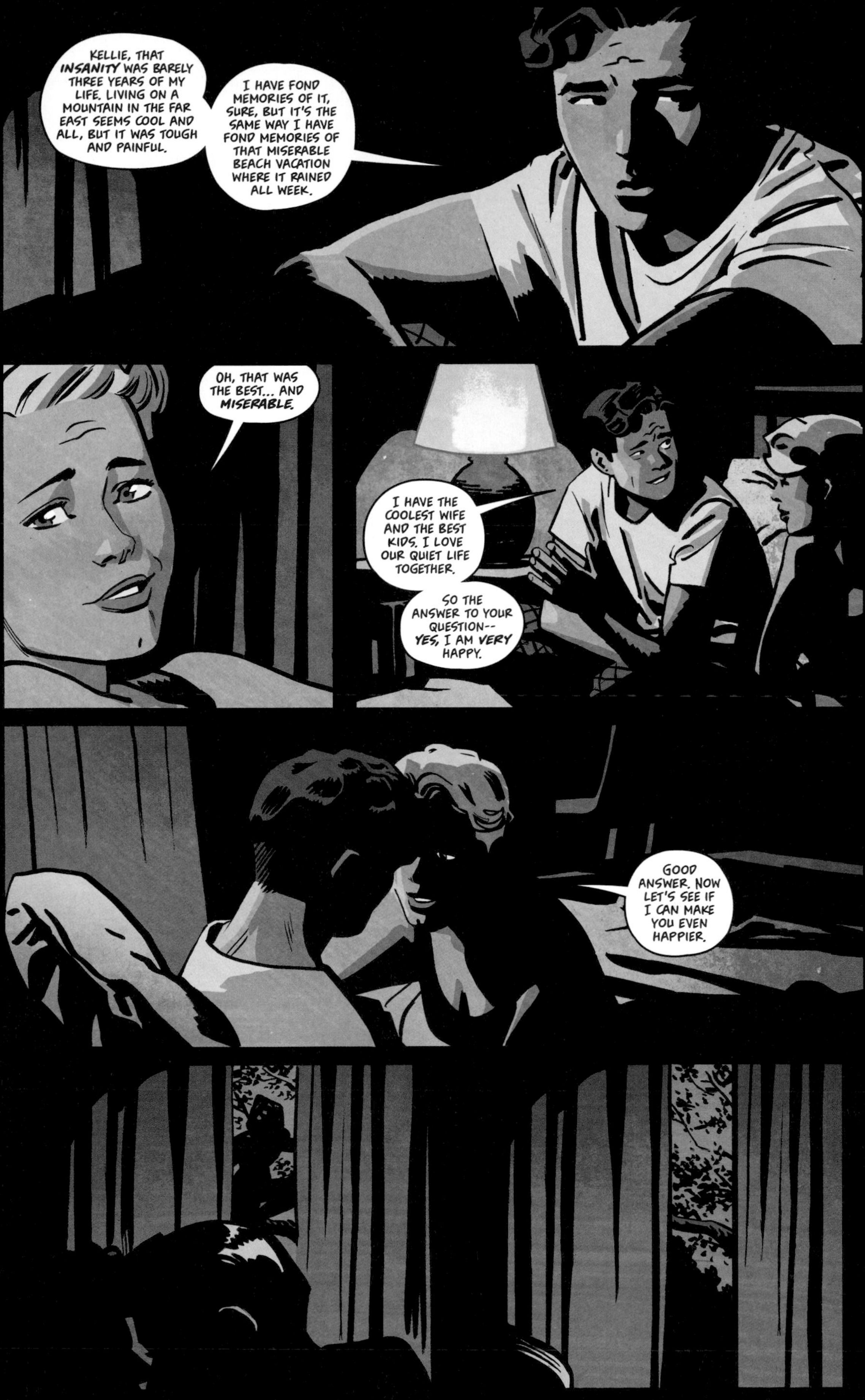
KELLIE, THAT INSANITY WAS BARELY THREE YEARS OF MY LIFE. LIVING ON A MOUNTAIN IN THE FAR EAST SEEMS COOL AND ALL, BUT IT WAS TOUGH AND PAINFUL.
I HAVE FOND MEMORIES OF IT, SURE, BUT IT'S THE SAME WAY I HAVE FOND MEMORIES OF THAT MISERABLE BEACH VACATION WHERE IT RAINED ALL WEEK.
OH, THAT WAS THE BEST... AND MISERABLE.
I HAVE THE COOLEST WIFE AND THE BEST KIDS. I LOVE OUR QUIET LIFE TOGETHER.
SO THE ANSWER TO YOUR QUESTION--YES, I AM VERY HAPPY.
GOOD ANSWER. NOW LET'S SEE IF I CAN MAKE YOU EVEN HAPPIER.

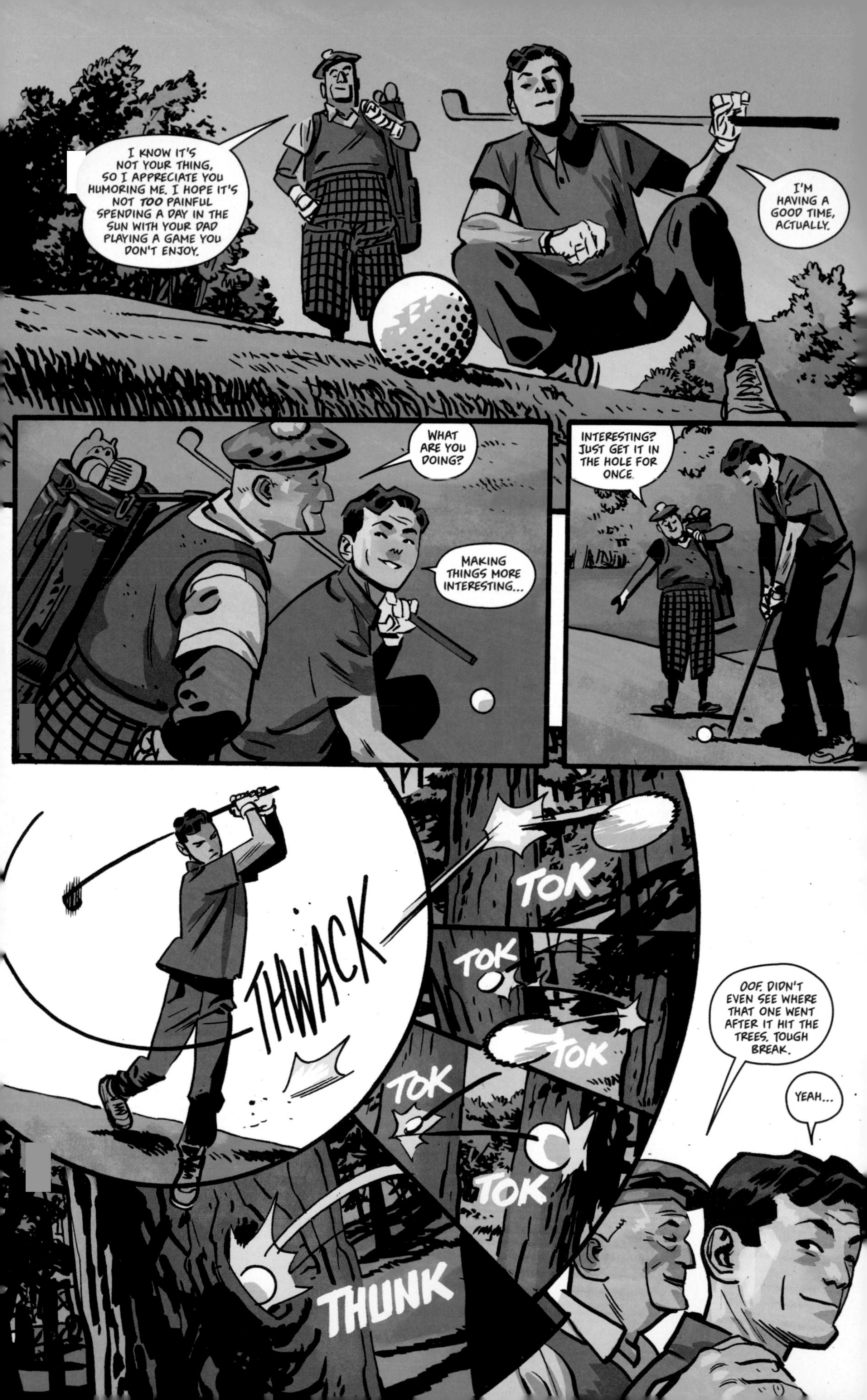
I KNOW IT'S NOT YOUR THING, SO I APPRECIATE YOU HUMORING ME. I HOPE IT'S NOT TOO PAINFUL SPENDING A DAY IN THE SUN WITH YOUR DAD PLAYING A GAME YOU DON'T ENJOY.
I'M HAVING A GOOD TIME, ACTUALLY.
WHAT ARE YOU DOING?
MAKING THINGS MORE INTERESTING...
INTERESTING? JUST GET IT IN THE HOLE FOR ONCE.
THWACK
TOK
TOK
TOK
TOK
TOK
THUNK
OOF. DIDN'T EVEN SEE WHERE THAT ONE WENT AFTER IT HIT THE TREES. TOUGH BREAK.
YEAH...

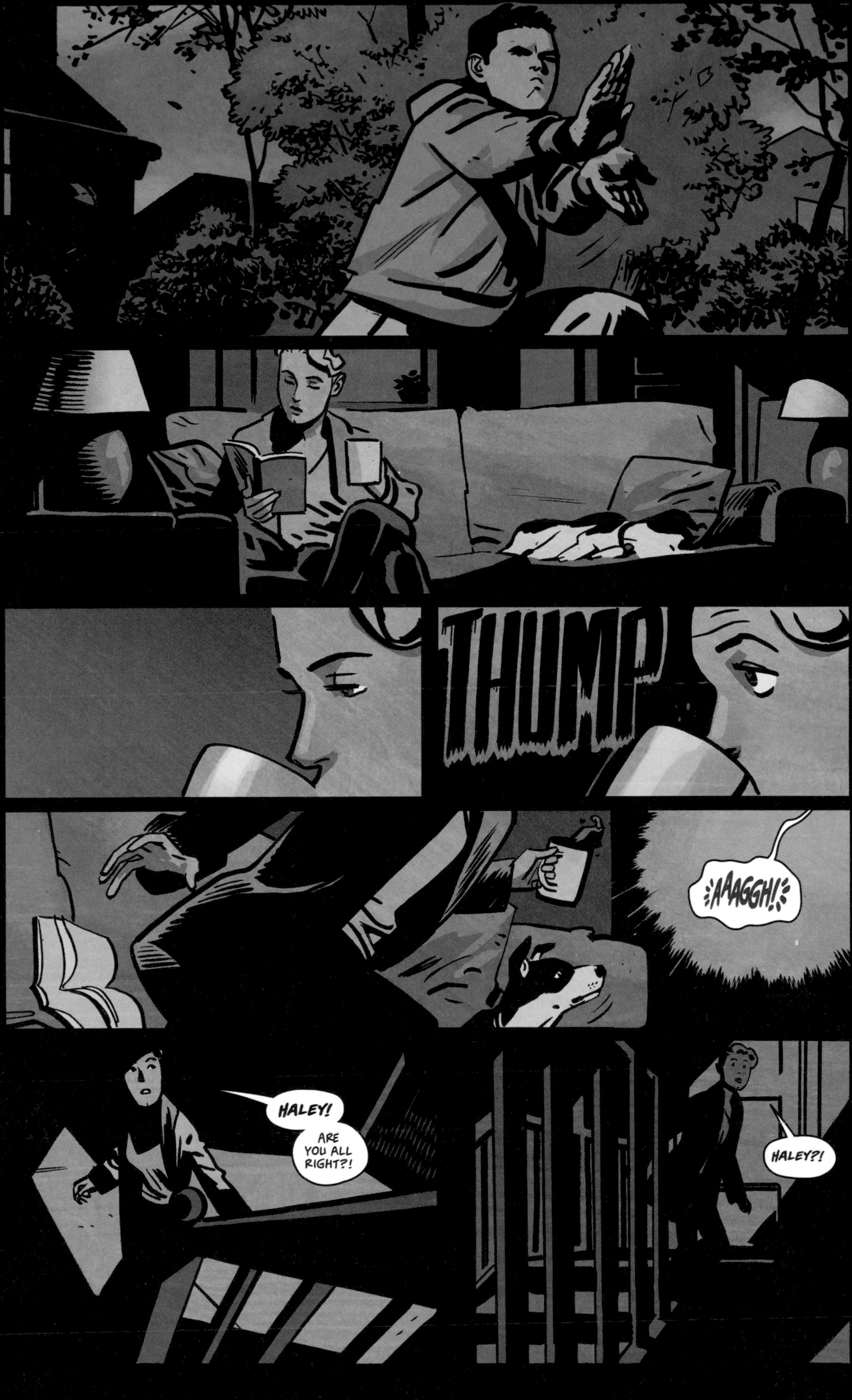
THUMP
AAAGGH!
HALEY!
ARE YOU ALL RIGHT?!
HALEY?!

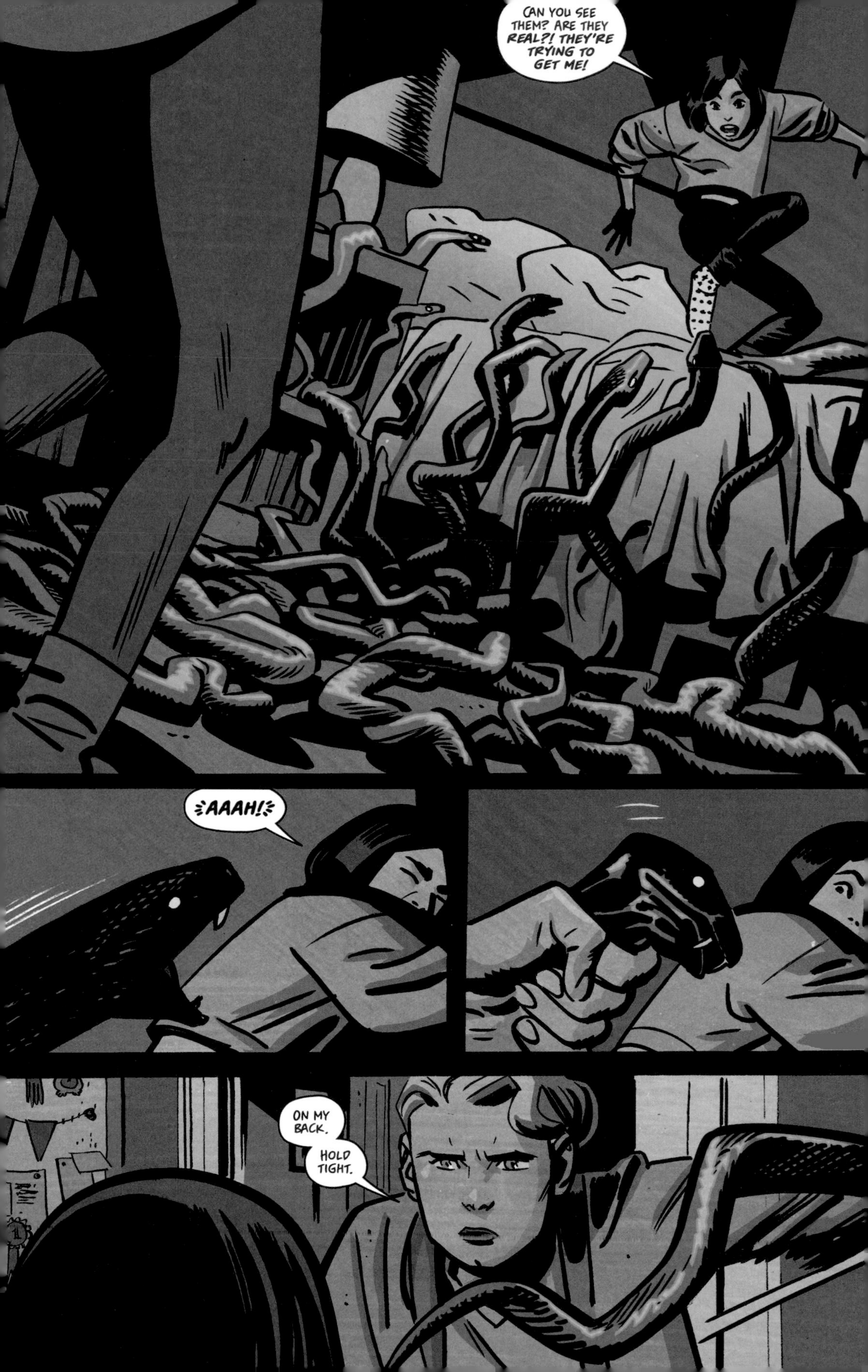
CAN YOU SEE THEM? ARE THEY REAL?! THEY'RE TRYING TO GET ME!
AAAH!
ON MY BACK.
HOLD TIGHT.

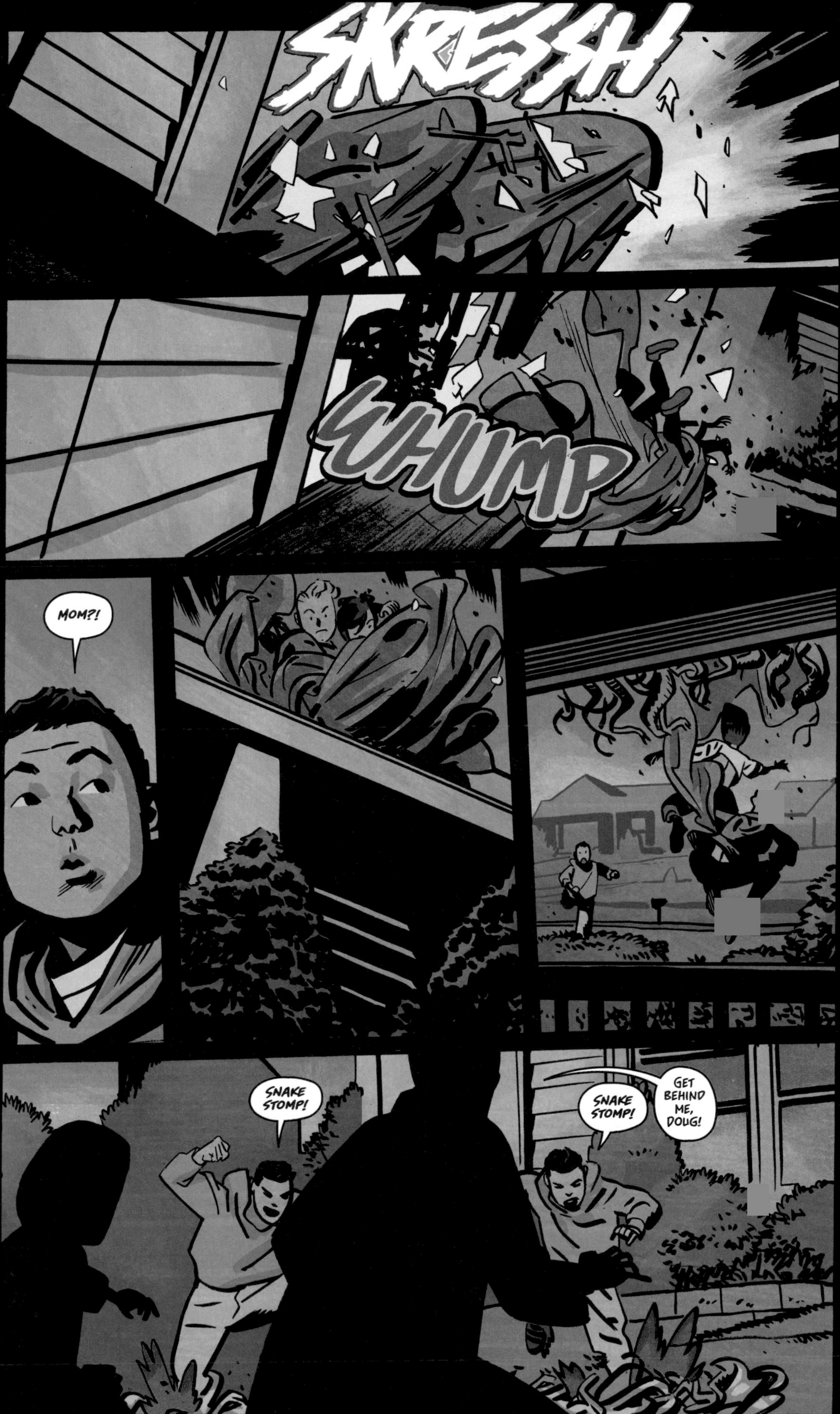
SKRESSH
WHUMP
MOM?!
SNAKE STOMP!
SNAKE STOMP!
GET BEHIND ME, DOUG!

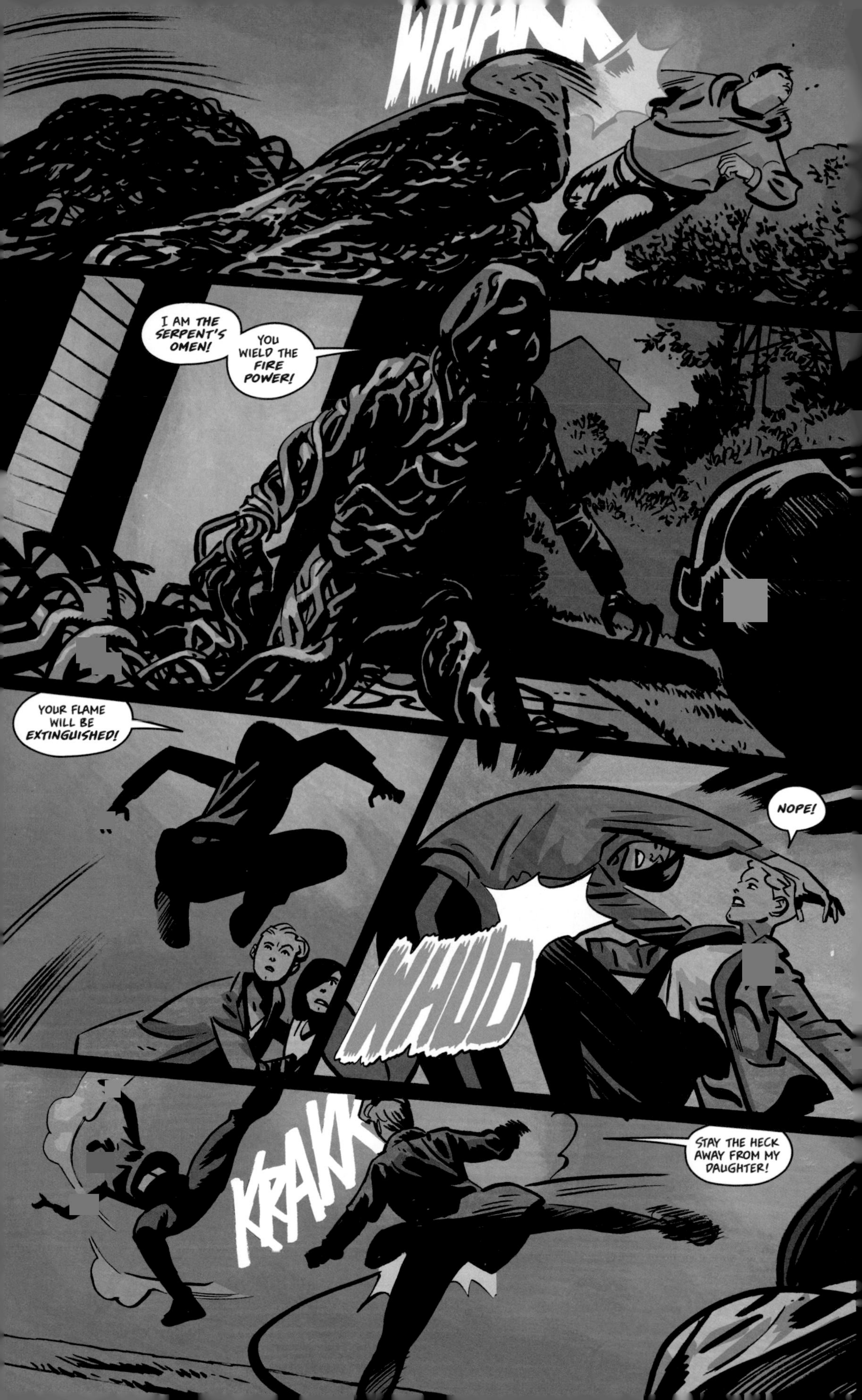
WHAKK
I AM THE SERPENT'S OMEN!
YOU WIELD THE FIRE POWER!
YOUR FLAME WILL BE EXTINGUISHED!
NOPE!
WHUD
KRAKK
STAY THE HECK AWAY FROM MY DAUGHTER!

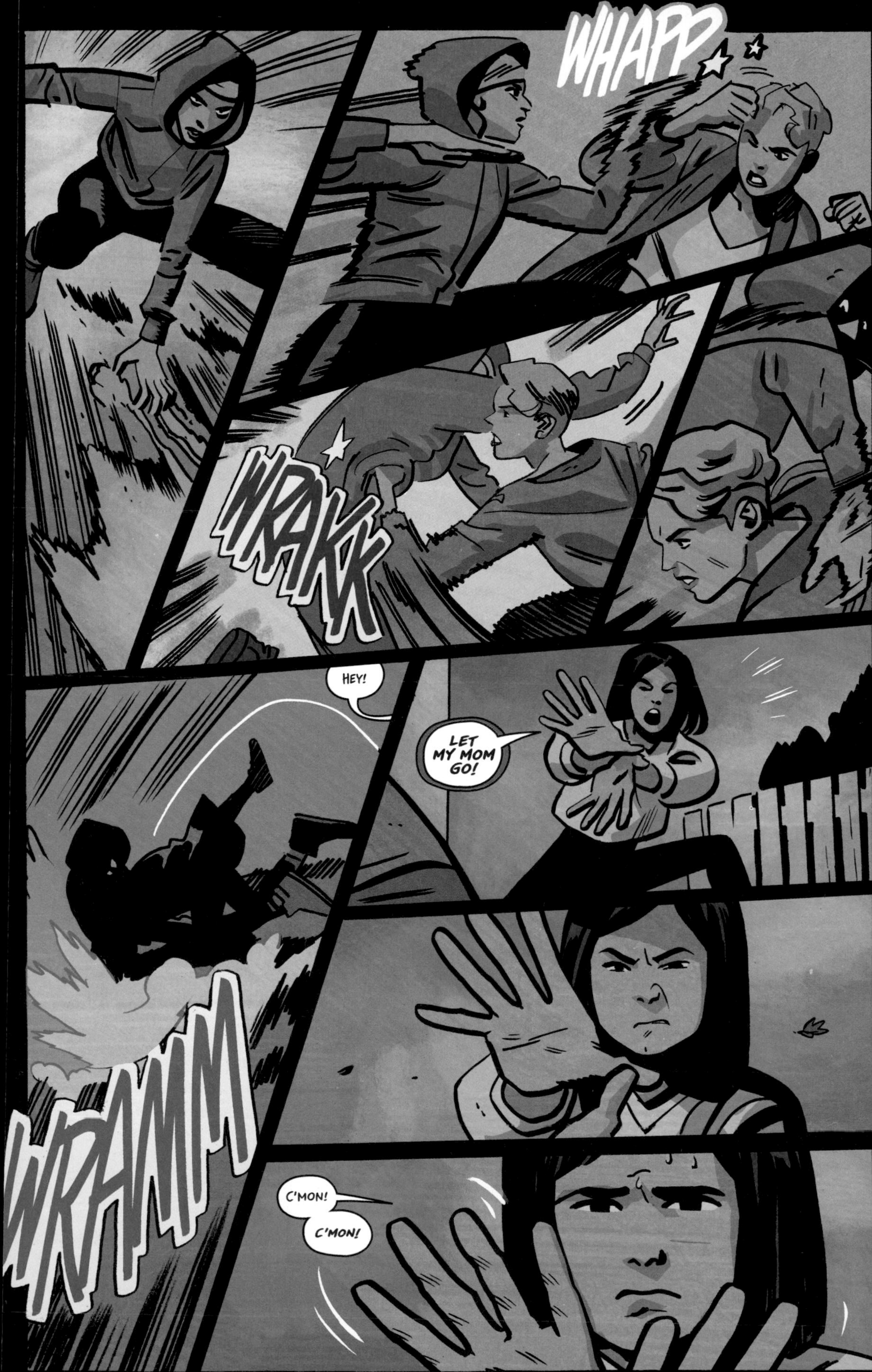
WHAPP
WRAKK
HEY!
WRAMM
LET MY MOM GO!
C'MON!
C'MON!

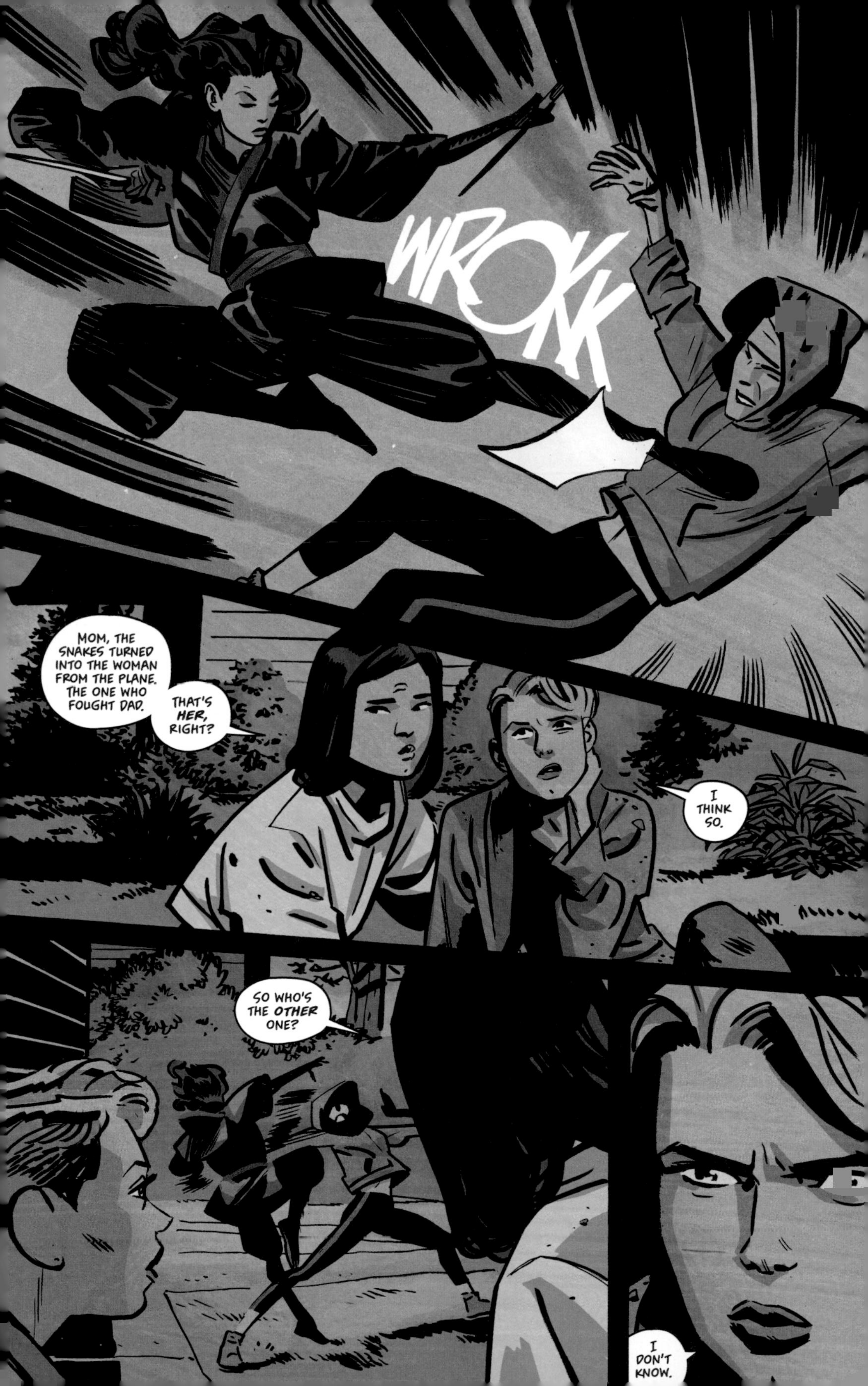
WROKK
MOM, THE SNAKES TURNED INTO THE WOMAN FROM THE PLANE. THE ONE WHO FOUGHT DAD.
THAT'S *HER*, RIGHT?
I THINK SO.
SO WHO'S THE *OTHER* ONE?
I DON'T KNOW.

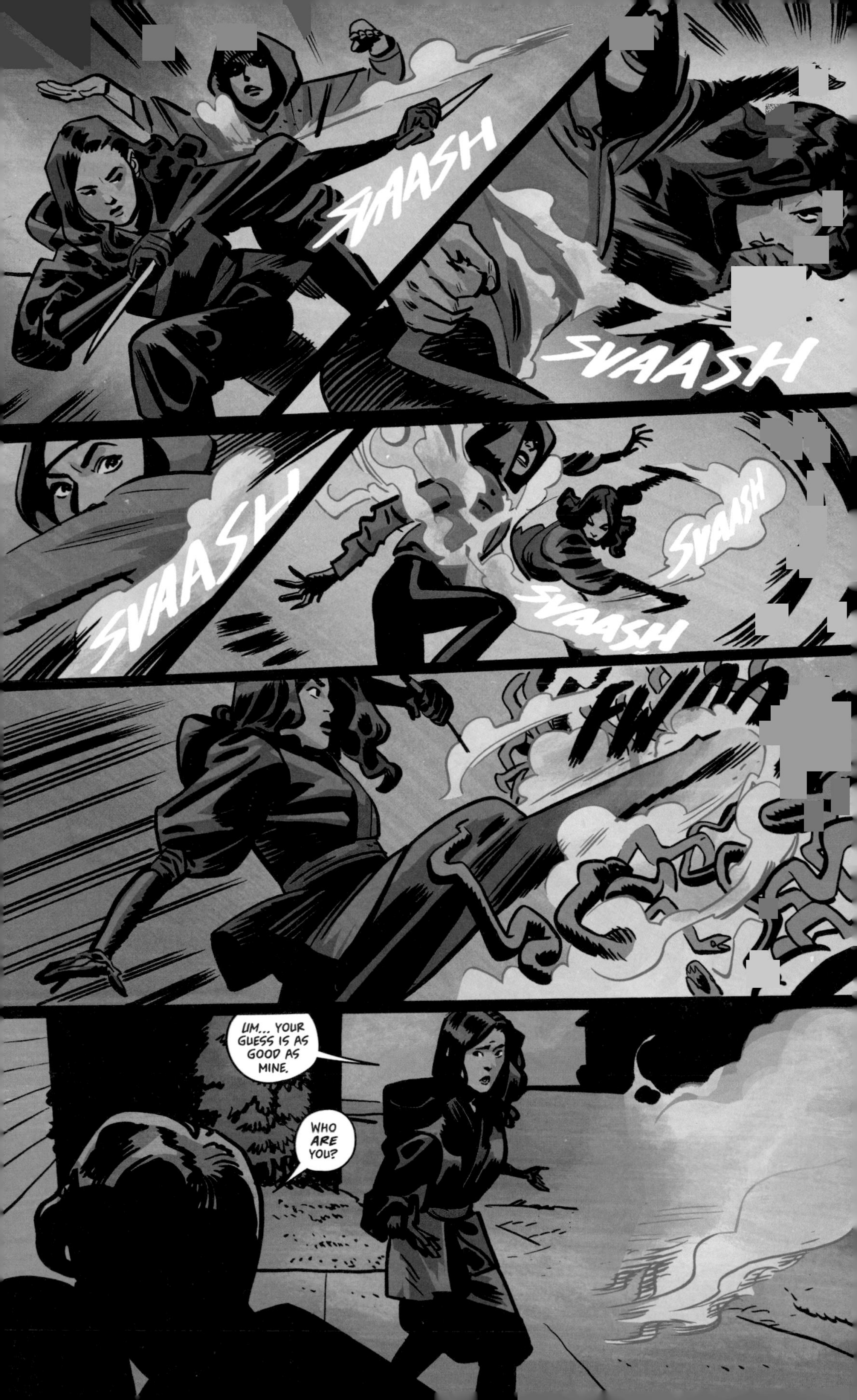
SVAASH
SVAASH
SVAASH
SVAASH
SVAASH
UM... YOUR GUESS IS AS GOOD AS MINE.
WHO ARE YOU?

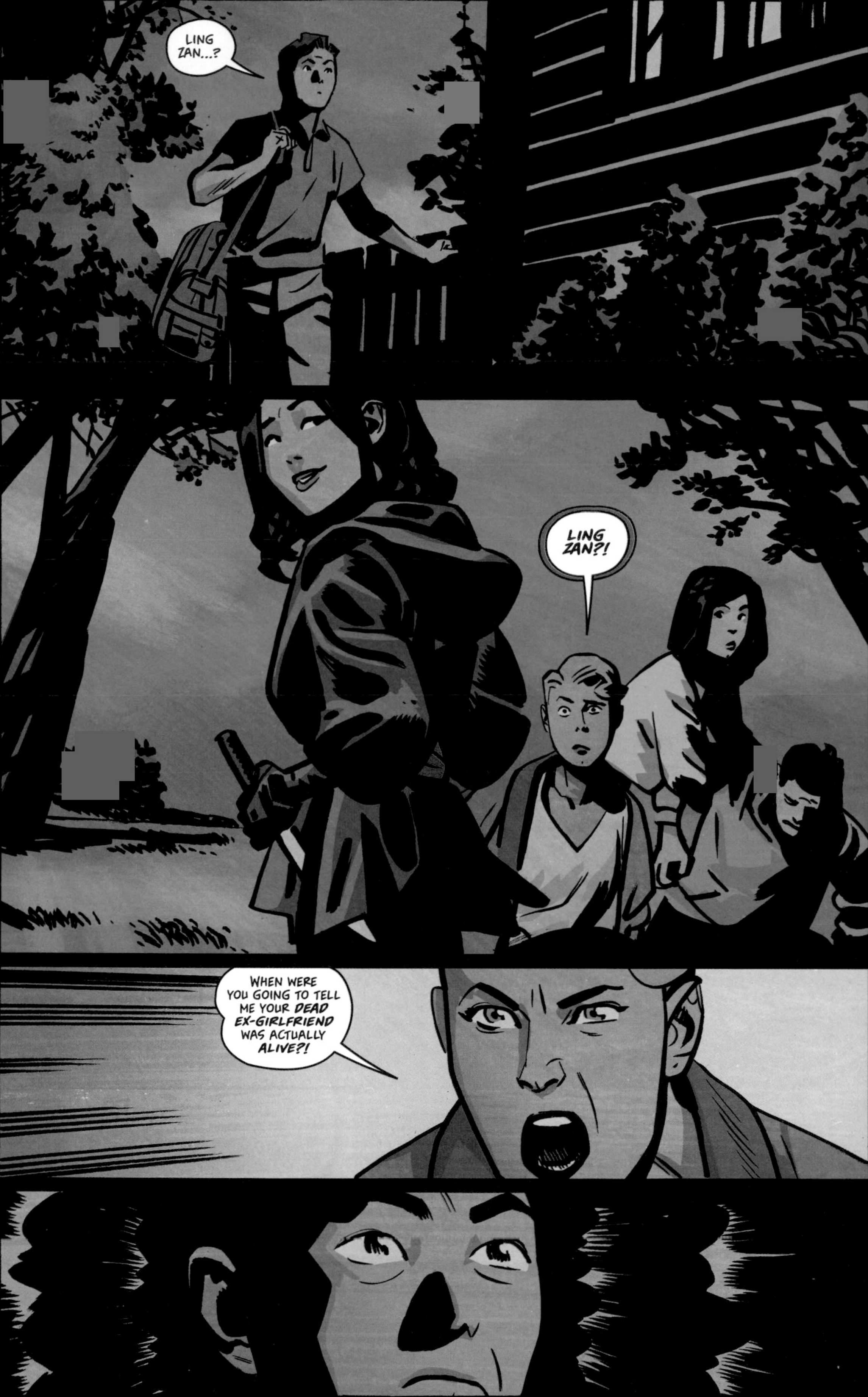
LING ZAN...?
LING ZAN?!
WHEN WERE YOU GOING TO TELL ME YOUR DEAD EX-GIRLFRIEND WAS ACTUALLY ALIVE?!

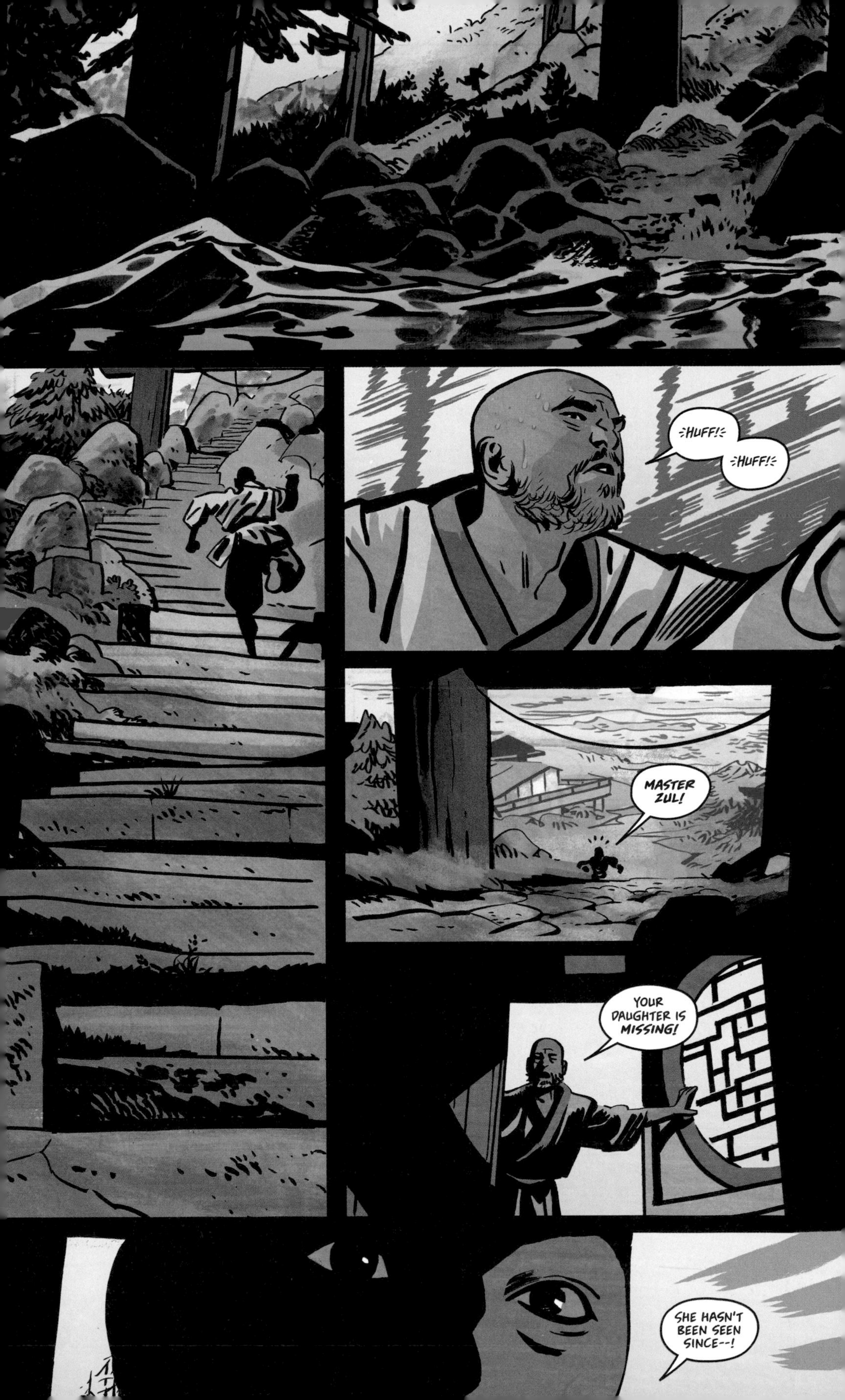
HUFF!
HUFF!
MASTER ZUL!
YOUR DAUGHTER IS MISSING!
SHE HASN'T BEEN SEEN SINCE--!

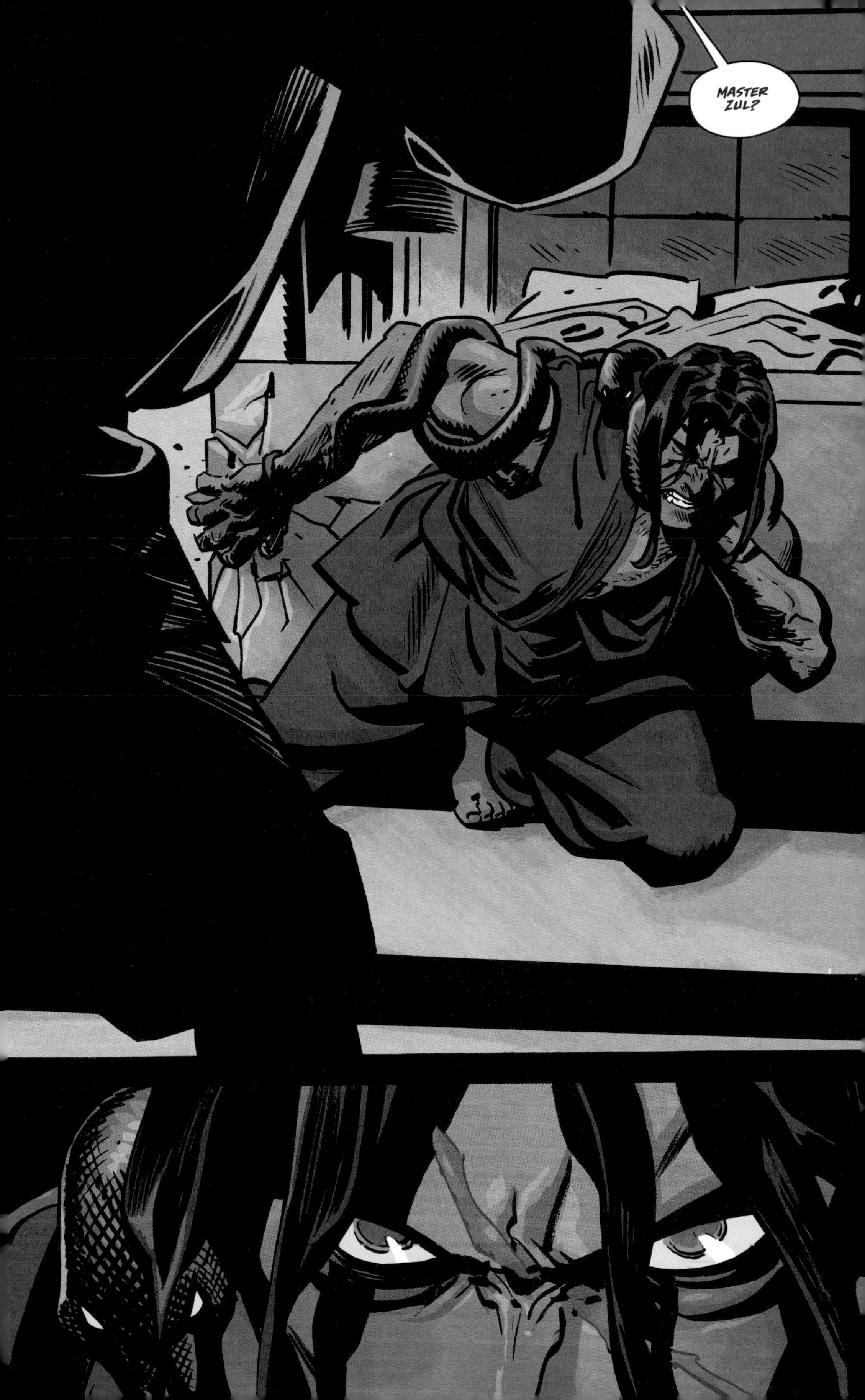
MASTER ZUL?

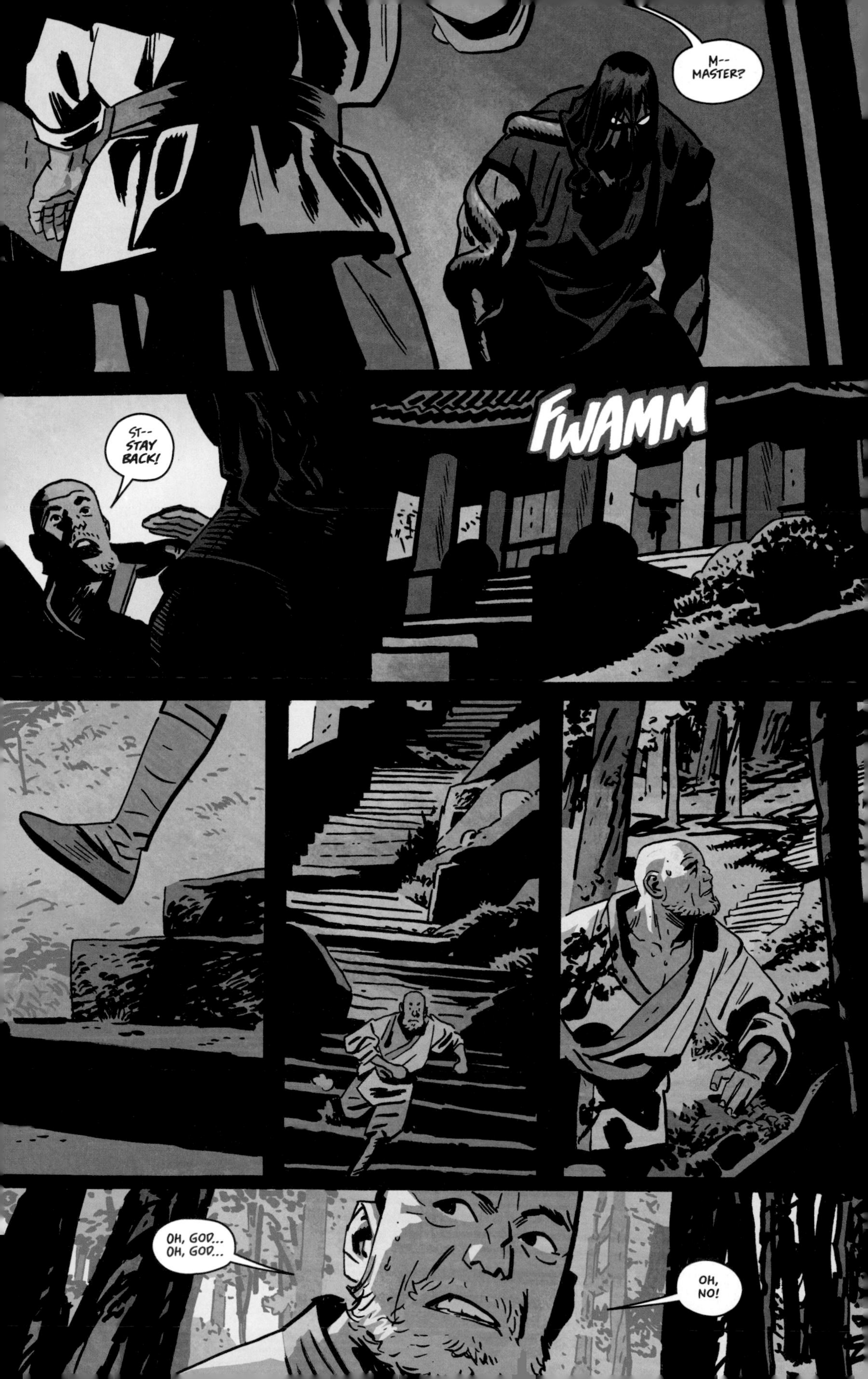
M--
MASTER?
ST--
STAY
BACK!
FWAMM
OH, GOD...
OH, GOD...
OH,
NO!

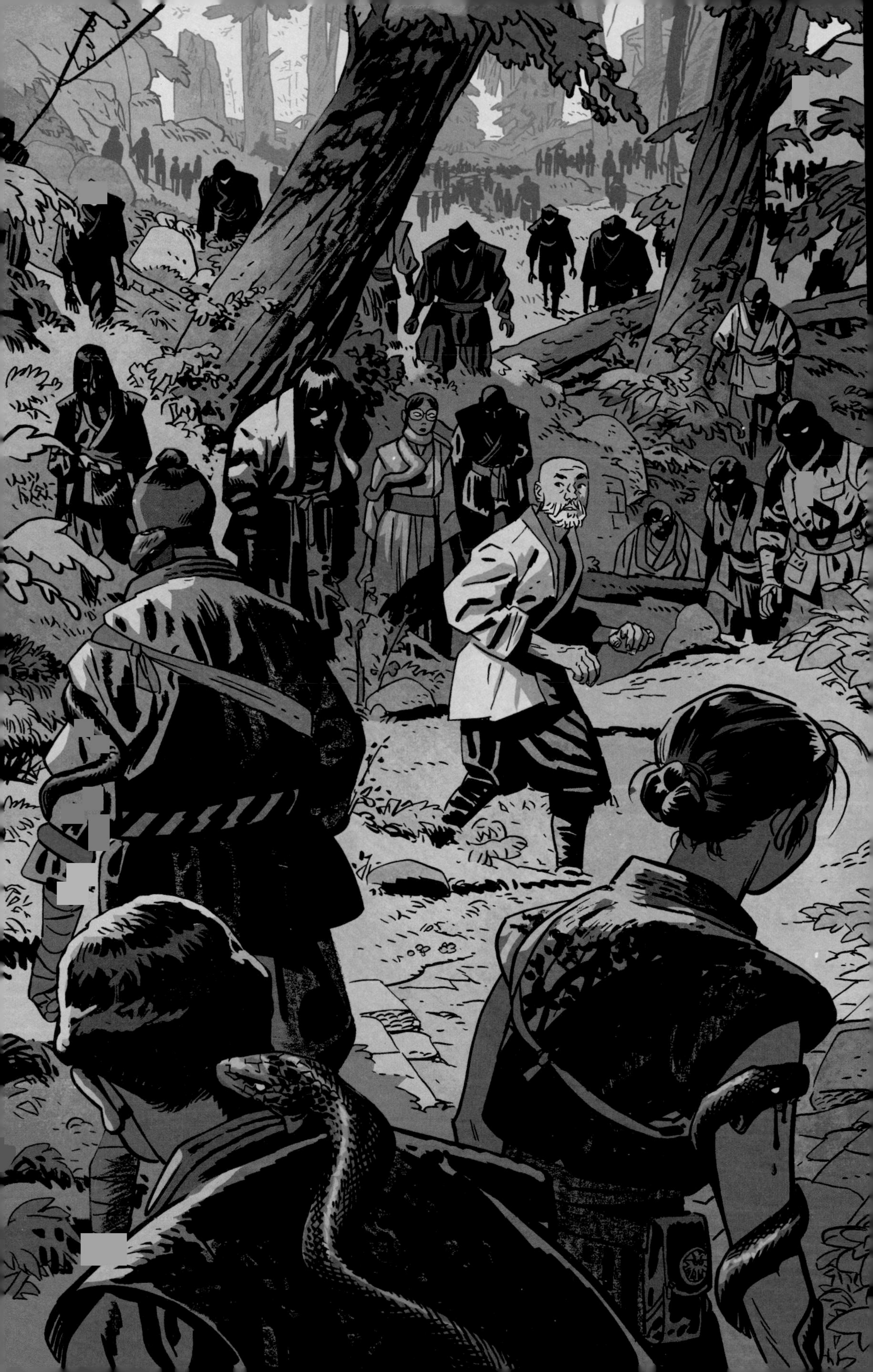

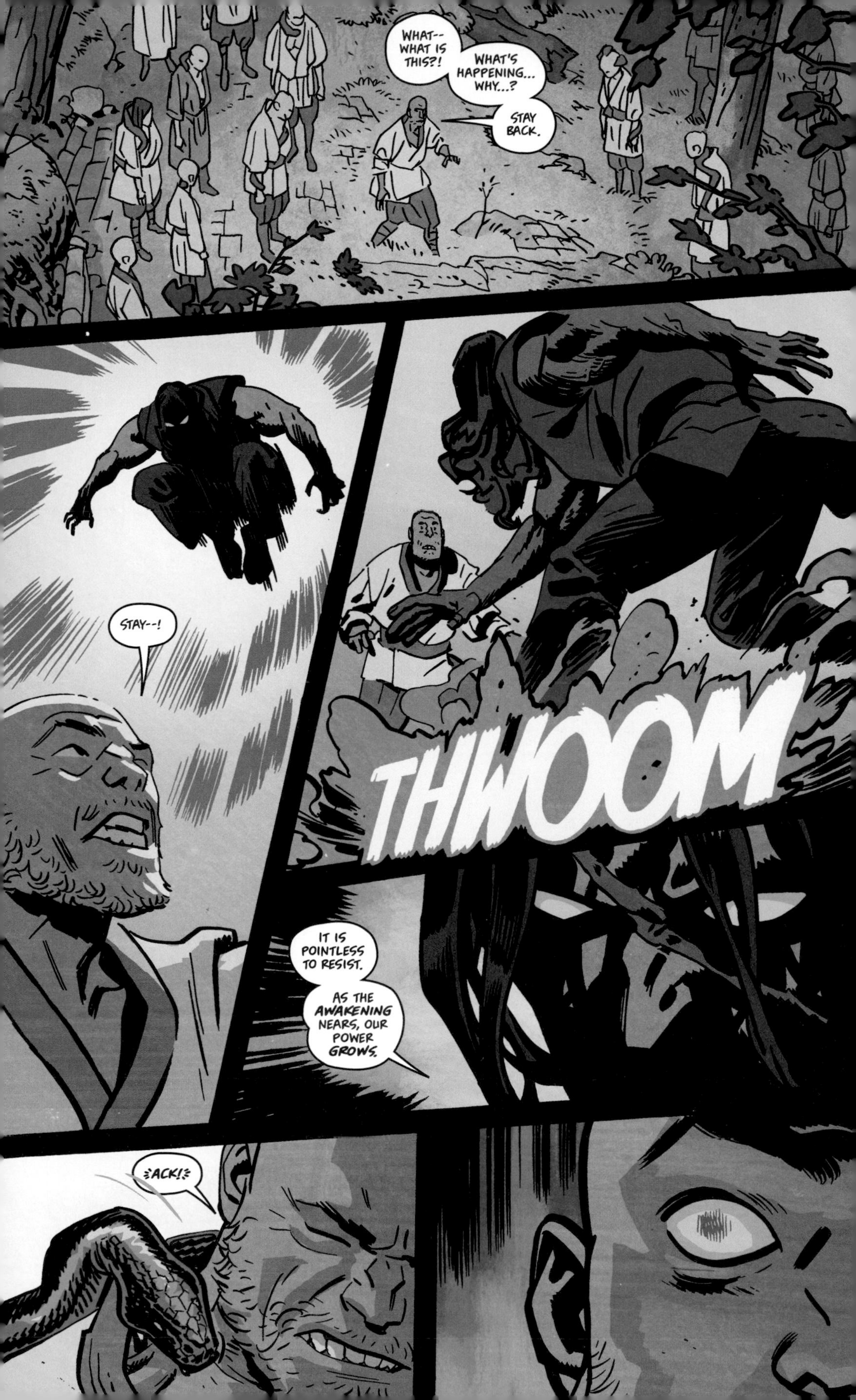
WHAT-- WHAT IS THIS?!
WHAT'S HAPPENING... WHY...?
STAY BACK.
STAY--!
THWOOM
IT IS POINTLESS TO RESIST.
AS THE AWAKENING NEARS, OUR POWER GROWS.
ACK!

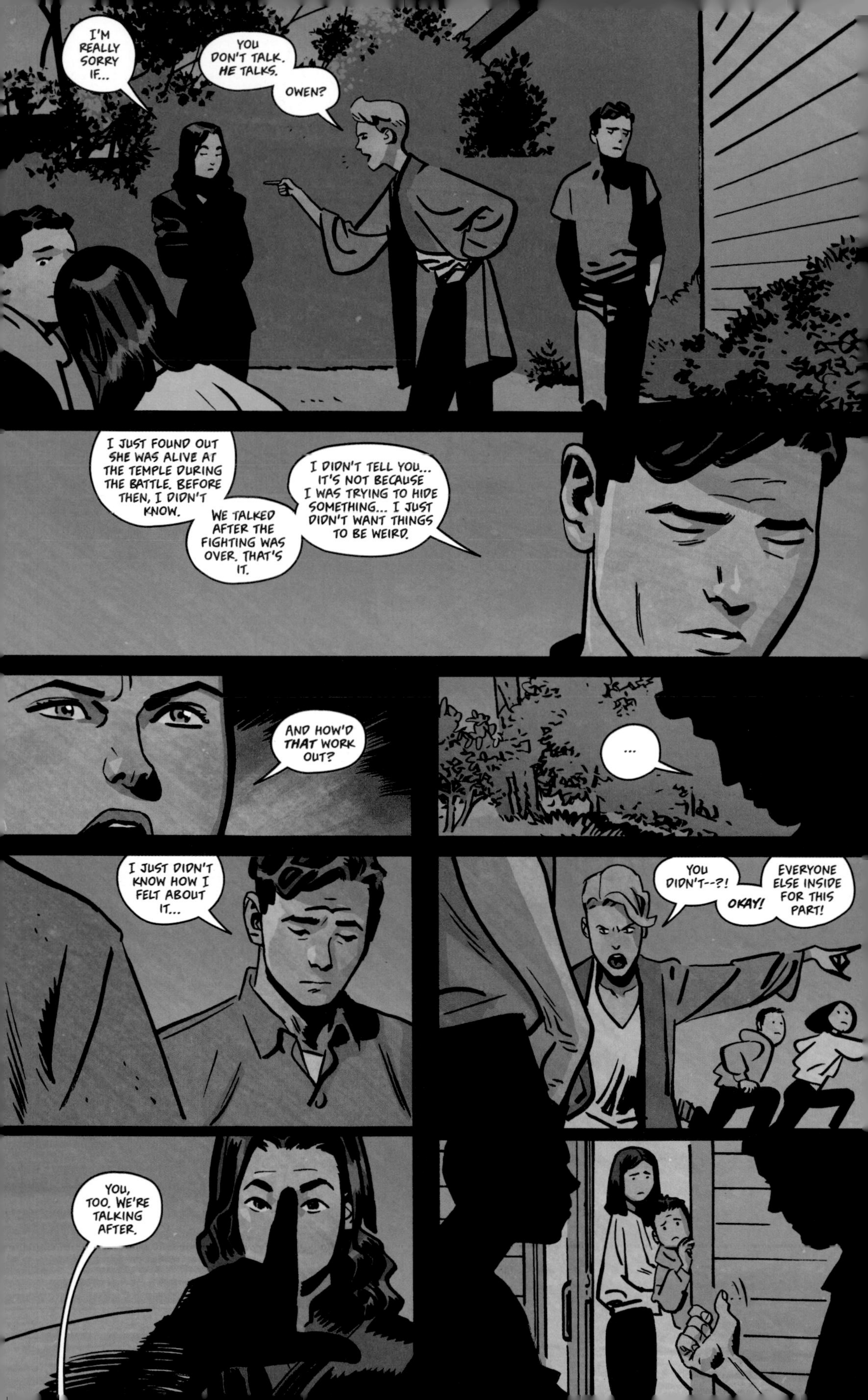
I'M REALLY SORRY IF...
YOU DON'T TALK. *HE* TALKS.
OWEN?
I JUST FOUND OUT SHE WAS ALIVE AT THE TEMPLE DURING THE BATTLE. BEFORE THEN, I DIDN'T KNOW.
WE TALKED AFTER THE FIGHTING WAS OVER. THAT'S IT.
I DIDN'T TELL YOU... IT'S NOT BECAUSE I WAS TRYING TO HIDE SOMETHING... I JUST DIDN'T WANT THINGS TO BE WEIRD.
AND HOW'D *THAT* WORK OUT?
...
I JUST DIDN'T KNOW HOW I FELT ABOUT IT...
YOU DIDN'T--?!
OKAY!
EVERYONE ELSE INSIDE FOR THIS PART!
YOU, TOO. WE'RE TALKING AFTER.

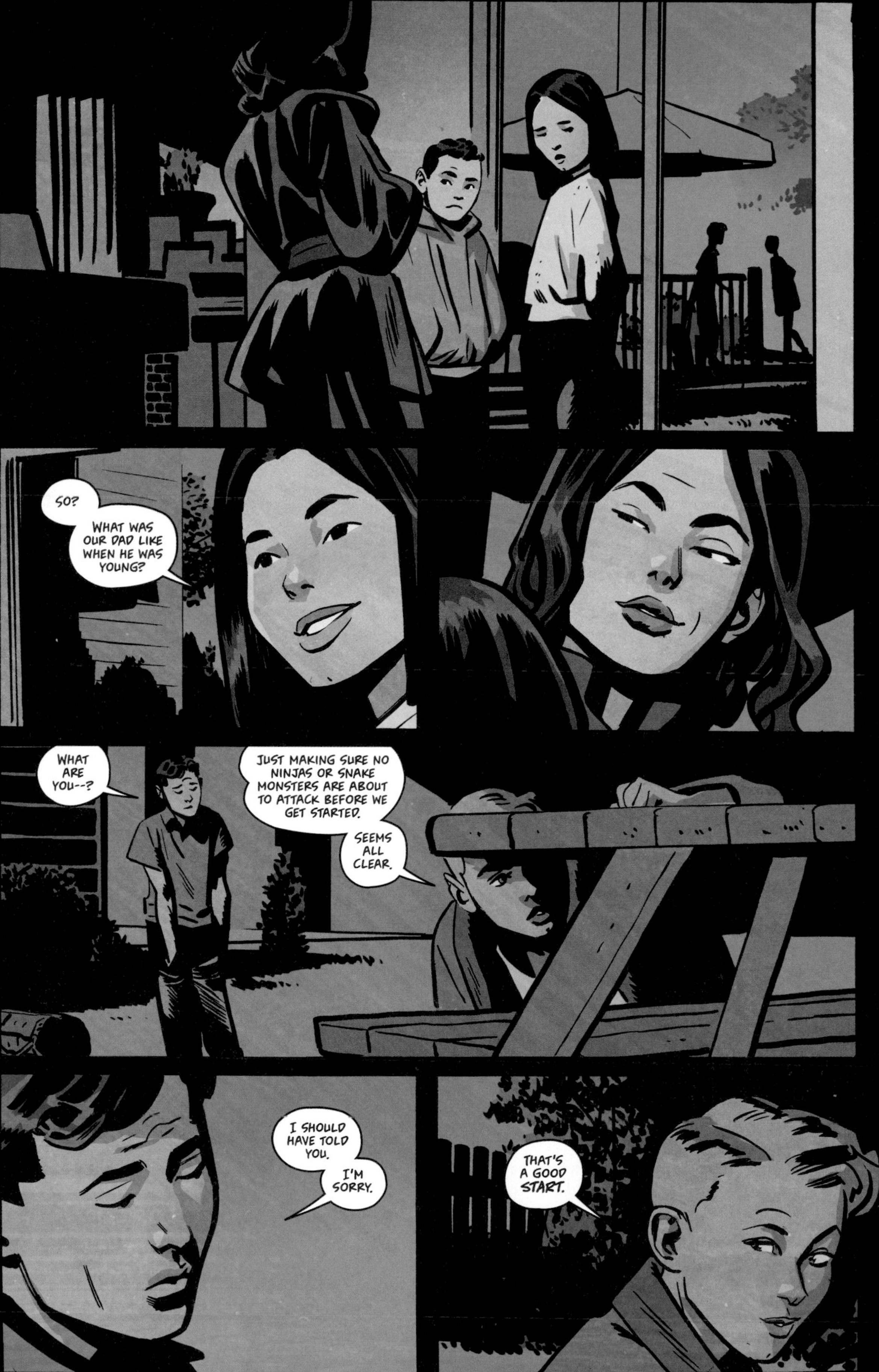
SO?
WHAT WAS OUR DAD LIKE WHEN HE WAS YOUNG?
WHAT ARE YOU--?
JUST MAKING SURE NO NINJAS OR SNAKE MONSTERS ARE ABOUT TO ATTACK BEFORE WE GET STARTED.
SEEMS ALL CLEAR.
I SHOULD HAVE TOLD YOU.
I'M SORRY.
THAT'S A GOOD START.

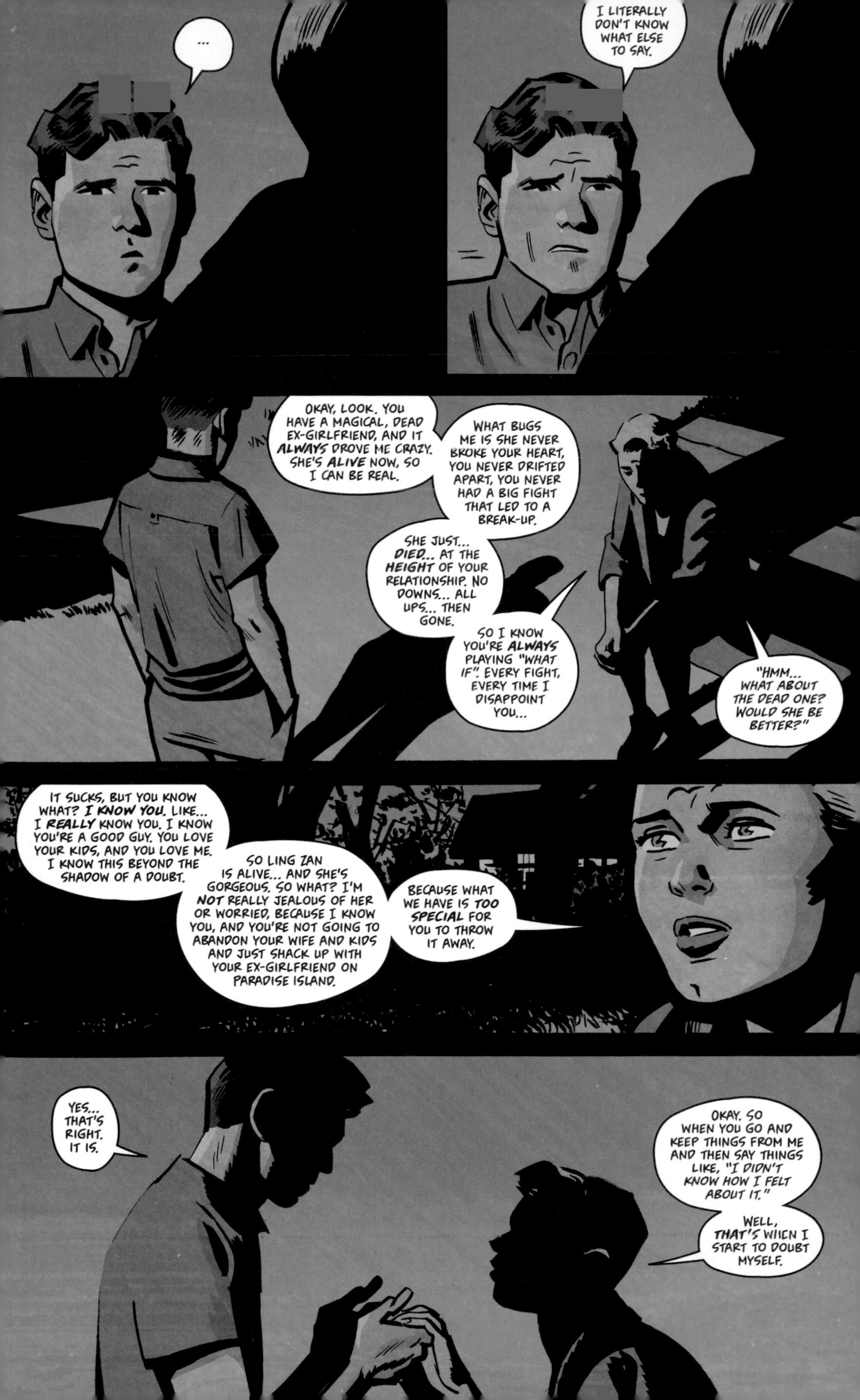
...
I LITERALLY DON'T KNOW WHAT ELSE TO SAY.
OKAY, LOOK. YOU HAVE A MAGICAL, DEAD EX-GIRLFRIEND, AND IT ALWAYS DROVE ME CRAZY. SHE'S ALIVE NOW, SO I CAN BE REAL.
WHAT BUGS ME IS SHE NEVER BROKE YOUR HEART, YOU NEVER DRIFTED APART, YOU NEVER HAD A BIG FIGHT THAT LED TO A BREAK-UP.
SHE JUST... DIED... AT THE HEIGHT OF YOUR RELATIONSHIP. NO DOWNS... ALL UPS... THEN GONE.
SO I KNOW YOU'RE ALWAYS PLAYING "WHAT IF". EVERY FIGHT, EVERY TIME I DISAPPOINT YOU...
"HMM... WHAT ABOUT THE DEAD ONE? WOULD SHE BE BETTER?"
IT SUCKS, BUT YOU KNOW WHAT? I KNOW YOU. LIKE... I REALLY KNOW YOU. I KNOW YOU'RE A GOOD GUY. YOU LOVE YOUR KIDS, AND YOU LOVE ME. I KNOW THIS BEYOND THE SHADOW OF A DOUBT.
SO LING ZAN IS ALIVE... AND SHE'S GORGEOUS. SO WHAT? I'M NOT REALLY JEALOUS OF HER OR WORRIED, BECAUSE I KNOW YOU, AND YOU'RE NOT GOING TO ABANDON YOUR WIFE AND KIDS AND JUST SHACK UP WITH YOUR EX-GIRLFRIEND ON PARADISE ISLAND.
BECAUSE WHAT WE HAVE IS TOO SPECIAL FOR YOU TO THROW IT AWAY.
YES... THAT'S RIGHT. IT IS.
OKAY. SO WHEN YOU GO AND KEEP THINGS FROM ME AND THEN SAY THINGS LIKE, "I DIDN'T KNOW HOW I FELT ABOUT IT."
WELL, THAT'S WHEN I START TO DOUBT MYSELF.

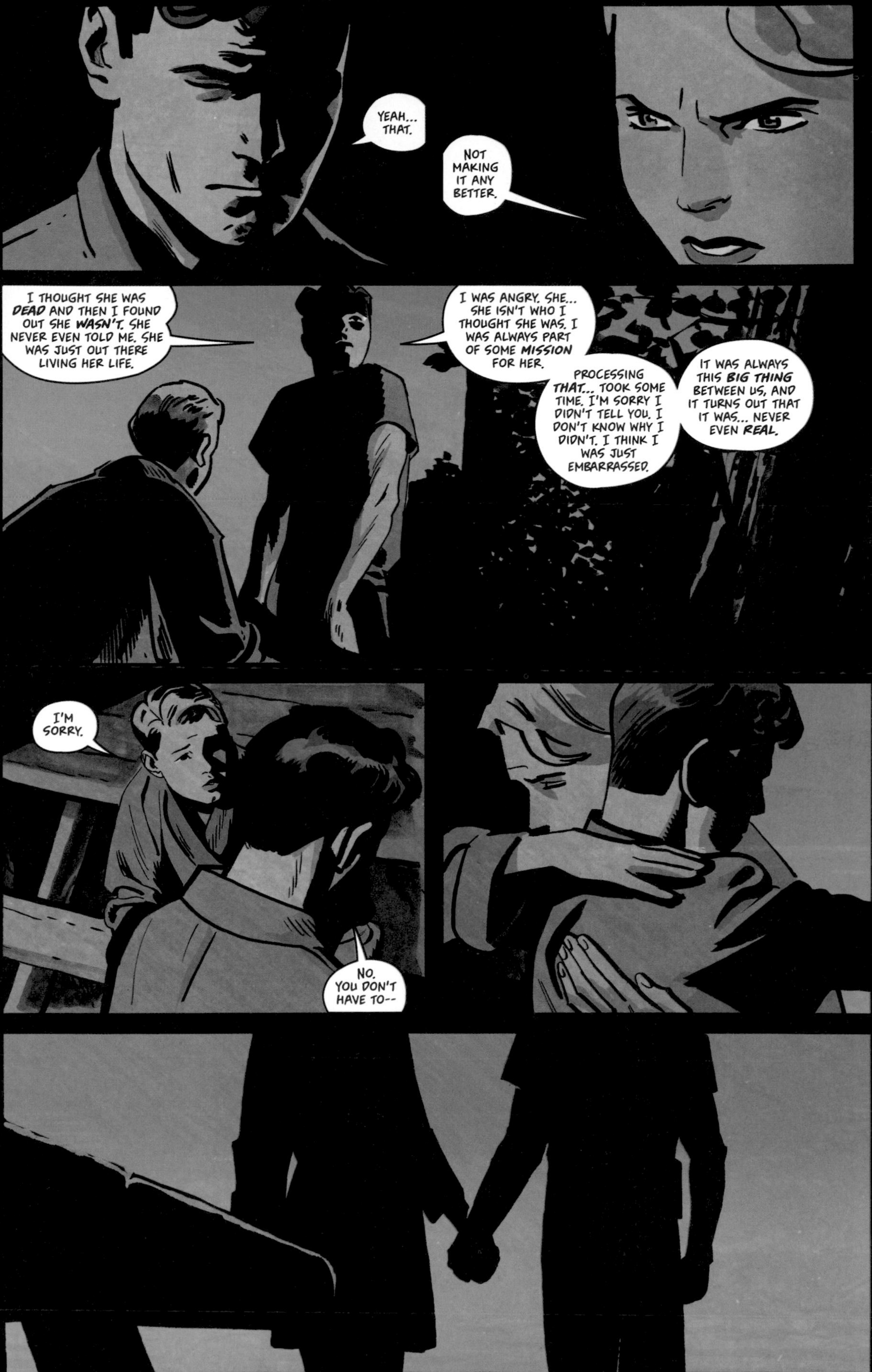
YEAH... THAT.
NOT MAKING IT ANY BETTER.
I THOUGHT SHE WAS **DEAD** AND THEN I FOUND OUT SHE **WASN'T**. SHE NEVER EVEN TOLD ME. SHE WAS JUST OUT THERE LIVING HER LIFE.
I WAS ANGRY. SHE... SHE ISN'T WHO I THOUGHT SHE WAS. I WAS ALWAYS PART OF SOME **MISSION** FOR HER.
PROCESSING **THAT...** TOOK SOME TIME. I'M SORRY I DIDN'T TELL YOU. I DON'T KNOW WHY I DIDN'T. I THINK I WAS JUST EMBARRASSED.
IT WAS ALWAYS THIS **BIG THING** BETWEEN US, AND IT TURNS OUT THAT IT WAS... NEVER EVEN **REAL**.
I'M SORRY.
NO. YOU DON'T HAVE TO--

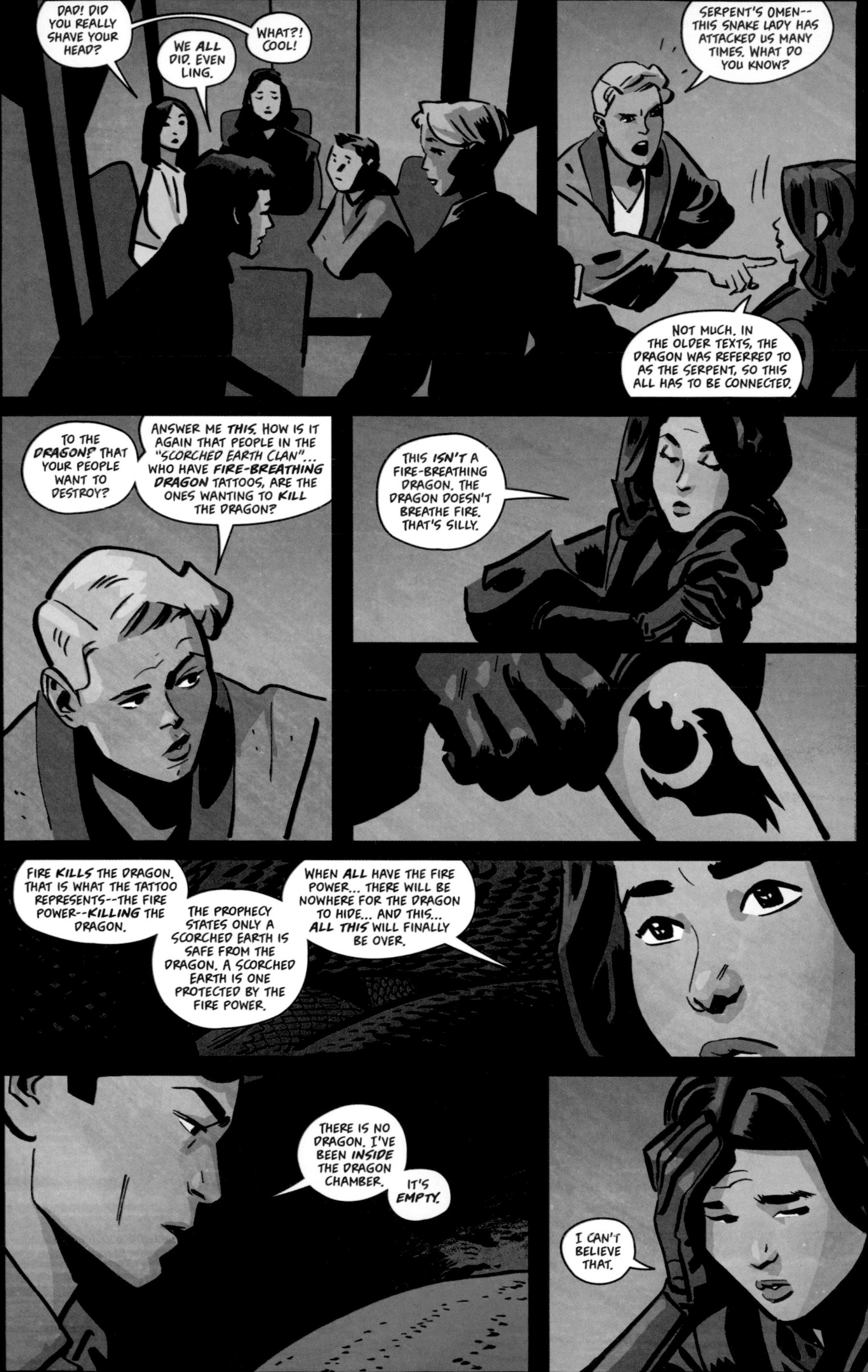
DAD! DID YOU REALLY SHAVE YOUR HEAD?
WE ALL DID. EVEN LING.
WHAT?! COOL!
SERPENT'S OMEN-- THIS SNAKE LADY HAS ATTACKED US MANY TIMES. WHAT DO YOU KNOW?
NOT MUCH. IN THE OLDER TEXTS, THE DRAGON WAS REFERRED TO AS THE SERPENT, SO THIS ALL HAS TO BE CONNECTED.
TO THE DRAGON? THAT YOUR PEOPLE WANT TO DESTROY?
ANSWER ME THIS. HOW IS IT AGAIN THAT PEOPLE IN THE "SCORCHED EARTH CLAN"... WHO HAVE FIRE-BREATHING DRAGON TATTOOS, ARE THE ONES WANTING TO KILL THE DRAGON?
THIS ISN'T A FIRE-BREATHING DRAGON. THE DRAGON DOESN'T BREATHE FIRE. THAT'S SILLY.
FIRE KILLS THE DRAGON. THAT IS WHAT THE TATTOO REPRESENTS--THE FIRE POWER--KILLING THE DRAGON.
THE PROPHECY STATES ONLY A SCORCHED EARTH IS SAFE FROM THE DRAGON. A SCORCHED EARTH IS ONE PROTECTED BY THE FIRE POWER.
WHEN ALL HAVE THE FIRE POWER... THERE WILL BE NOWHERE FOR THE DRAGON TO HIDE... AND THIS... ALL THIS WILL FINALLY BE OVER.
THERE IS NO DRAGON. I'VE BEEN INSIDE THE DRAGON CHAMBER.
IT'S EMPTY.
I CAN'T BELIEVE THAT.

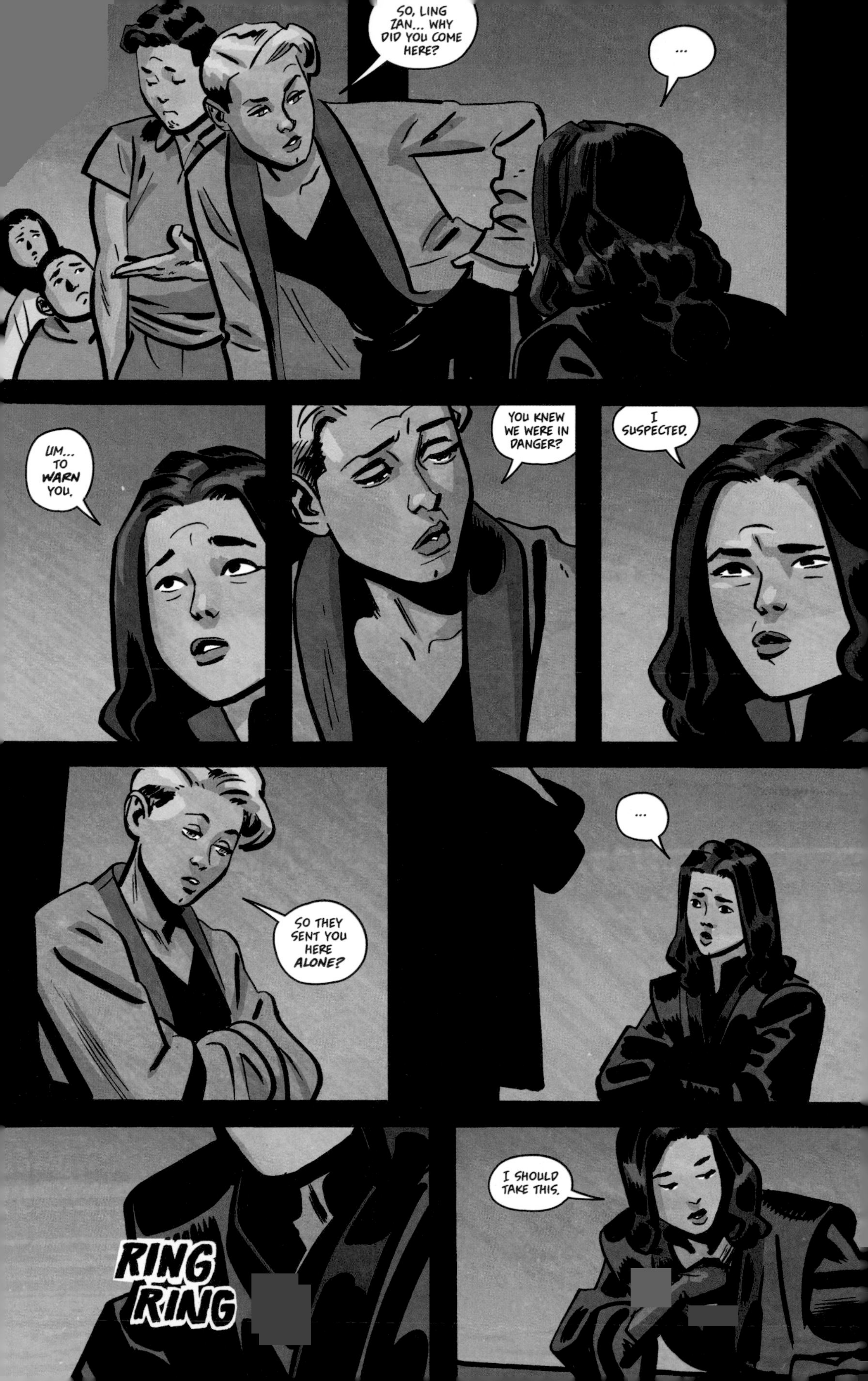
SO, LING ZAN... WHY DID YOU COME HERE?
...
UM... TO WARN YOU.
YOU KNEW WE WERE IN DANGER?
I SUSPECTED.
SO THEY SENT YOU HERE ALONE?
...
RING
RING
I SHOULD TAKE THIS.

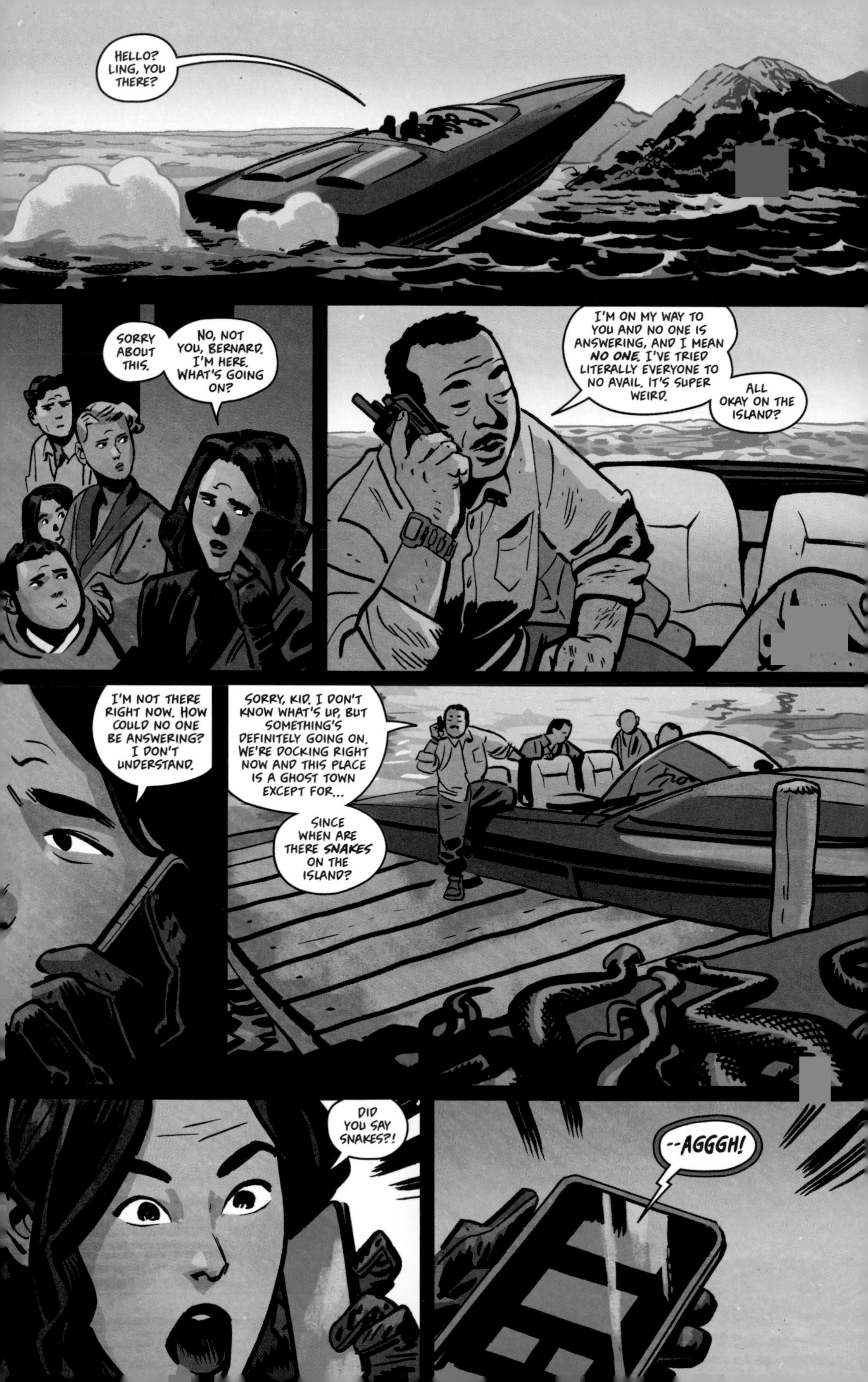
HELLO? LING, YOU THERE?
SORRY ABOUT THIS.
NO, NOT YOU, BERNARD. I'M HERE. WHAT'S GOING ON?
I'M ON MY WAY TO YOU AND NO ONE IS ANSWERING, AND I MEAN *NO ONE*. I'VE TRIED LITERALLY EVERYONE TO NO AVAIL. IT'S SUPER WEIRD.
ALL OKAY ON THE ISLAND?
I'M NOT THERE RIGHT NOW. HOW COULD NO ONE BE ANSWERING? I DON'T UNDERSTAND.
SORRY, KID. I DON'T KNOW WHAT'S UP, BUT SOMETHING'S DEFINITELY GOING ON. WE'RE DOCKING RIGHT NOW AND THIS PLACE IS A GHOST TOWN EXCEPT FOR...
SINCE WHEN ARE THERE *SNAKES* ON THE ISLAND?
DID YOU SAY SNAKES?!
--AGGGH!

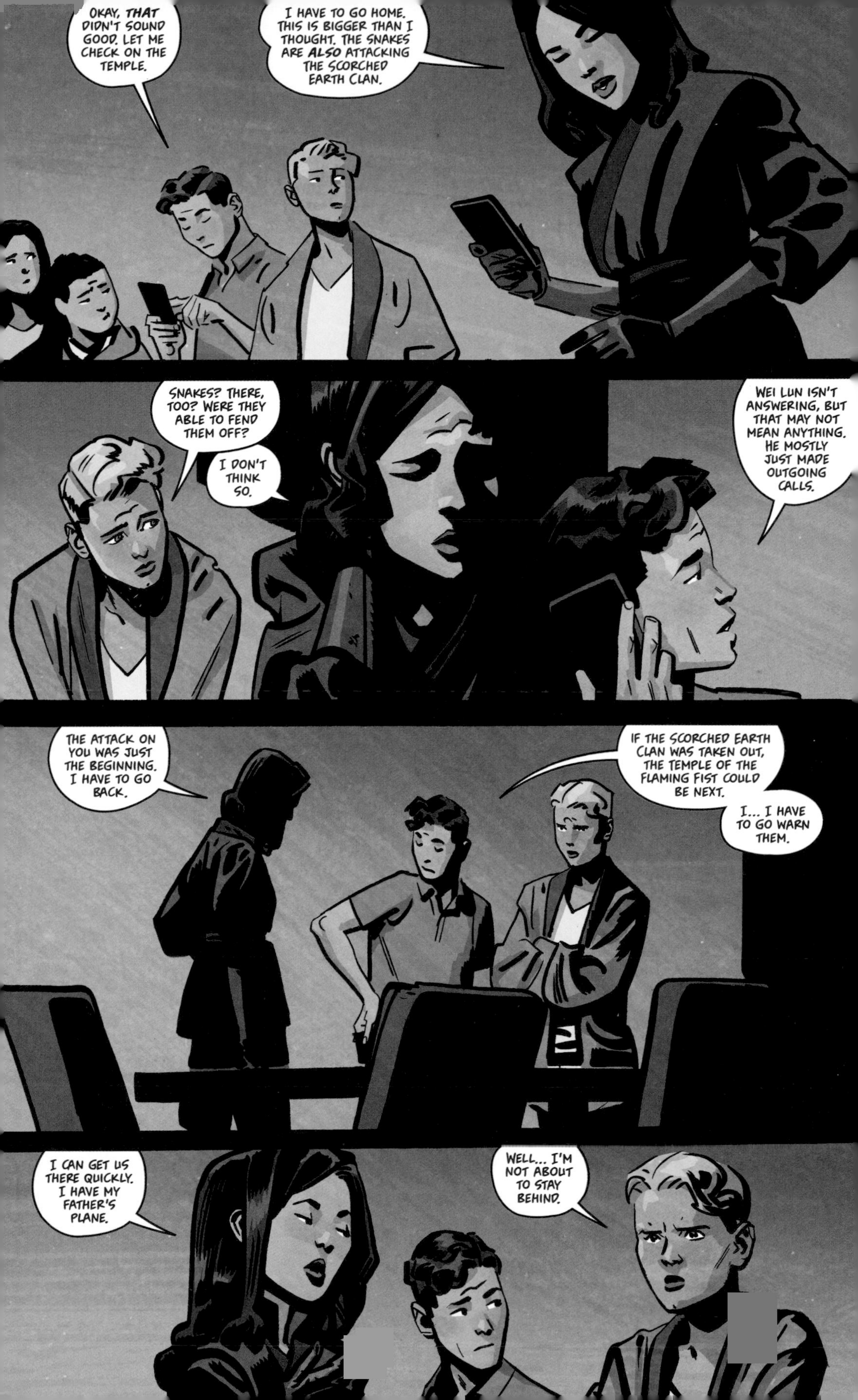
OKAY, THAT DIDN'T SOUND GOOD. LET ME CHECK ON THE TEMPLE.
I HAVE TO GO HOME. THIS IS BIGGER THAN I THOUGHT. THE SNAKES ARE ALSO ATTACKING THE SCORCHED EARTH CLAN.
SNAKES? THERE, TOO? WERE THEY ABLE TO FEND THEM OFF?
I DON'T THINK SO.
WEI LUN ISN'T ANSWERING, BUT THAT MAY NOT MEAN ANYTHING. HE MOSTLY JUST MADE OUTGOING CALLS.
THE ATTACK ON YOU WAS JUST THE BEGINNING. I HAVE TO GO BACK.
IF THE SCORCHED EARTH CLAN WAS TAKEN OUT, THE TEMPLE OF THE FLAMING FIST COULD BE NEXT.
I... I HAVE TO GO WARN THEM.
I CAN GET US THERE QUICKLY. I HAVE MY FATHER'S PLANE.
WELL... I'M NOT ABOUT TO STAY BEHIND.

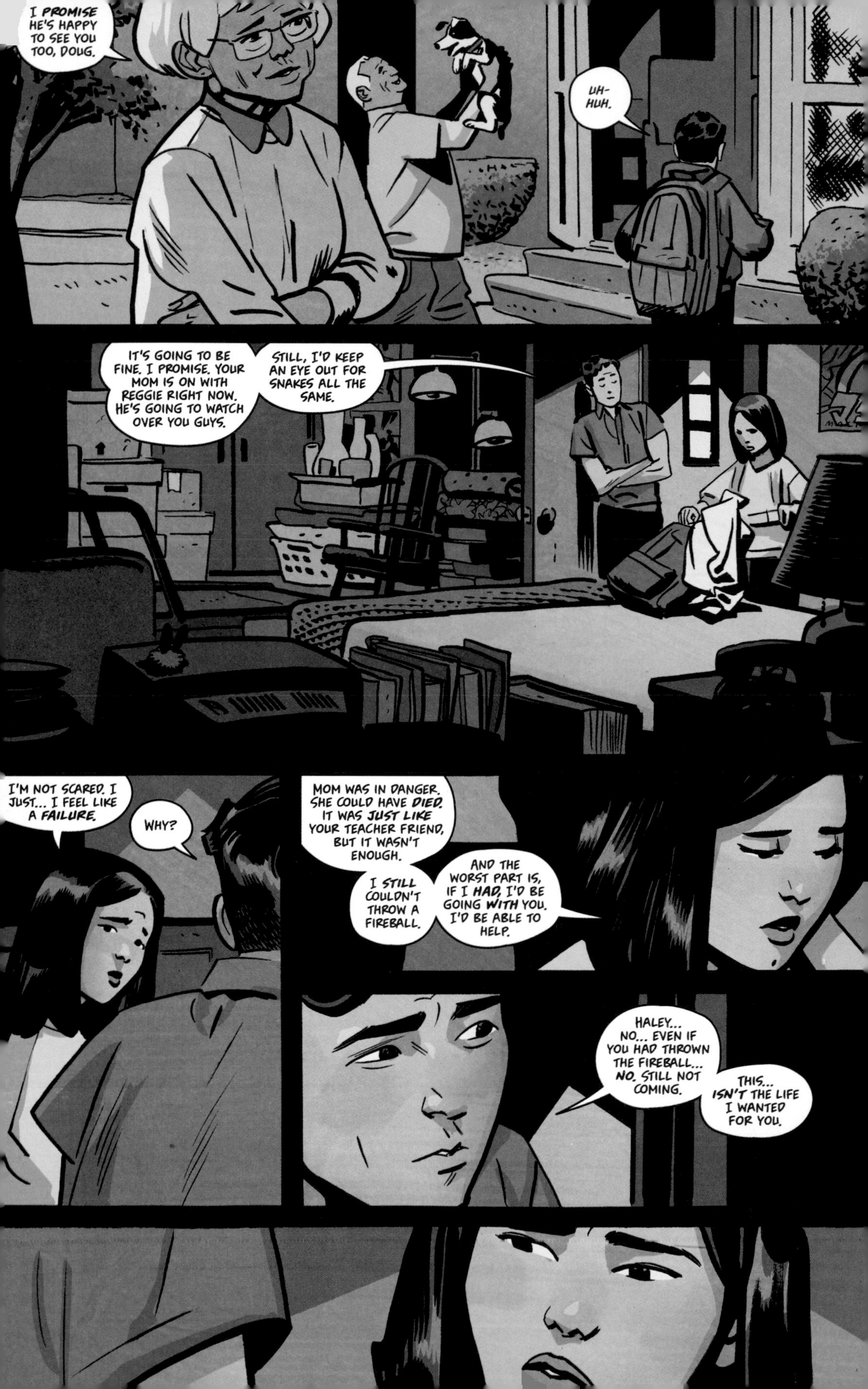
I PROMISE HE'S HAPPY TO SEE YOU TOO, DOUG.
UH-HUH.
IT'S GOING TO BE FINE. I PROMISE. YOUR MOM IS ON WITH REGGIE RIGHT NOW. HE'S GOING TO WATCH OVER YOU GUYS.
STILL, I'D KEEP AN EYE OUT FOR SNAKES ALL THE SAME.
I'M NOT SCARED. I JUST... I FEEL LIKE A FAILURE.
WHY?
MOM WAS IN DANGER. SHE COULD HAVE DIED. IT WAS JUST LIKE YOUR TEACHER FRIEND, BUT IT WASN'T ENOUGH.
I STILL COULDN'T THROW A FIREBALL.
AND THE WORST PART IS, IF I HAD, I'D BE GOING WITH YOU. I'D BE ABLE TO HELP.
HALEY... NO... EVEN IF YOU HAD THROWN THE FIREBALL... NO. STILL NOT COMING.
THIS... ISN'T THE LIFE I WANTED FOR YOU.

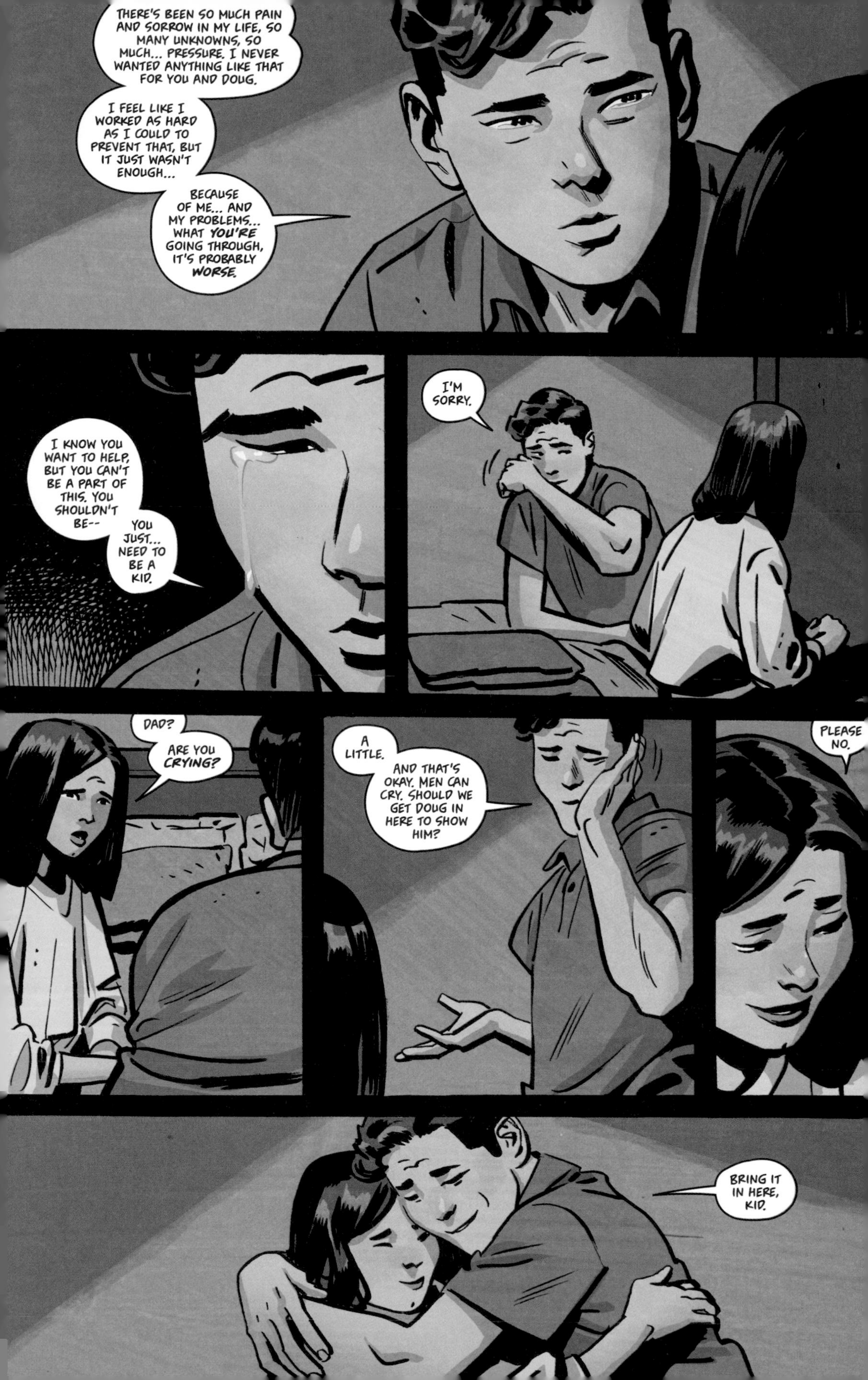
THERE'S BEEN SO MUCH PAIN AND SORROW IN MY LIFE, SO MANY UNKNOWNS, SO MUCH... PRESSURE. I NEVER WANTED ANYTHING LIKE THAT FOR YOU AND DOUG.
I FEEL LIKE I WORKED AS HARD AS I COULD TO PREVENT THAT, BUT IT JUST WASN'T ENOUGH...
BECAUSE OF ME... AND MY PROBLEMS... WHAT YOU'RE GOING THROUGH, IT'S PROBABLY WORSE.
I KNOW YOU WANT TO HELP, BUT YOU CAN'T BE A PART OF THIS. YOU SHOULDN'T BE--
YOU JUST... NEED TO BE A KID.
I'M SORRY.
DAD?
ARE YOU CRYING?
A LITTLE.
AND THAT'S OKAY. MEN CAN CRY. SHOULD WE GET DOUG IN HERE TO SHOW HIM?
PLEASE NO.
BRING IT IN HERE, KID.

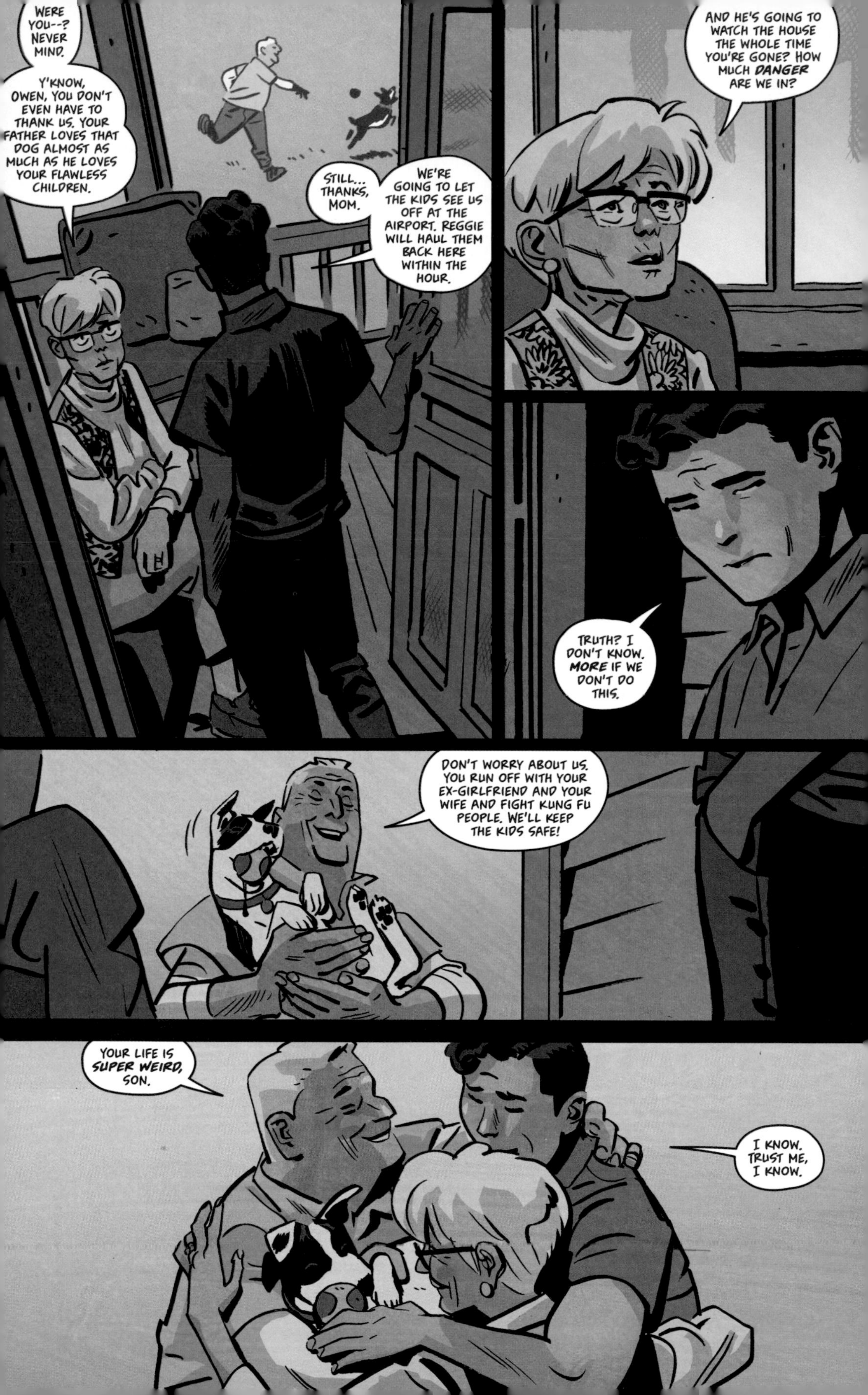
WERE YOU--? NEVER MIND.
Y'KNOW, OWEN, YOU DON'T EVEN HAVE TO THANK US. YOUR FATHER LOVES THAT DOG ALMOST AS MUCH AS HE LOVES YOUR FLAWLESS CHILDREN.
STILL... THANKS, MOM.
WE'RE GOING TO LET THE KIDS SEE US OFF AT THE AIRPORT. REGGIE WILL HAUL THEM BACK HERE WITHIN THE HOUR.
AND HE'S GOING TO WATCH THE HOUSE THE WHOLE TIME YOU'RE GONE? HOW MUCH DANGER ARE WE IN?
TRUTH? I DON'T KNOW. MORE IF WE DON'T DO THIS.
DON'T WORRY ABOUT US. YOU RUN OFF WITH YOUR EX-GIRLFRIEND AND YOUR WIFE AND FIGHT KUNG FU PEOPLE. WE'LL KEEP THE KIDS SAFE!
YOUR LIFE IS SUPER WEIRD, SON.
I KNOW. TRUST ME, I KNOW.

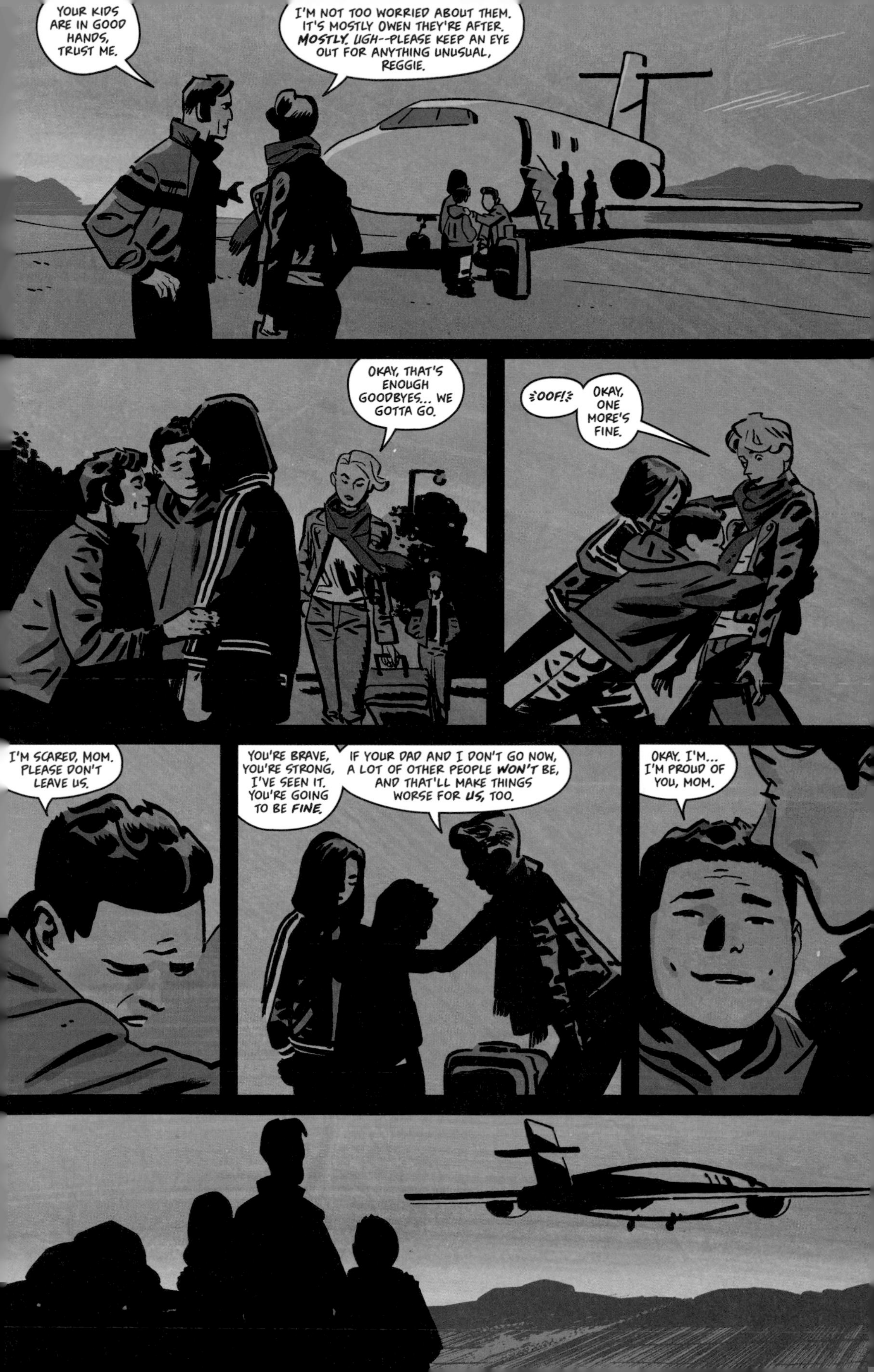
YOUR KIDS ARE IN GOOD HANDS, TRUST ME.
I'M NOT TOO WORRIED ABOUT THEM. IT'S MOSTLY OWEN THEY'RE AFTER. MOSTLY. UGH--PLEASE KEEP AN EYE OUT FOR ANYTHING UNUSUAL, REGGIE.
OKAY, THAT'S ENOUGH GOODBYES... WE GOTTA GO.
OOF!
OKAY, ONE MORE'S FINE.
I'M SCARED, MOM. PLEASE DON'T LEAVE US.
YOU'RE BRAVE, YOU'RE STRONG, I'VE SEEN IT. YOU'RE GOING TO BE FINE.
IF YOUR DAD AND I DON'T GO NOW, A LOT OF OTHER PEOPLE WON'T BE, AND THAT'LL MAKE THINGS WORSE FOR US, TOO.
OKAY. I'M... I'M PROUD OF YOU, MOM.

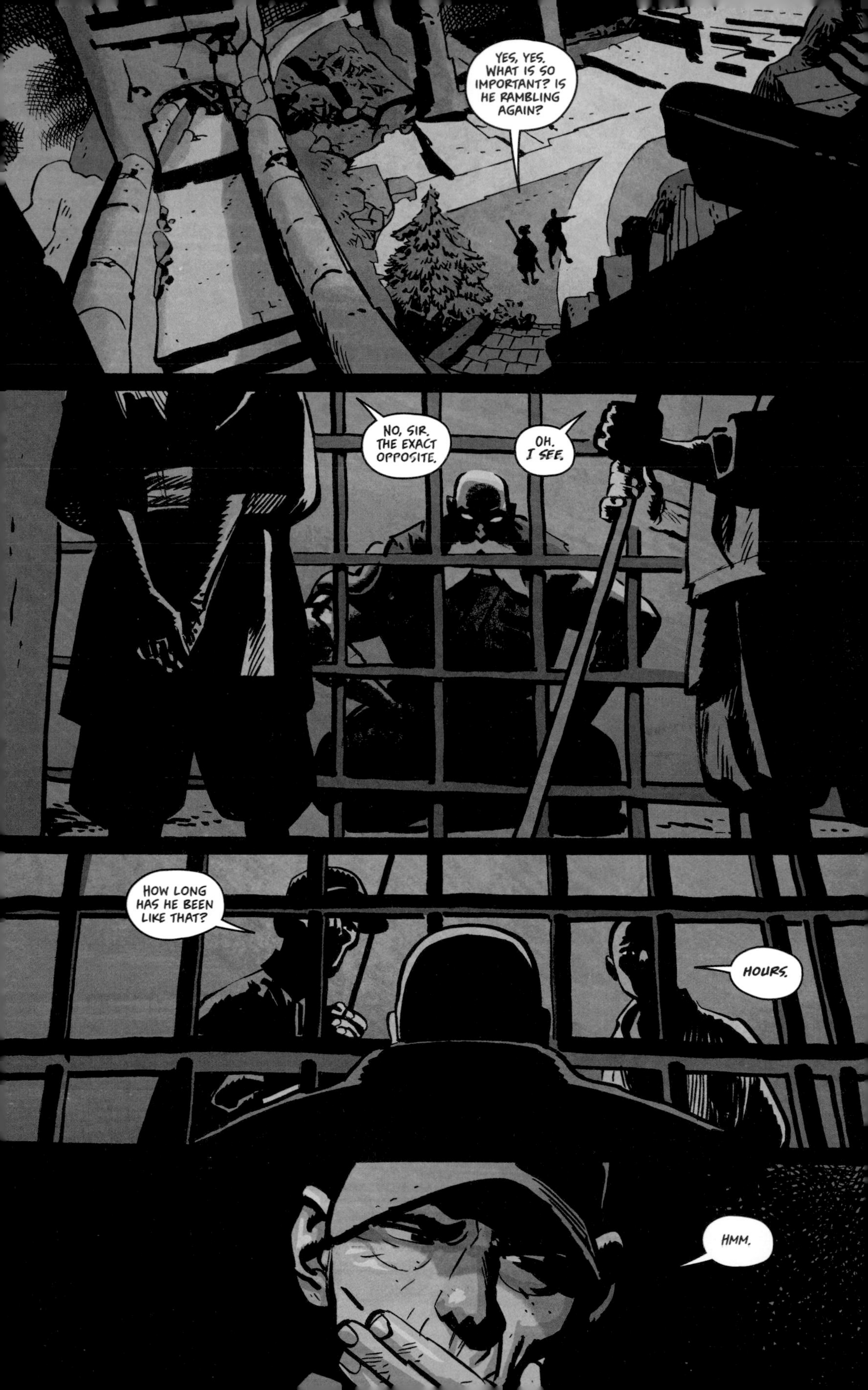
YES, YES. WHAT IS SO IMPORTANT? IS HE RAMBLING AGAIN?
NO, SIR. THE EXACT OPPOSITE.
OH. I SEE.
HOW LONG HAS HE BEEN LIKE THAT?
HOURS.
HMM.

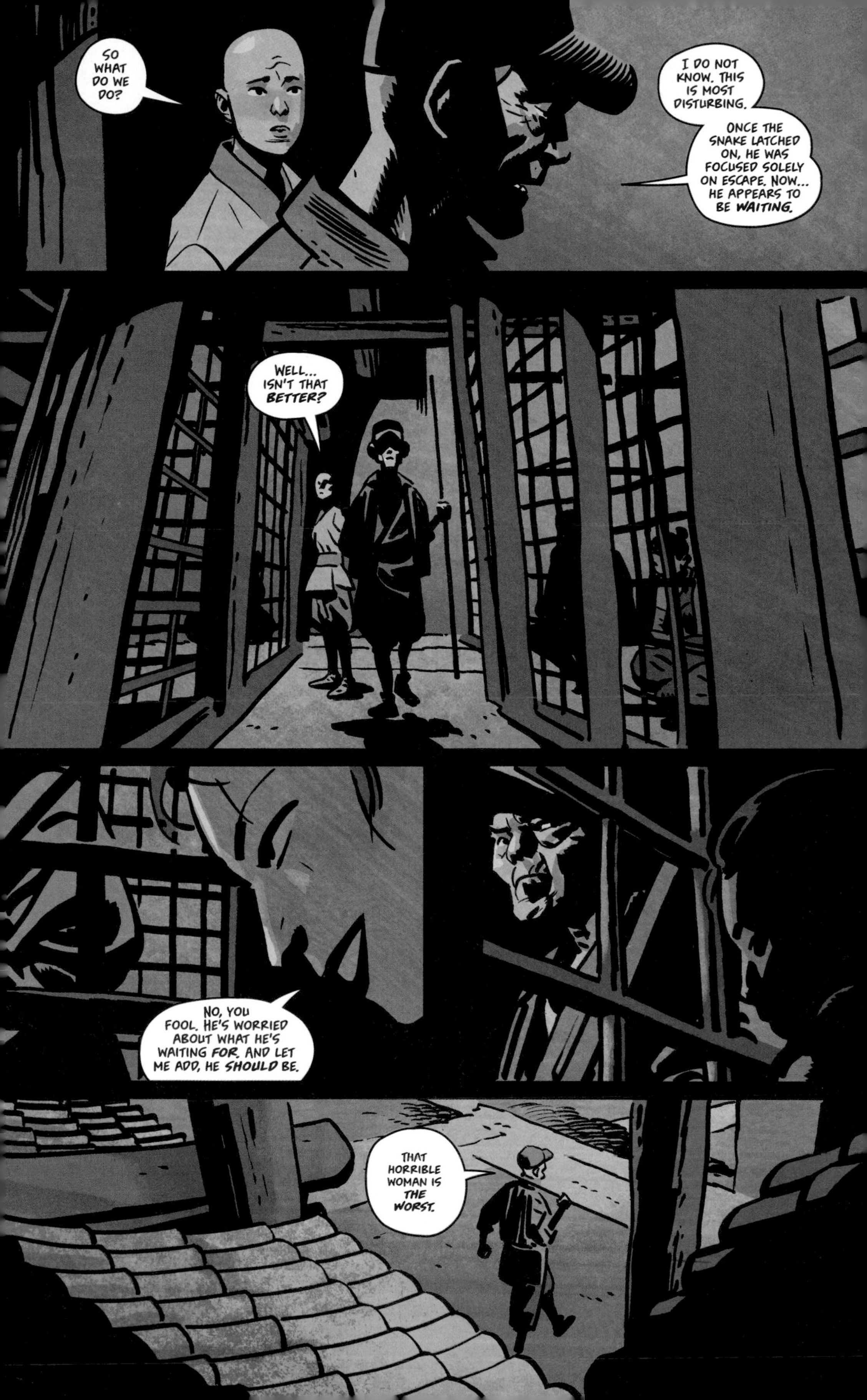
SO WHAT DO WE DO?
I DO NOT KNOW. THIS IS MOST DISTURBING.
ONCE THE SNAKE LATCHED ON, HE WAS FOCUSED SOLELY ON ESCAPE. NOW... HE APPEARS TO BE WAITING.
WELL... ISN'T THAT BETTER?
NO, YOU FOOL. HE'S WORRIED ABOUT WHAT HE'S WAITING FOR. AND LET ME ADD, HE SHOULD BE.
THAT HORRIBLE WOMAN IS THE WORST.

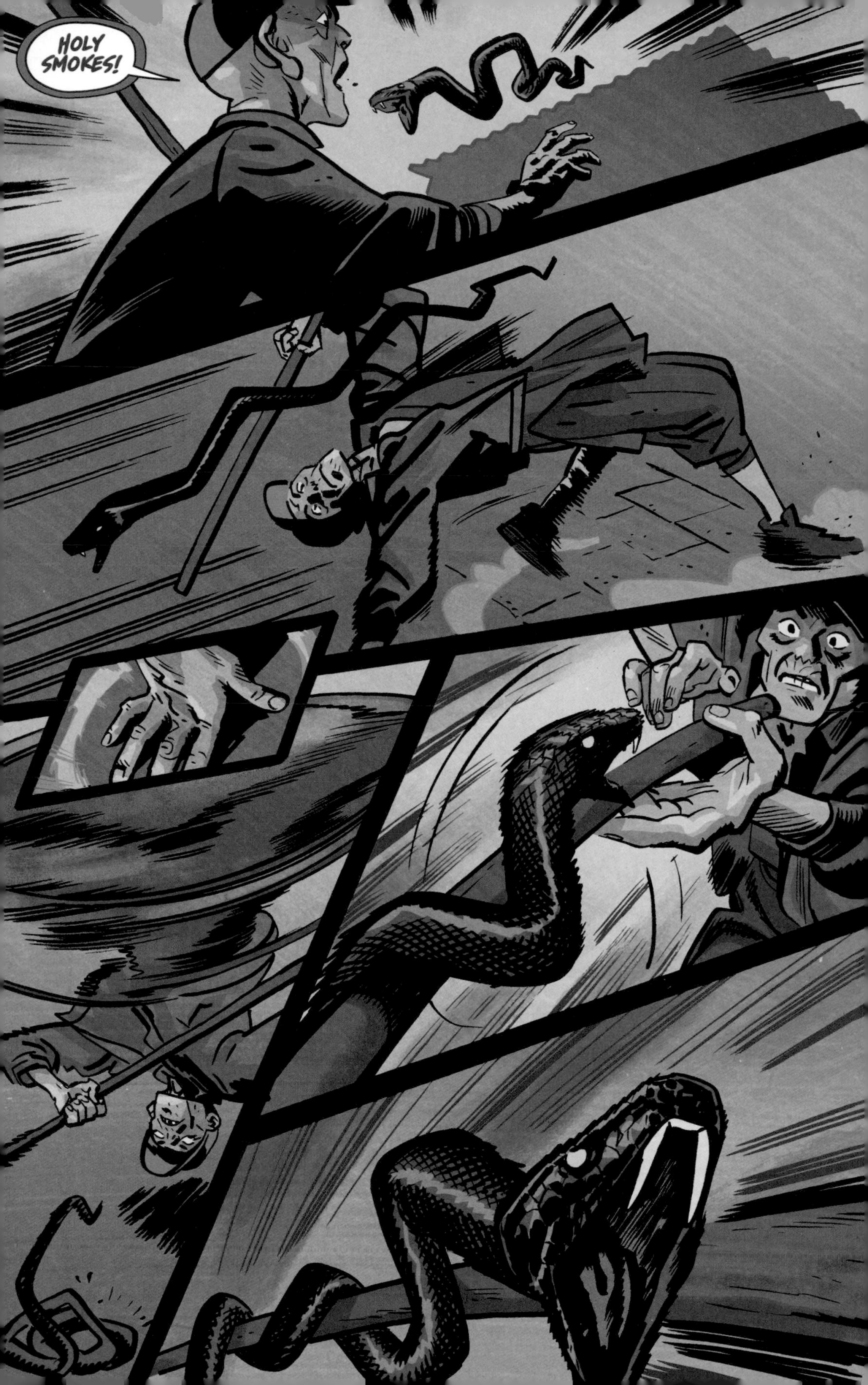
HOLY SMOKES!

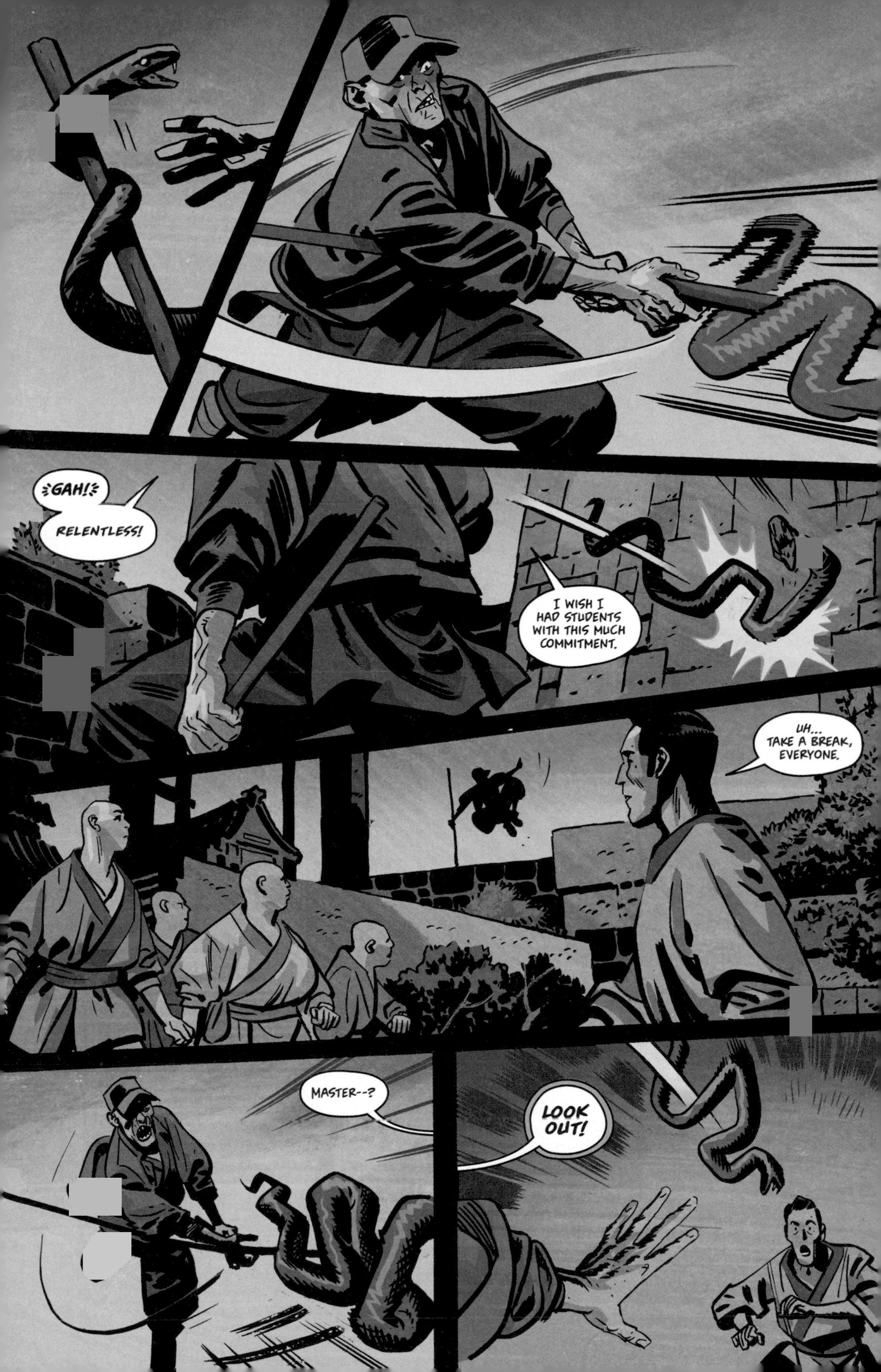
GAH!
RELENTLESS!
I WISH I HAD STUDENTS WITH THIS MUCH COMMITMENT.
UH... TAKE A BREAK, EVERYONE.
MASTER--?
LOOK OUT!

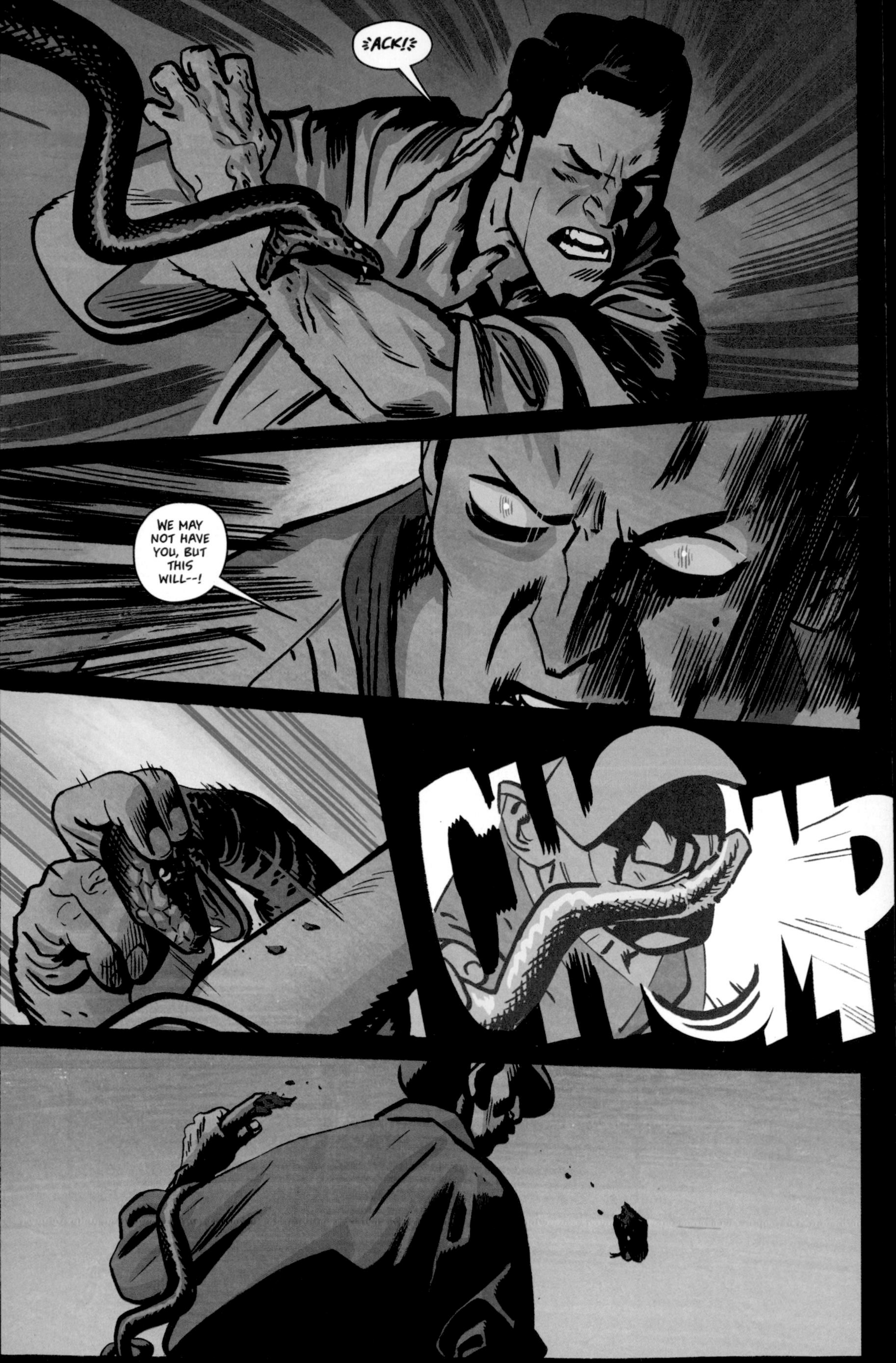
ACK!
WE MAY NOT HAVE YOU, BUT THIS WILL--!
CHOMP

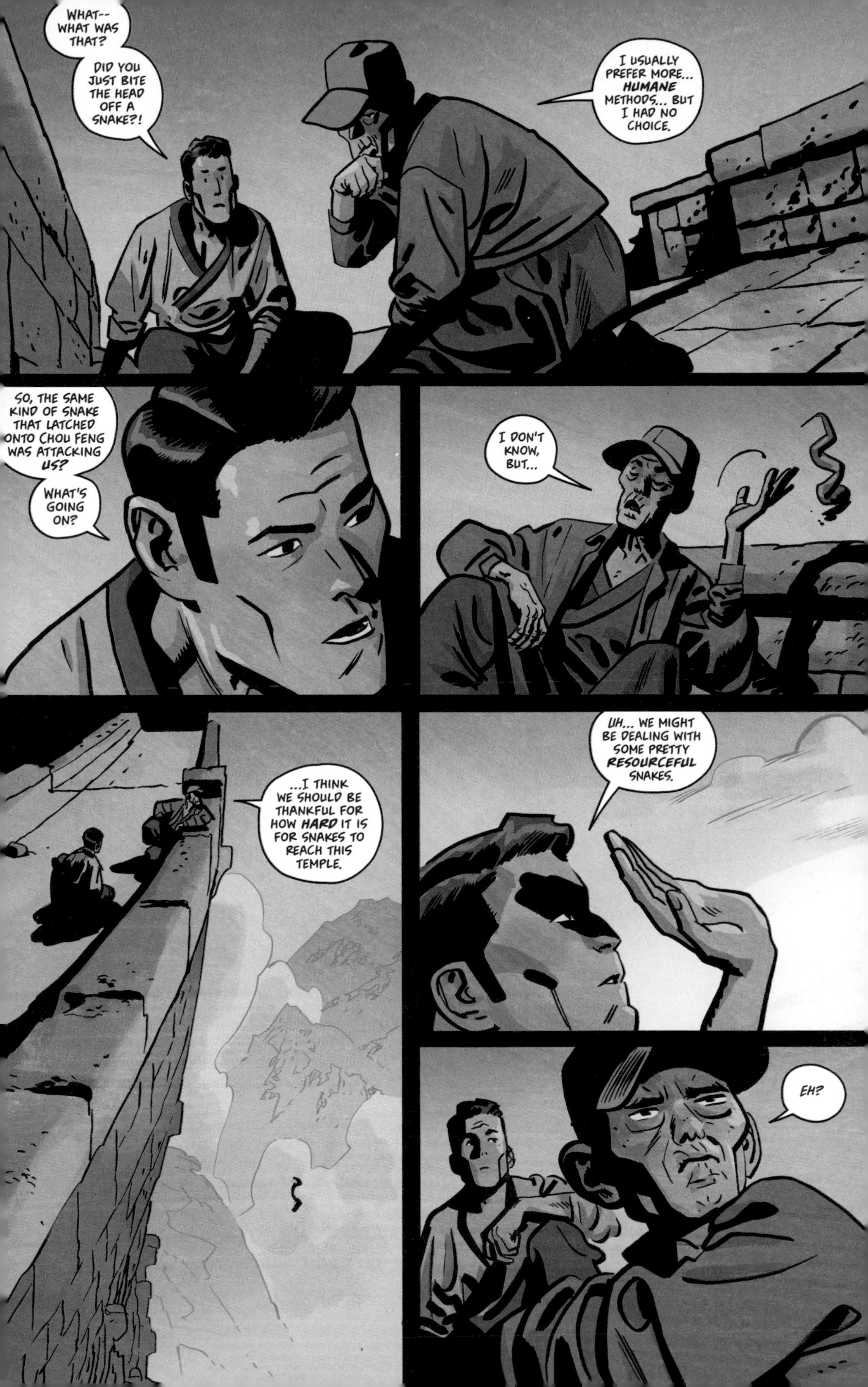
WHAT-- WHAT WAS THAT?
DID YOU JUST BITE THE HEAD OFF A SNAKE?!
I USUALLY PREFER MORE... HUMANE METHODS... BUT I HAD NO CHOICE.
SO, THE SAME KIND OF SNAKE THAT LATCHED ONTO CHOU FENG WAS ATTACKING US?
WHAT'S GOING ON?
I DON'T KNOW, BUT...
...I THINK WE SHOULD BE THANKFUL FOR HOW HARD IT IS FOR SNAKES TO REACH THIS TEMPLE.
UH... WE MIGHT BE DEALING WITH SOME PRETTY RESOURCEFUL SNAKES.
EH?

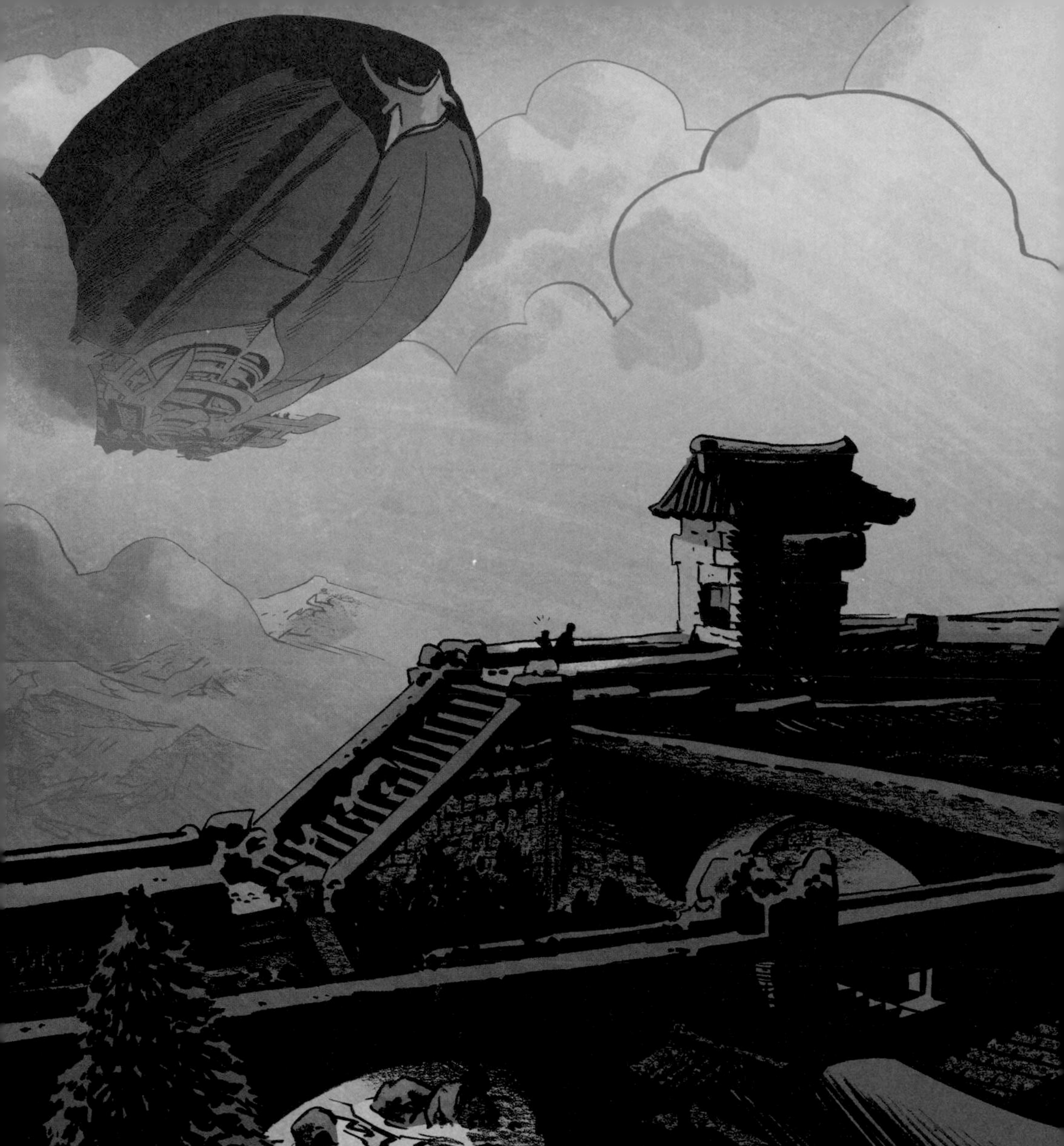

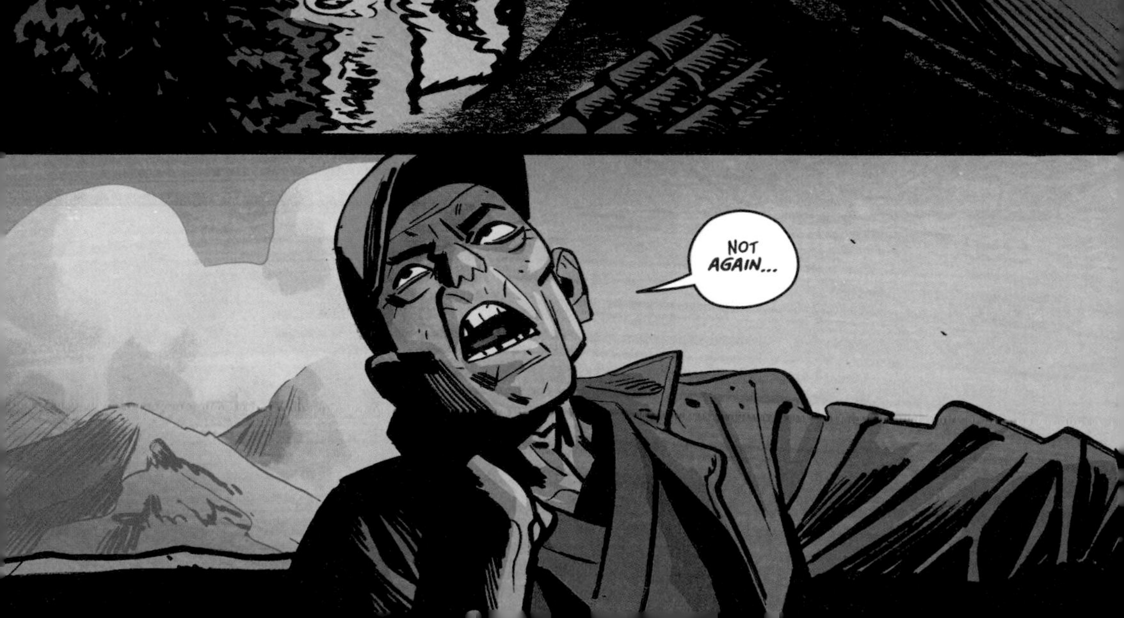
NOT AGAIN...

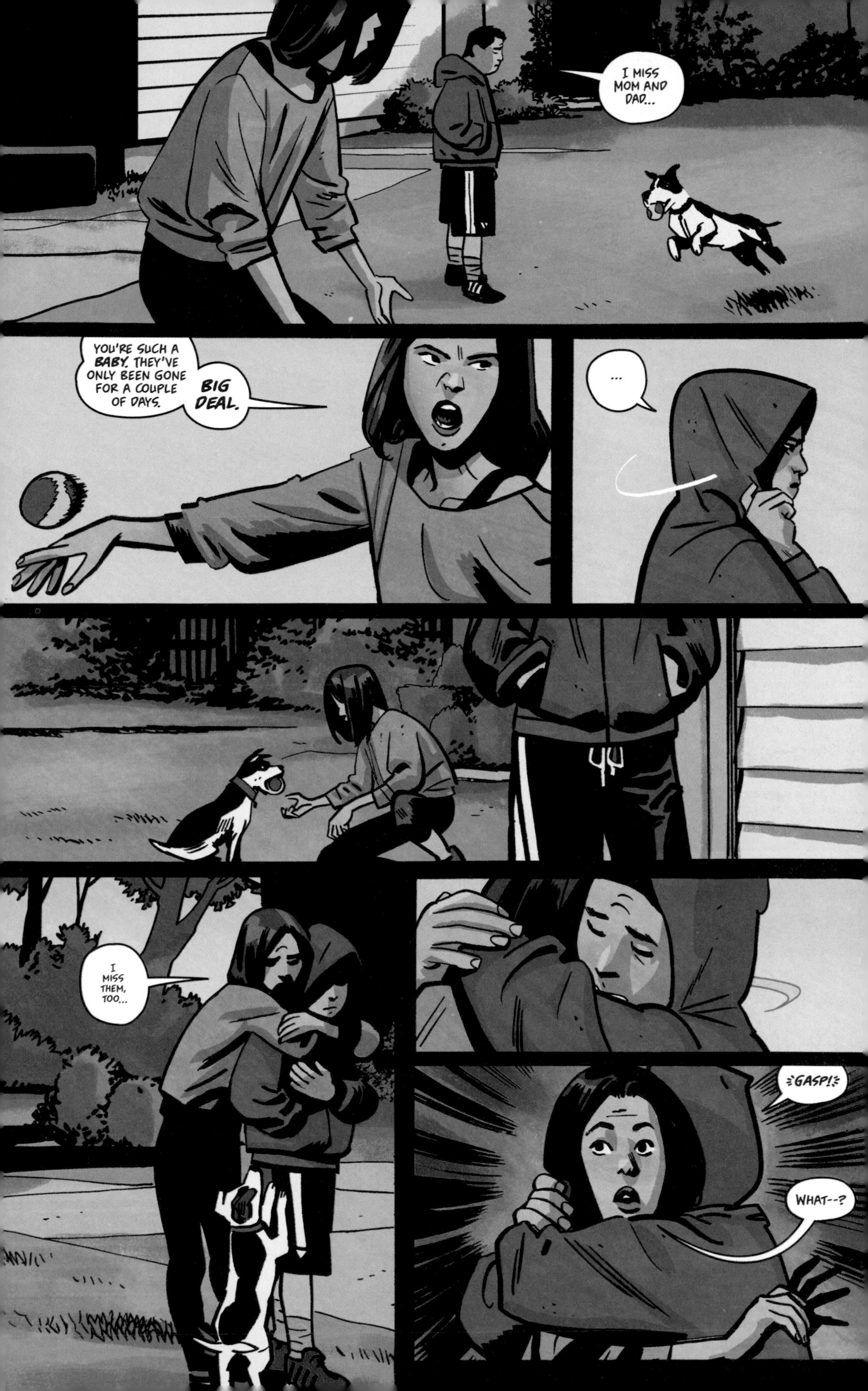
I MISS MOM AND DAD...
YOU'RE SUCH A BABY. THEY'VE ONLY BEEN GONE FOR A COUPLE OF DAYS.
BIG DEAL.
...
I MISS THEM, TOO...
GASP!
WHAT--?

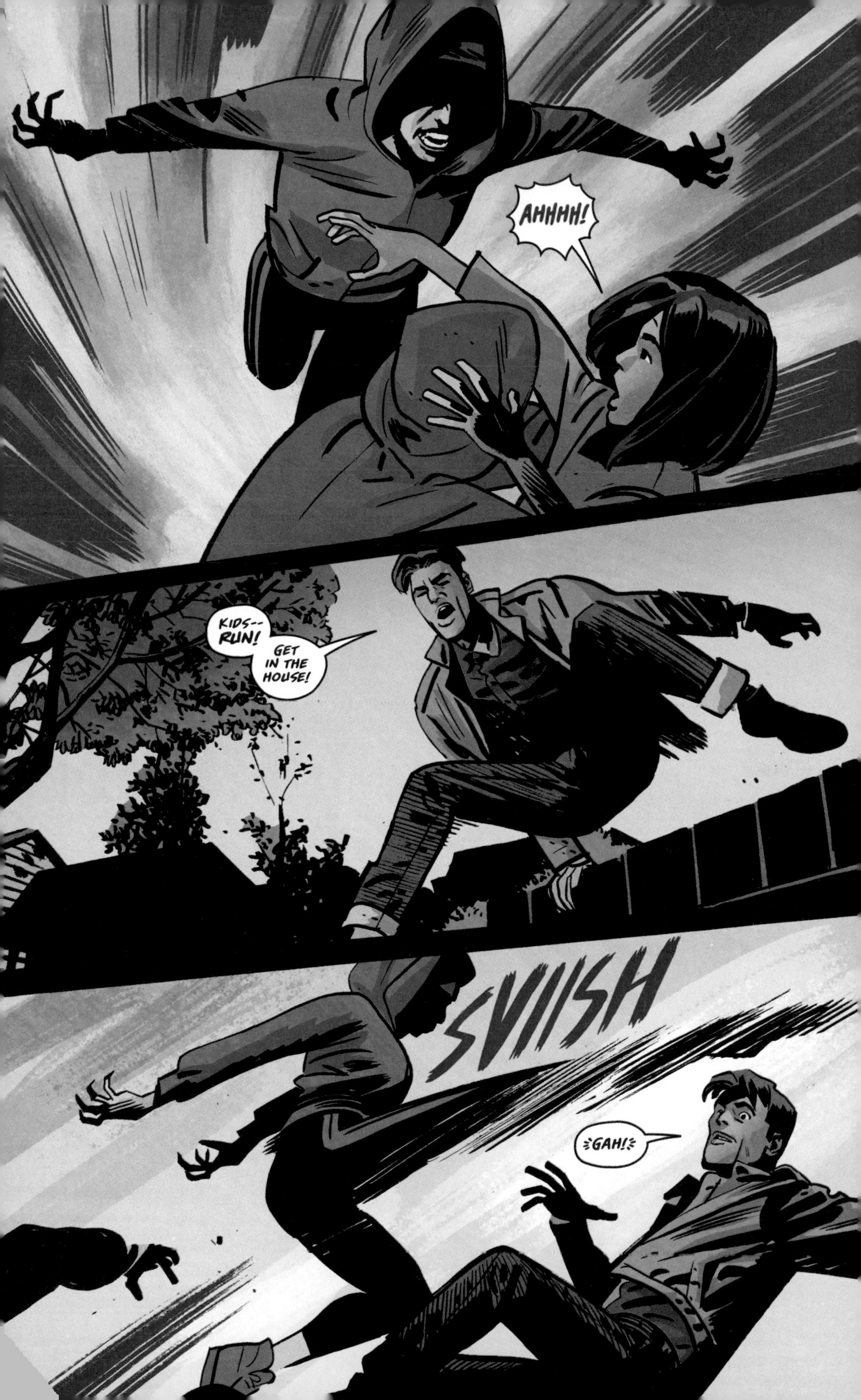
AHHHH!
KIDS--
RUN!
GET IN THE HOUSE!
SVIISH
GAH!

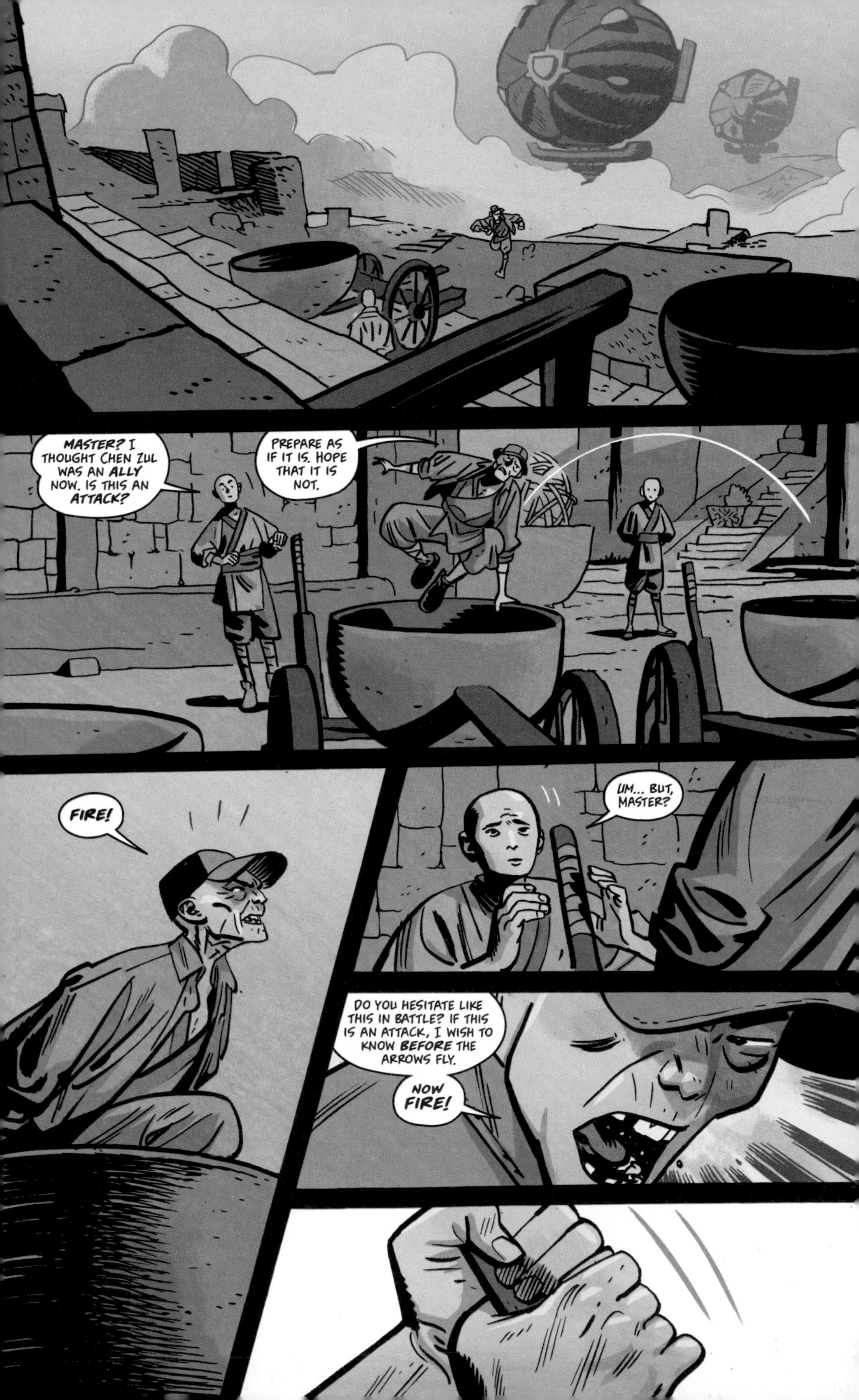
MASTER? I THOUGHT CHEN ZUL WAS AN ALLY NOW. IS THIS AN ATTACK?
PREPARE AS IF IT IS. HOPE THAT IT IS NOT.
FIRE!
UM... BUT, MASTER?
DO YOU HESITATE LIKE THIS IN BATTLE? IF THIS IS AN ATTACK, I WISH TO KNOW BEFORE THE ARROWS FLY.
NOW FIRE!

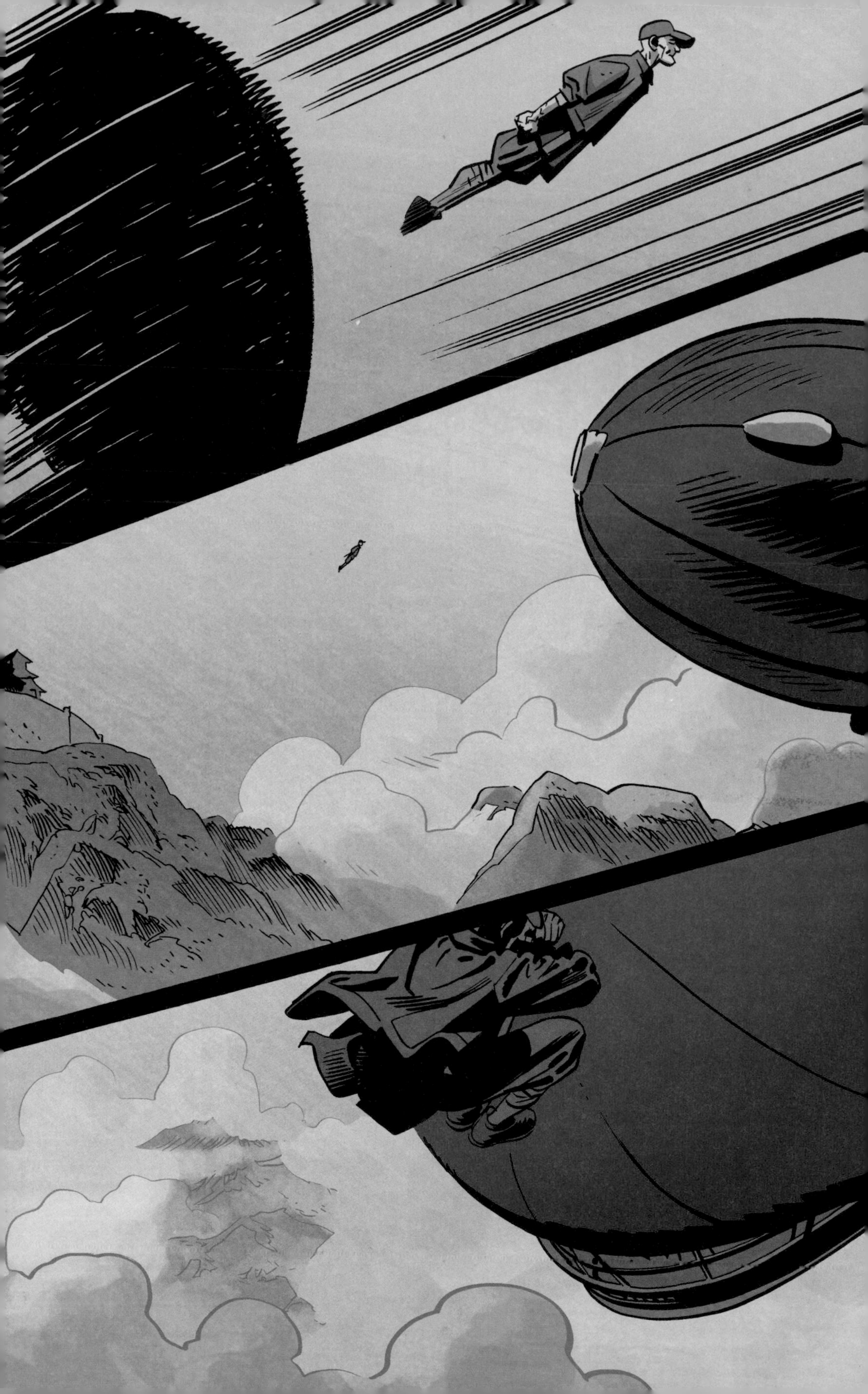

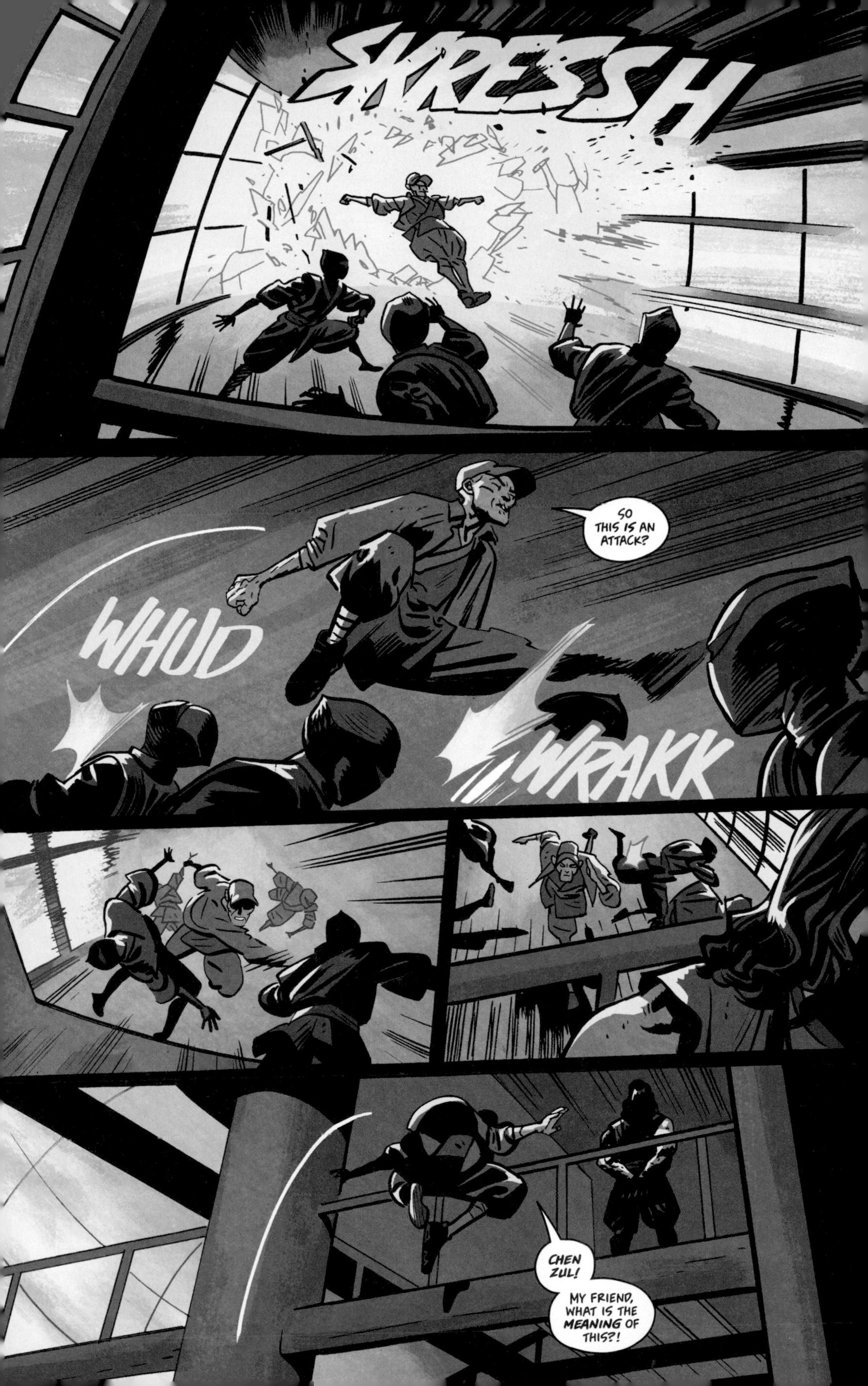
SKRESSH
SO THIS IS AN ATTACK?
WHUD
WRAKK
CHEN ZUL!
MY FRIEND, WHAT IS THE MEANING OF THIS?!

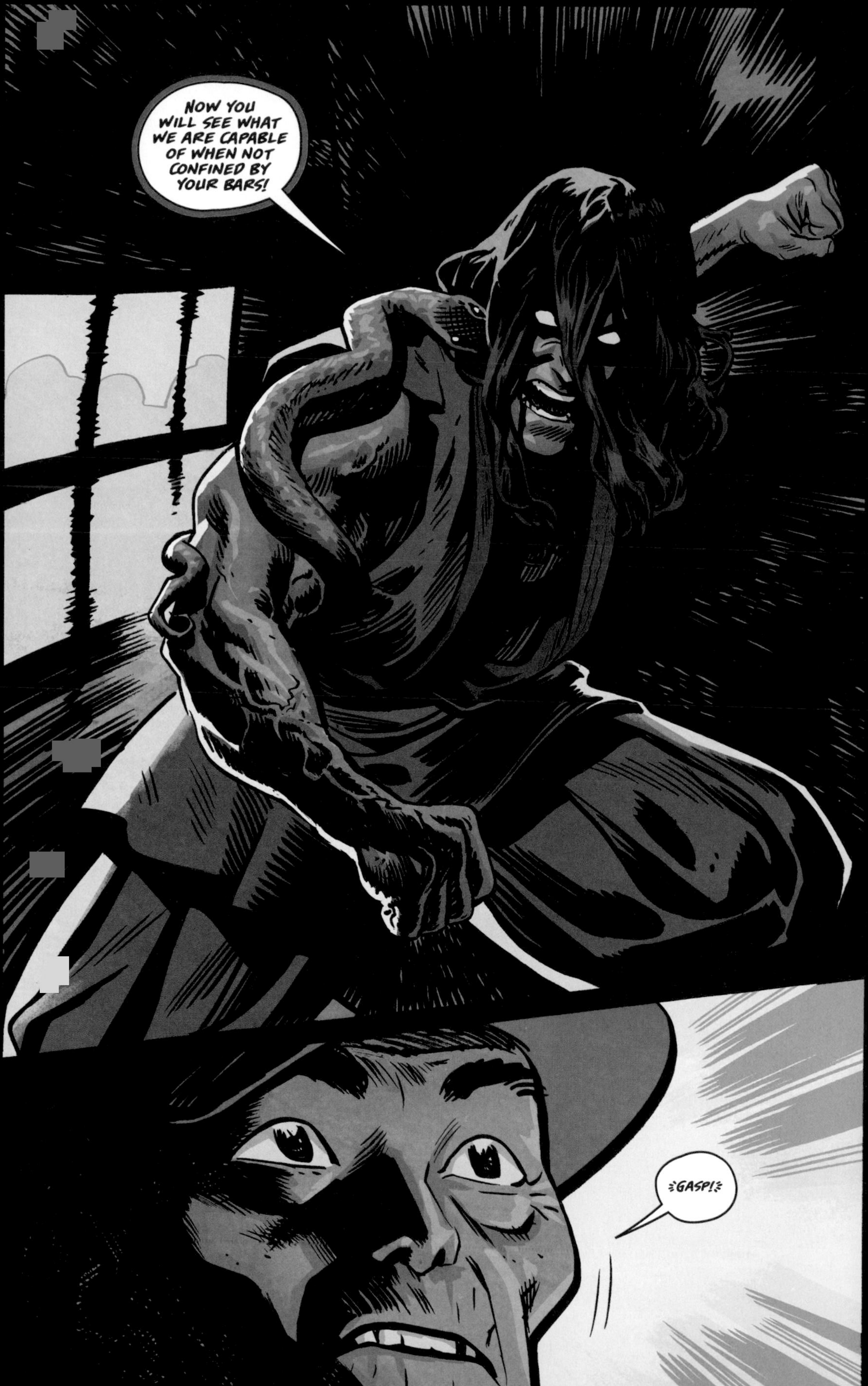
NOW YOU WILL SEE WHAT WE ARE CAPABLE OF WHEN NOT CONFINED BY YOUR BARS!
GASP!

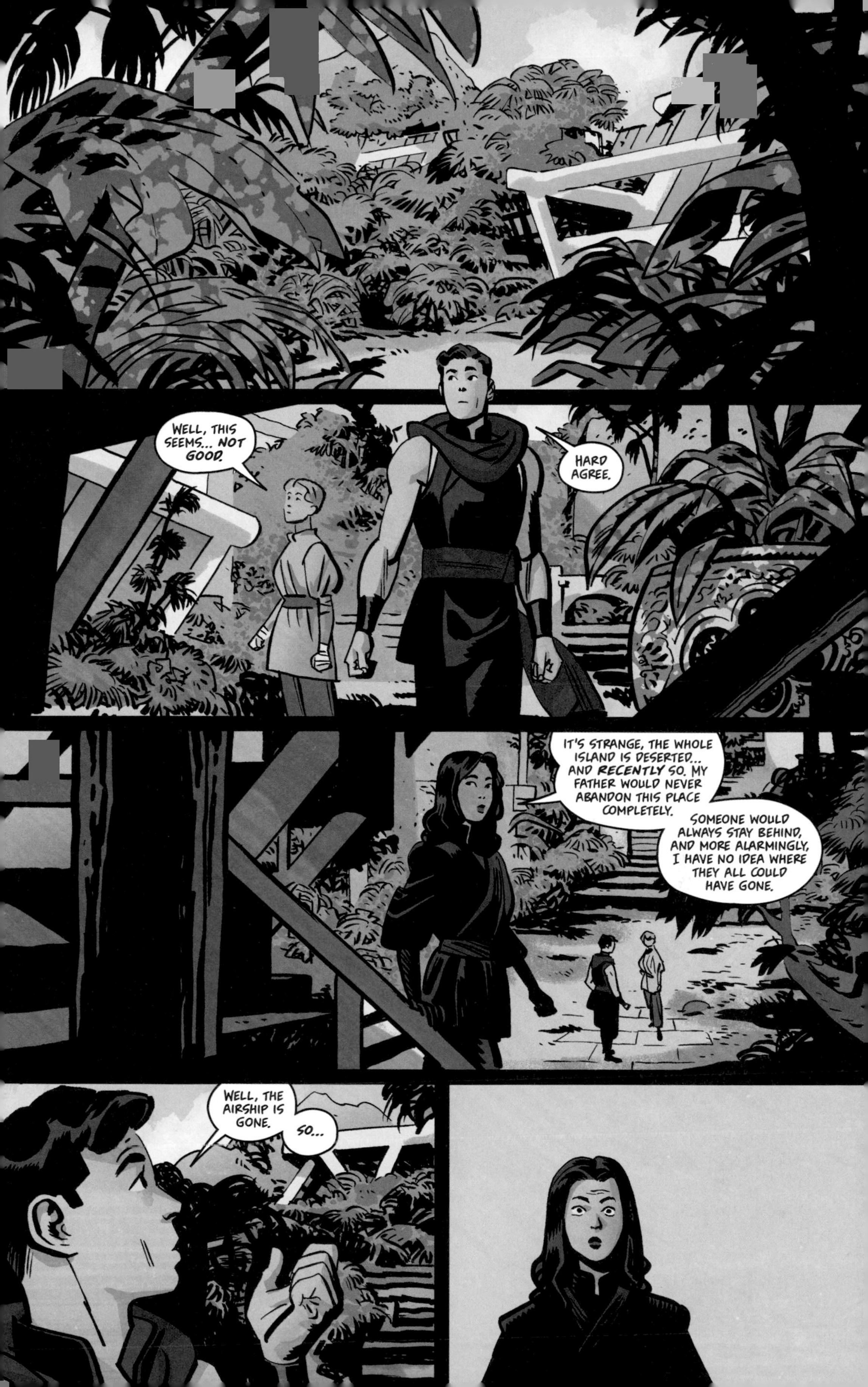
WELL, THIS SEEMS... NOT GOOD.
HARD AGREE.
IT'S STRANGE, THE WHOLE ISLAND IS DESERTED... AND RECENTLY SO. MY FATHER WOULD NEVER ABANDON THIS PLACE COMPLETELY.
SOMEONE WOULD ALWAYS STAY BEHIND, AND MORE ALARMINGLY, I HAVE NO IDEA WHERE THEY ALL COULD HAVE GONE.
WELL, THE AIRSHIP IS GONE.
SO...

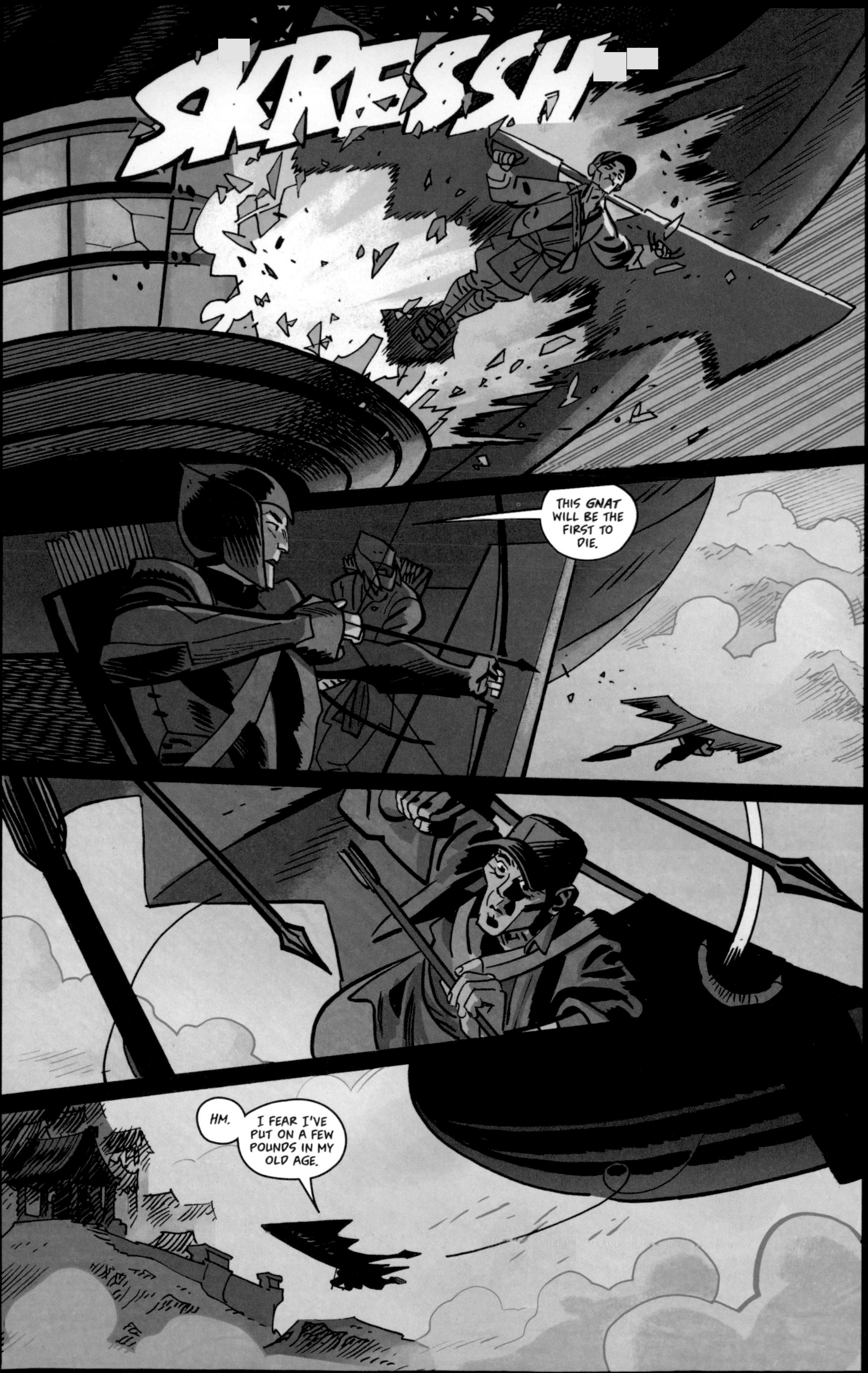
SKRESCH
THIS GNAT WILL BE THE FIRST TO DIE.
HM.
I FEAR I'VE PUT ON A FEW POUNDS IN MY OLD AGE.

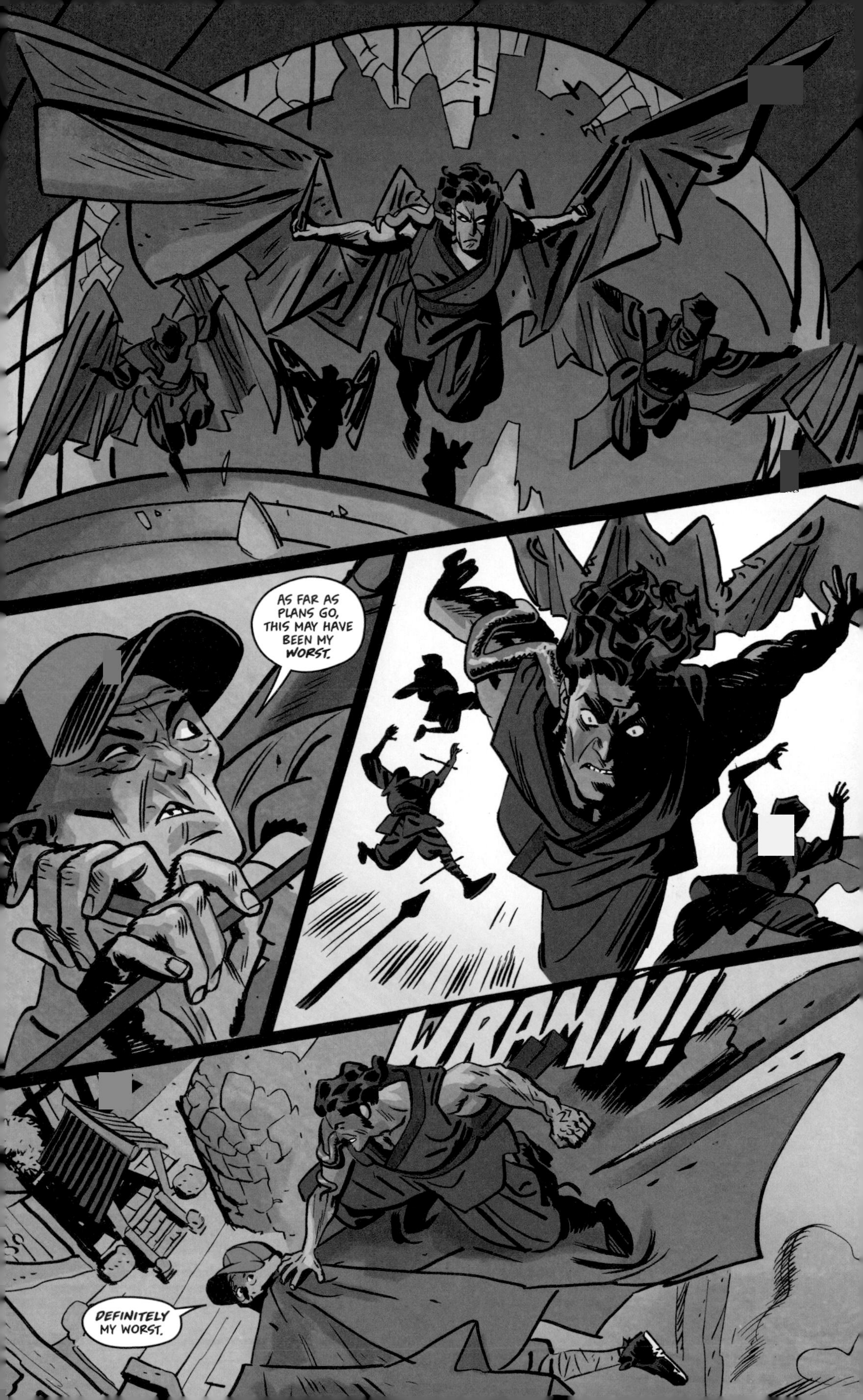
AS FAR AS PLANS GO, THIS MAY HAVE BEEN MY WORST.
WRAMM!
DEFINITELY MY WORST.

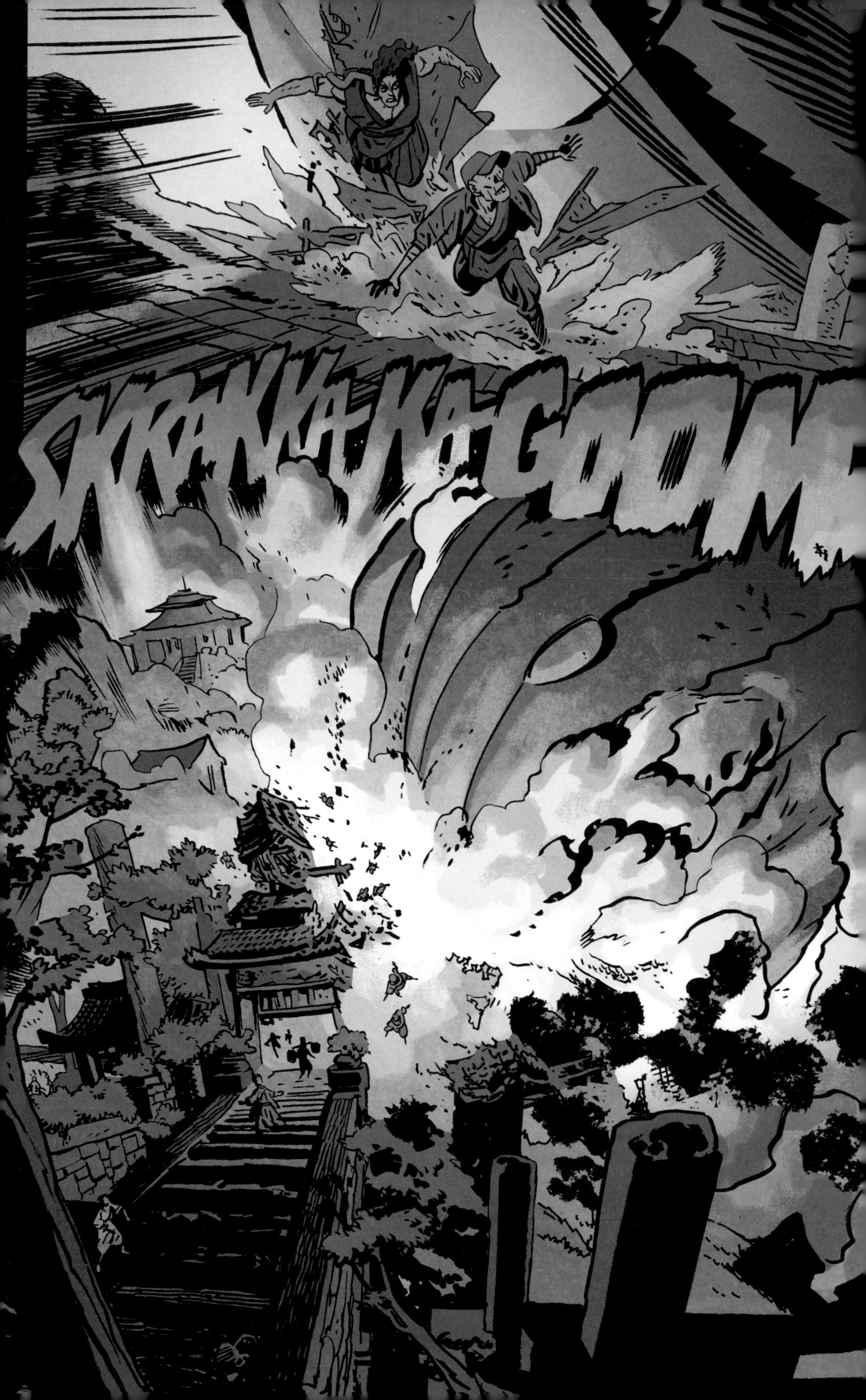

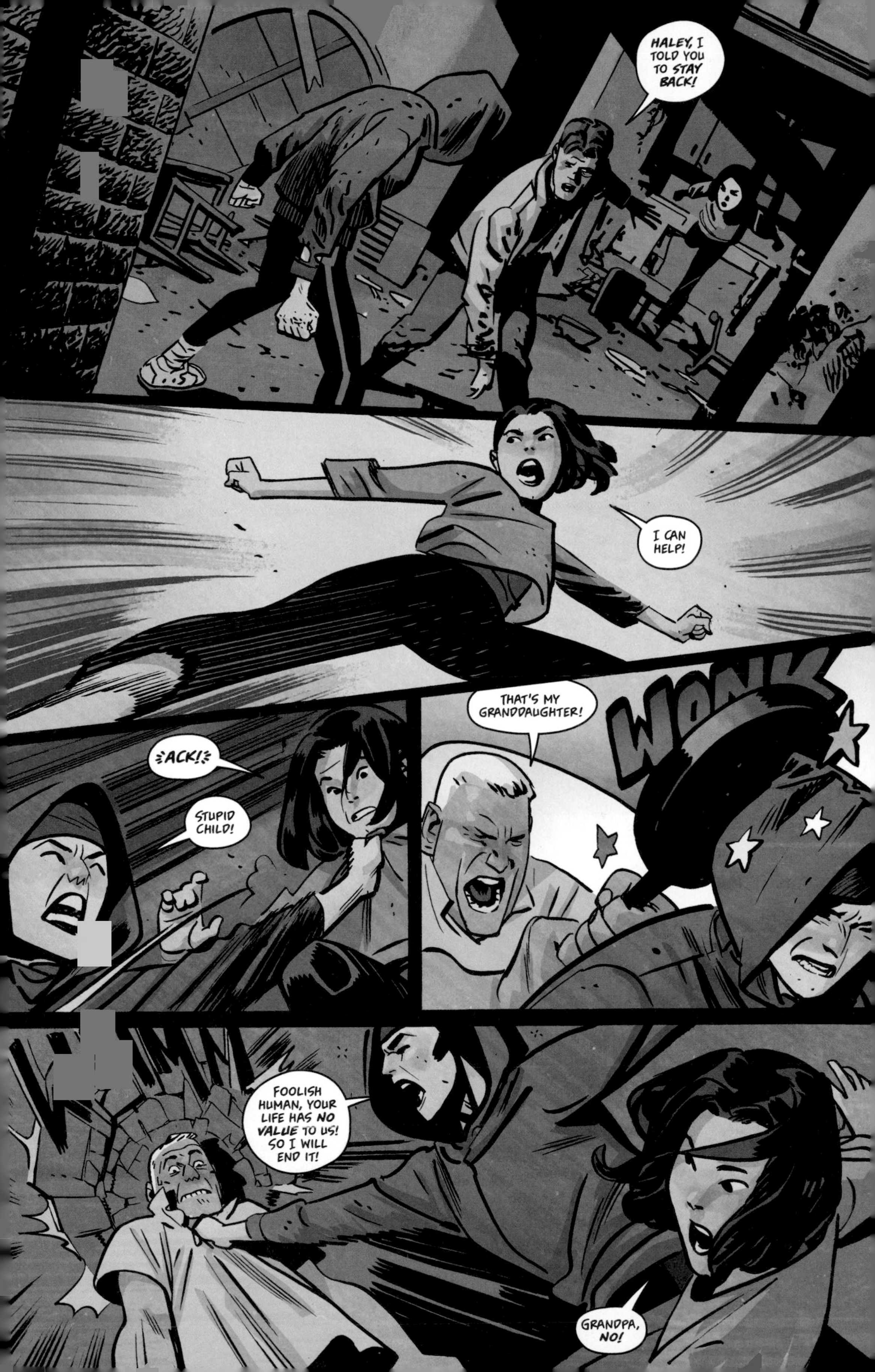

HALEY, I TOLD YOU TO STAY BACK!
I CAN HELP!
ACK!
STUPID CHILD!
THAT'S MY GRANDDAUGHTER!
WONK
FOOLISH HUMAN, YOUR LIFE HAS NO VALUE TO US! SO I WILL END IT!
GRANDPA, NO!

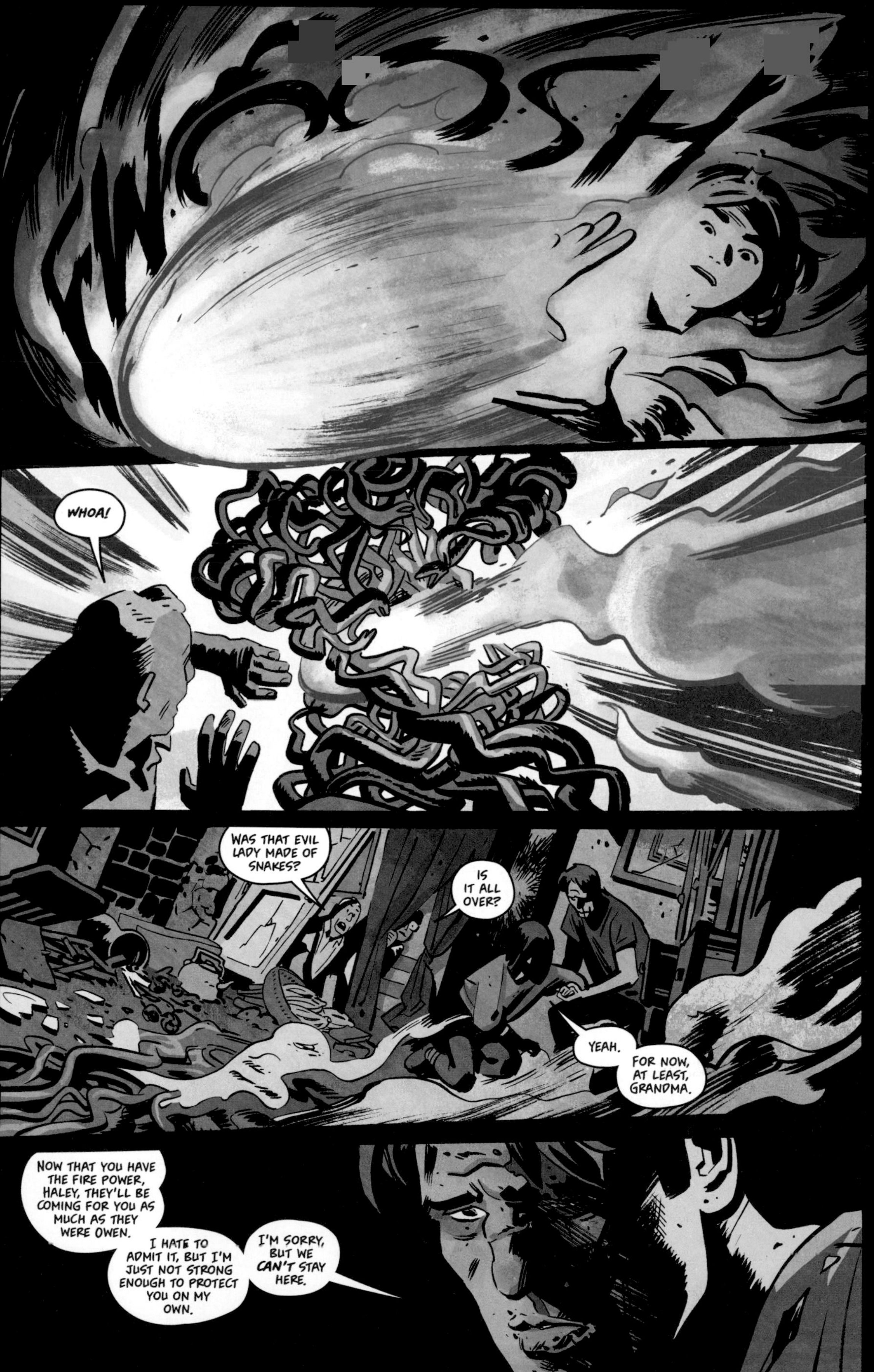
WHOA!
WAS THAT EVIL LADY MADE OF SNAKES?
IS IT ALL OVER?
YEAH.
FOR NOW, AT LEAST, GRANDMA.
NOW THAT YOU HAVE THE FIRE POWER, HALEY, THEY'LL BE COMING FOR YOU AS MUCH AS THEY WERE OWEN.
I HATE TO ADMIT IT, BUT I'M JUST NOT STRONG ENOUGH TO PROTECT YOU ON MY OWN.
I'M SORRY, BUT WE CAN'T STAY HERE.

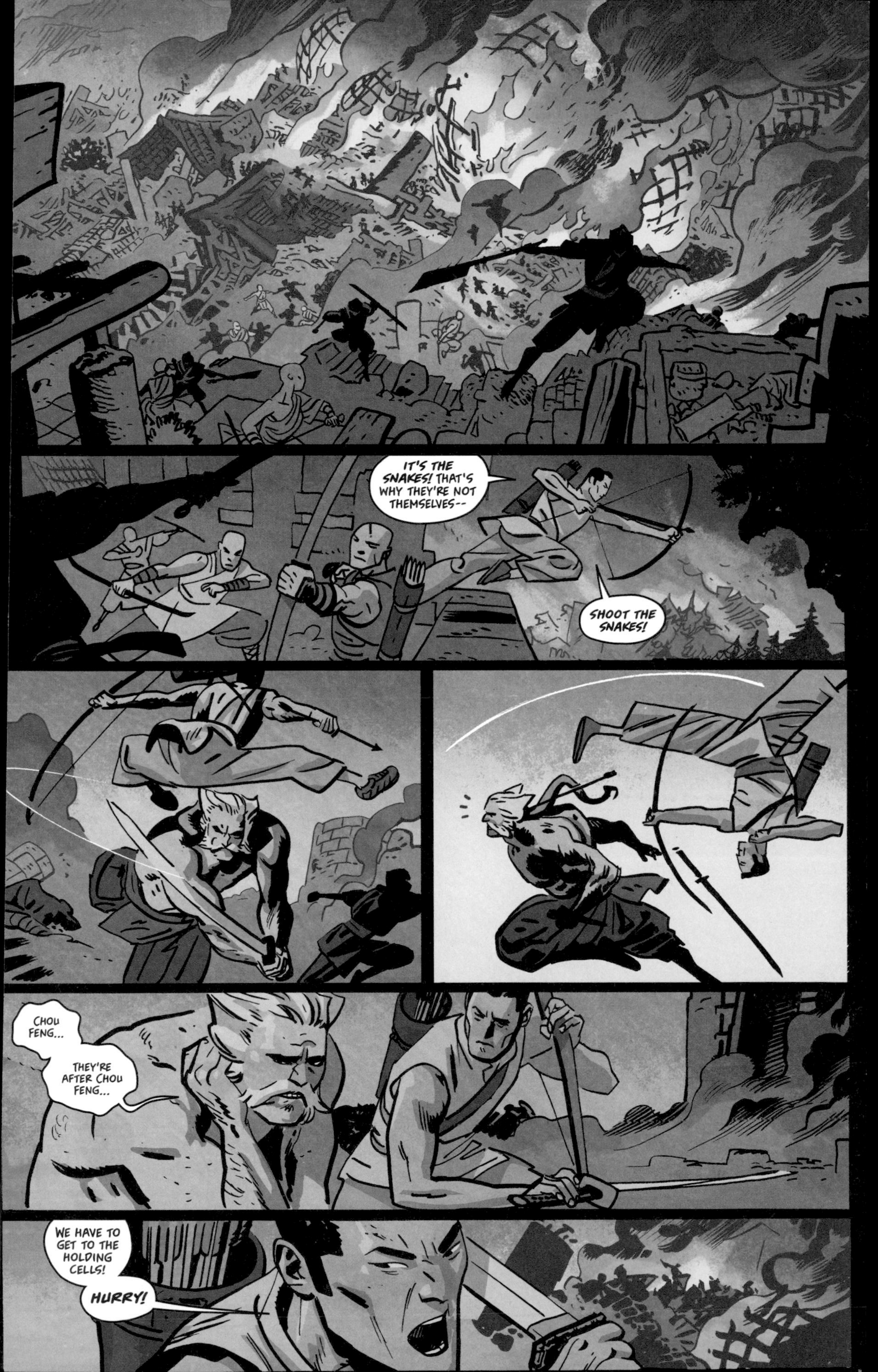
IT'S THE SNAKES! THAT'S WHY THEY'RE NOT THEMSELVES--
SHOOT THE SNAKES!
CHOU FENG...
THEY'RE AFTER CHOU FENG...
WE HAVE TO GET TO THE HOLDING CELLS!
HURRY!

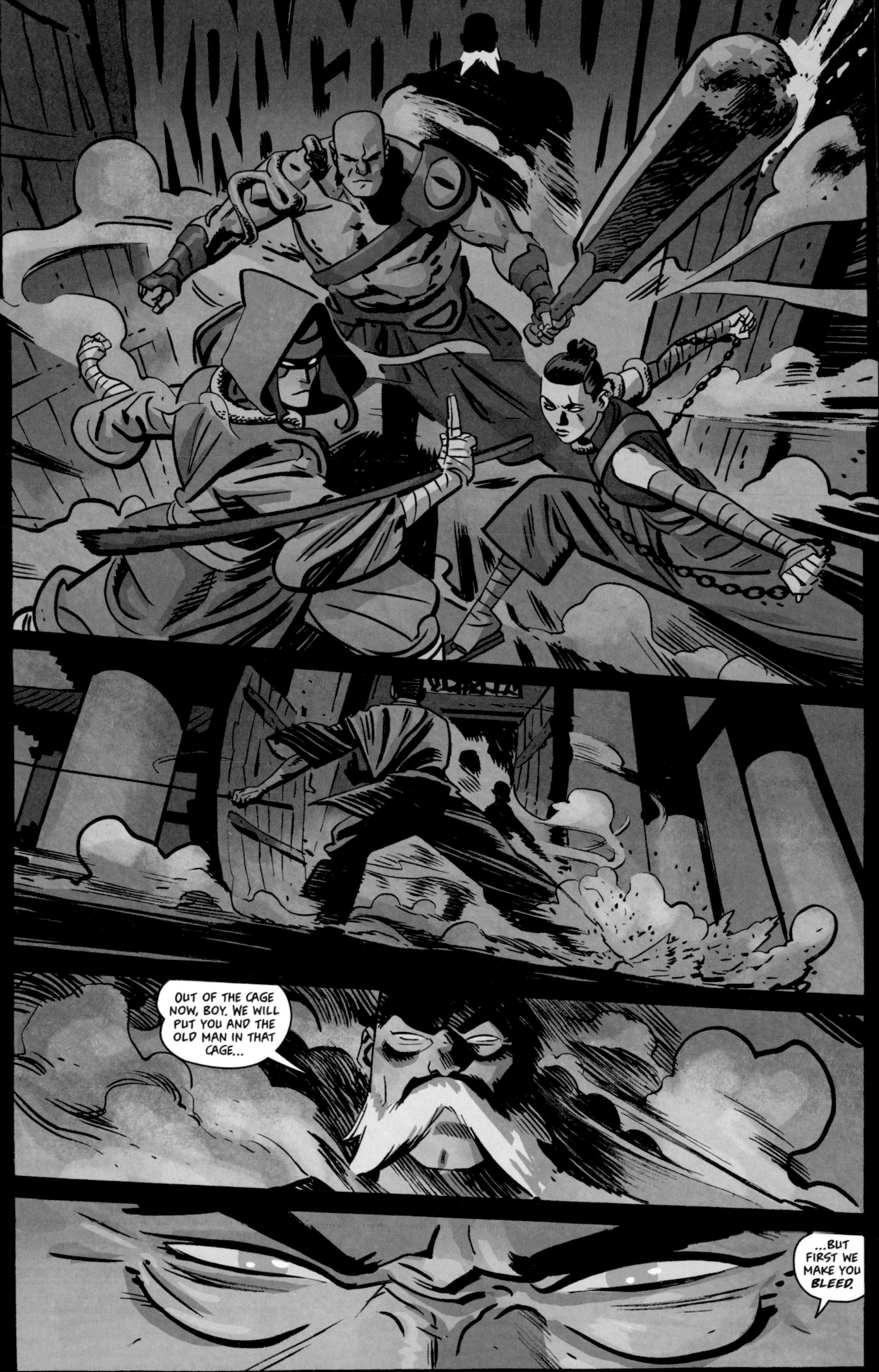
OUT OF THE CAGE NOW, BOY. WE WILL PUT YOU AND THE OLD MAN IN THAT CAGE...
...BUT FIRST WE MAKE YOU *BLEED.*

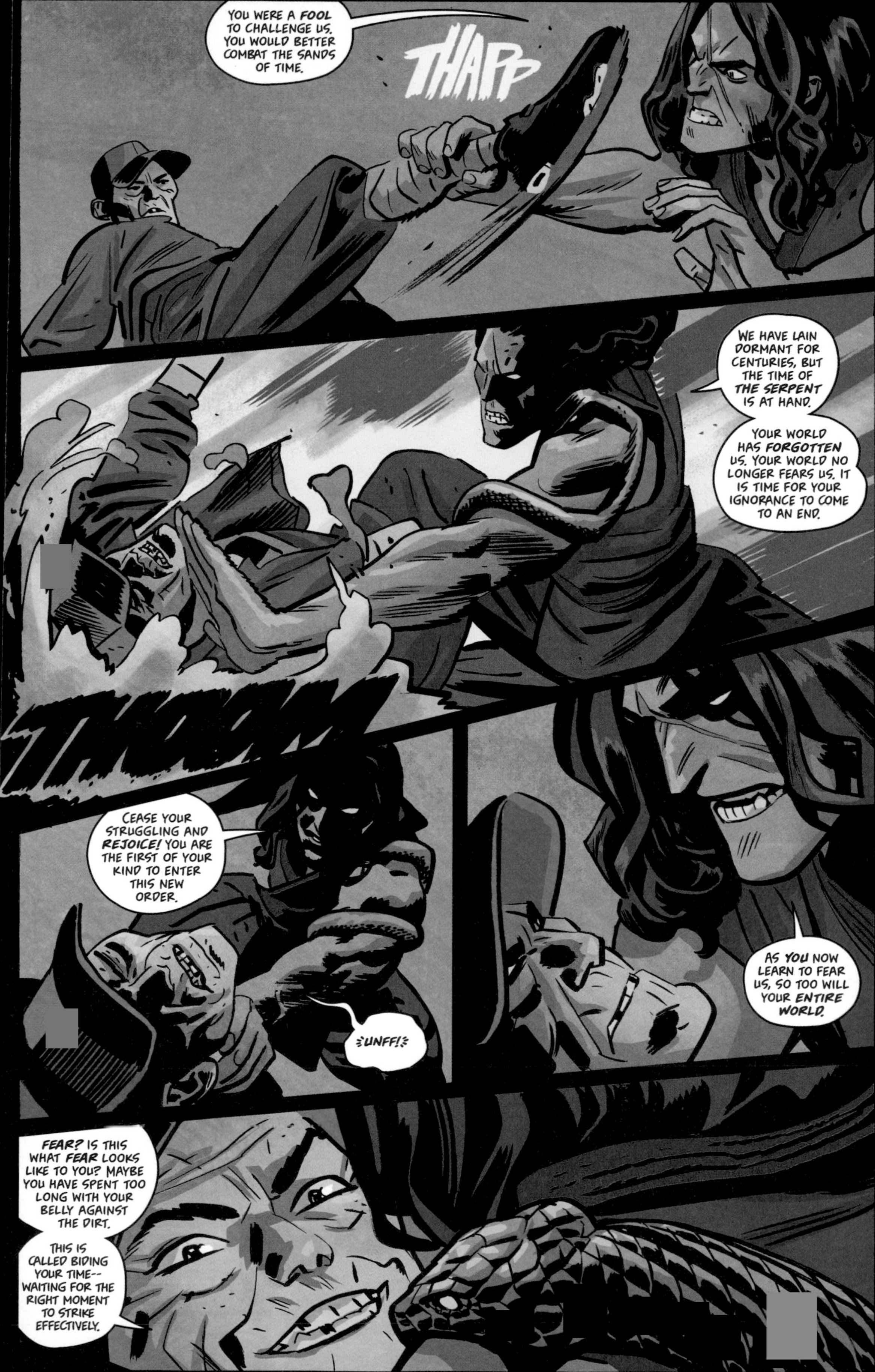
YOU WERE A FOOL TO CHALLENGE US. YOU WOULD BETTER COMBAT THE SANDS OF TIME.
THAPP
WE HAVE LAIN DORMANT FOR CENTURIES, BUT THE TIME OF THE SERPENT IS AT HAND.
YOUR WORLD HAS FORGOTTEN US. YOUR WORLD NO LONGER FEARS US. IT IS TIME FOR YOUR IGNORANCE TO COME TO AN END.
CEASE YOUR STRUGGLING AND REJOICE! YOU ARE THE FIRST OF YOUR KIND TO ENTER THIS NEW ORDER.
UNFF!
AS YOU NOW LEARN TO FEAR US, SO TOO WILL YOUR ENTIRE WORLD.
FEAR? IS THIS WHAT FEAR LOOKS LIKE TO YOU? MAYBE YOU HAVE SPENT TOO LONG WITH YOUR BELLY AGAINST THE DIRT.
THIS IS CALLED BIDING YOUR TIME-- WAITING FOR THE RIGHT MOMENT TO STRIKE EFFECTIVELY.

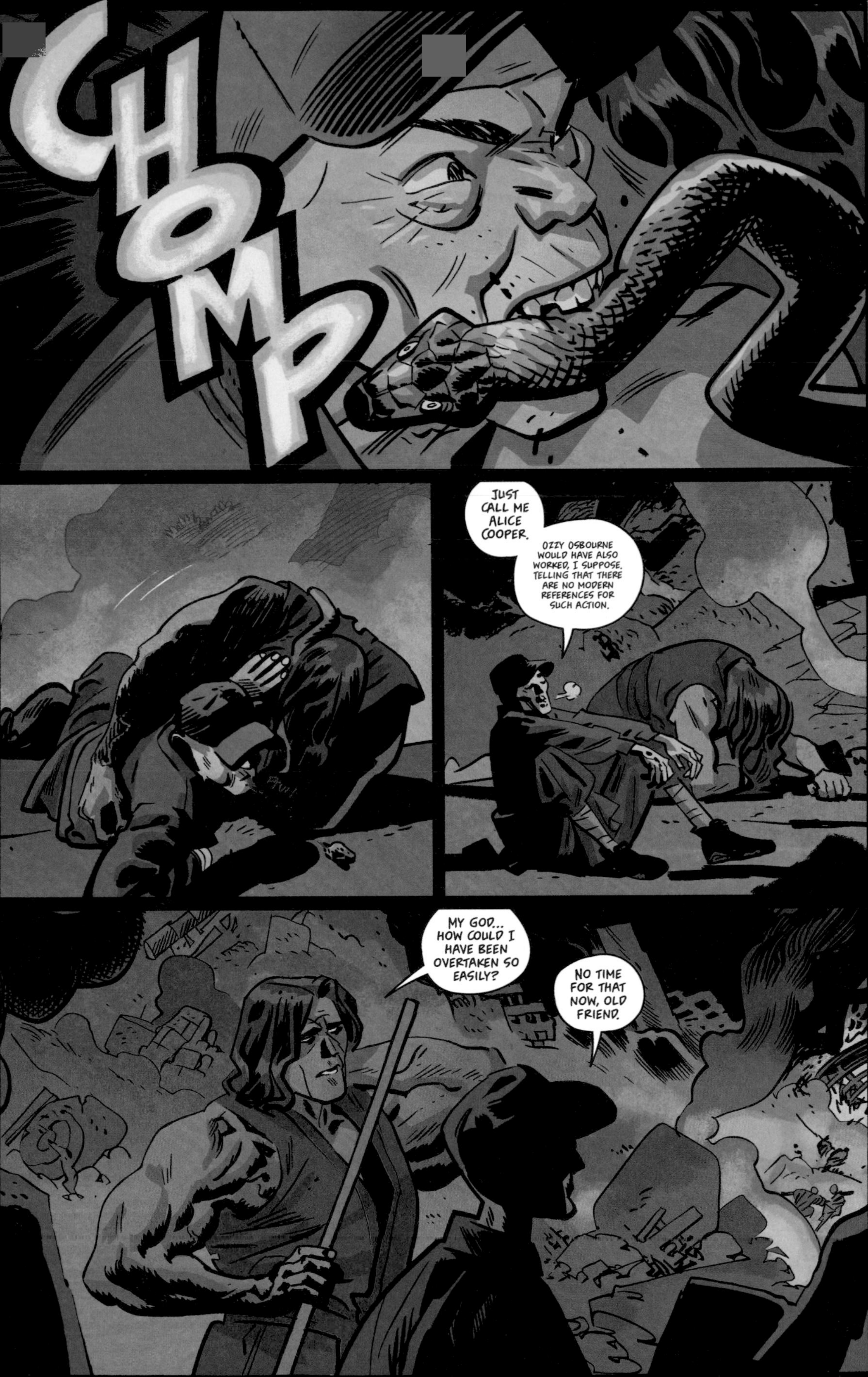
CHOMP
JUST CALL ME ALICE COOPER.
OZZY OSBOURNE WOULD HAVE ALSO WORKED, I SUPPOSE. TELLING THAT THERE ARE NO MODERN REFERENCES FOR SUCH ACTION.
MY GOD... HOW COULD I HAVE BEEN OVERTAKEN SO EASILY?
NO TIME FOR THAT NOW, OLD FRIEND.

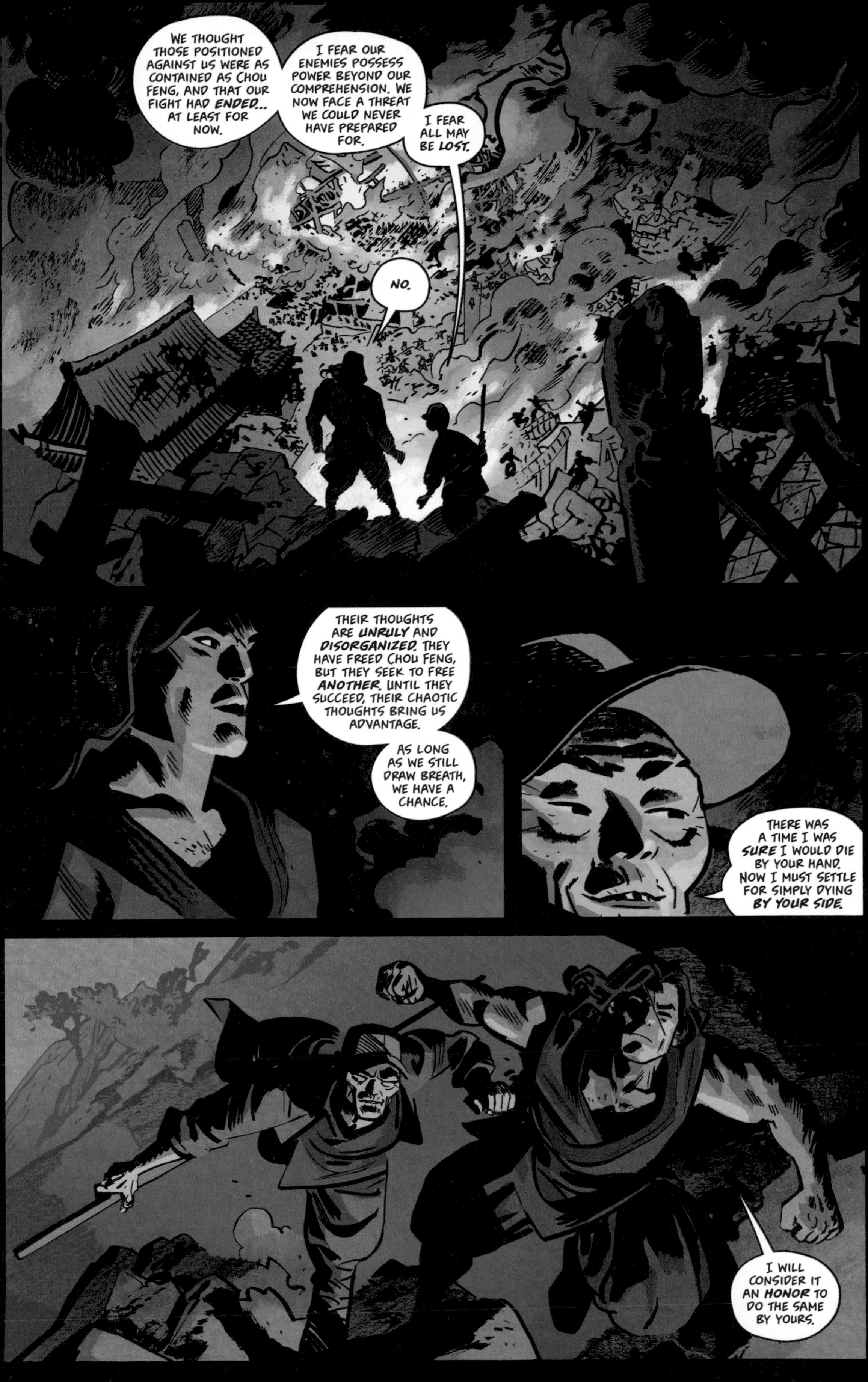
WE THOUGHT THOSE POSITIONED AGAINST US WERE AS CONTAINED AS CHOU FENG, AND THAT OUR FIGHT HAD ENDED... AT LEAST FOR NOW.
I FEAR OUR ENEMIES POSSESS POWER BEYOND OUR COMPREHENSION. WE NOW FACE A THREAT WE COULD NEVER HAVE PREPARED FOR.
I FEAR ALL MAY BE LOST.
NO.
THEIR THOUGHTS ARE UNRULY AND DISORGANIZED. THEY HAVE FREED CHOU FENG, BUT THEY SEEK TO FREE ANOTHER. UNTIL THEY SUCCEED, THEIR CHAOTIC THOUGHTS BRING US ADVANTAGE.
AS LONG AS WE STILL DRAW BREATH, WE HAVE A CHANCE.
THERE WAS A TIME I WAS SURE I WOULD DIE BY YOUR HAND. NOW I MUST SETTLE FOR SIMPLY DYING BY YOUR SIDE.
I WILL CONSIDER IT AN HONOR TO DO THE SAME BY YOURS.

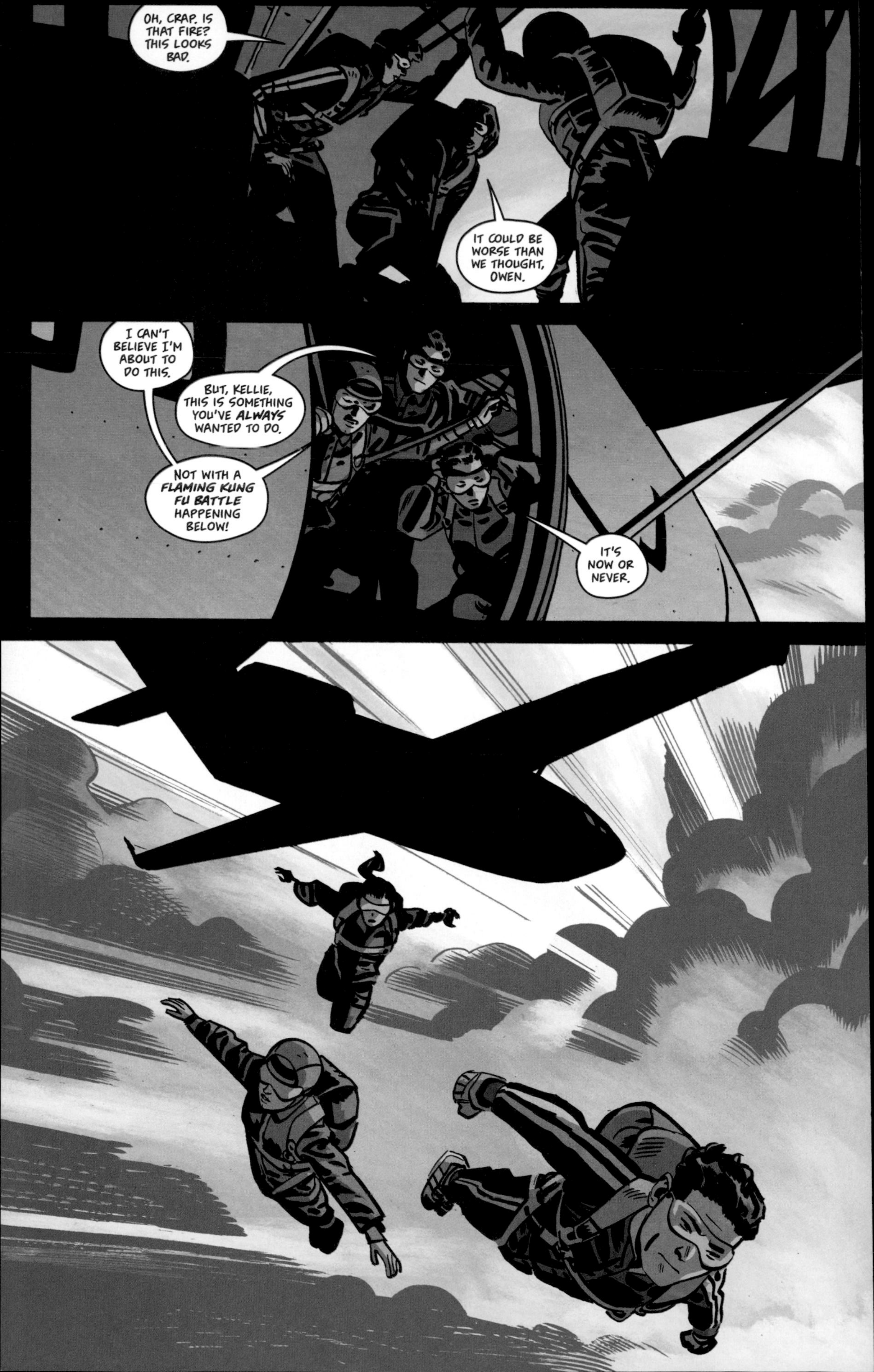
OH, CRAP. IS THAT FIRE? THIS LOOKS BAD.
IT COULD BE WORSE THAN WE THOUGHT, OWEN.
I CAN'T BELIEVE I'M ABOUT TO DO THIS.
BUT, KELLIE, THIS IS SOMETHING YOU'VE ALWAYS WANTED TO DO.
NOT WITH A FLAMING KUNG FU BATTLE HAPPENING BELOW!
IT'S NOW OR NEVER.

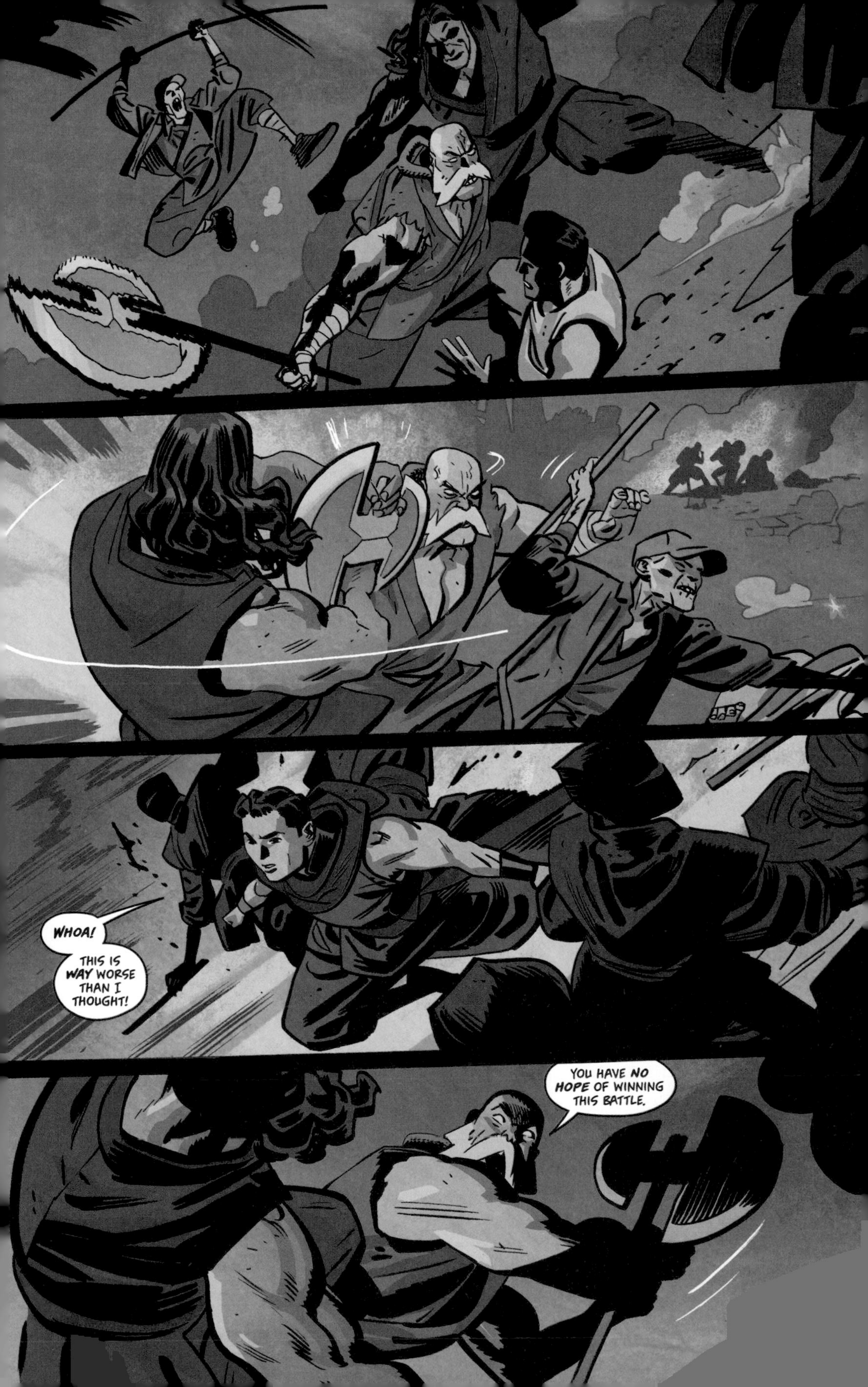
WHOA!
THIS IS WAY WORSE THAN I THOUGHT!
YOU HAVE NO HOPE OF WINNING THIS BATTLE.

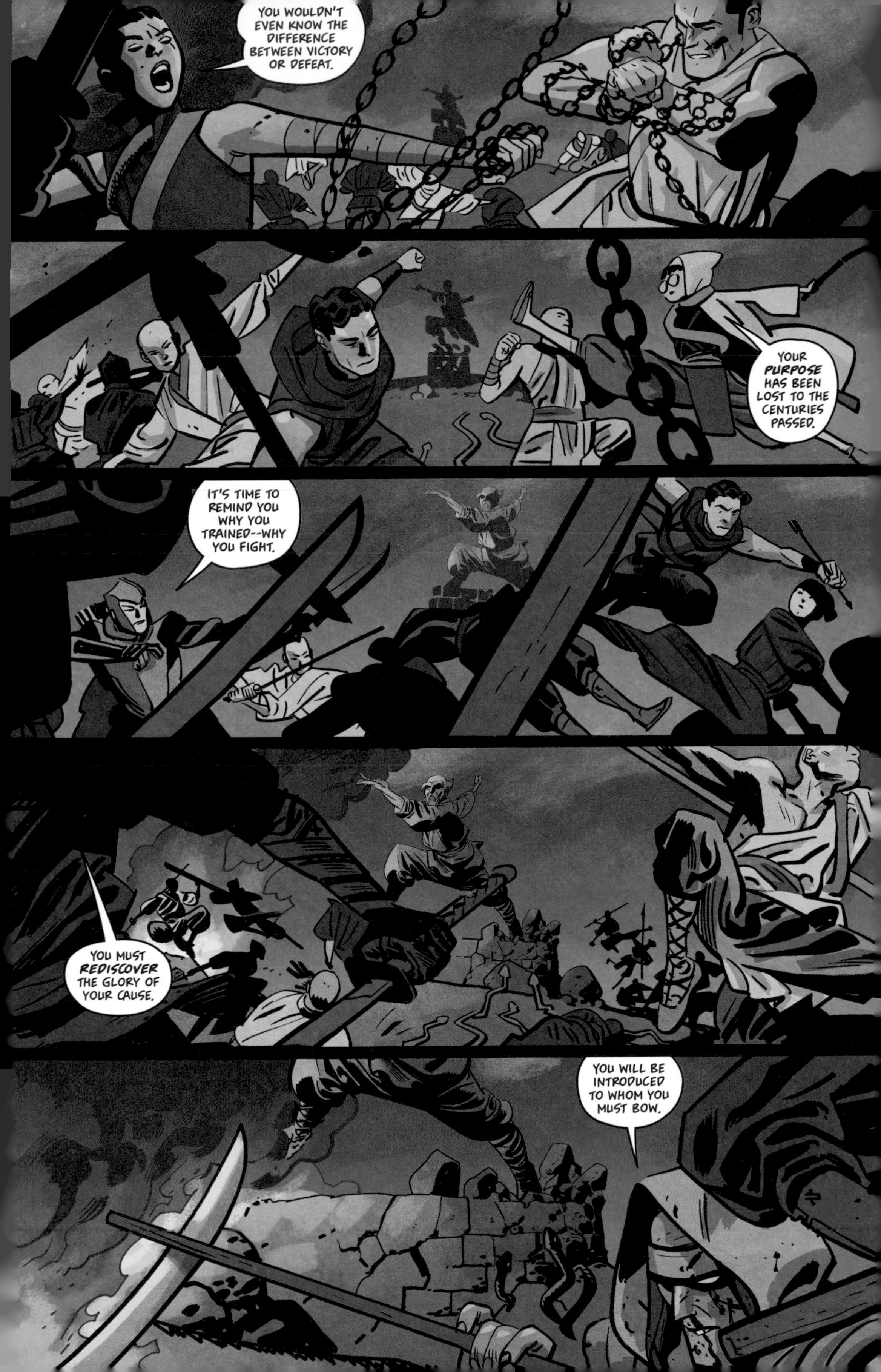
YOU WOULDN'T EVEN KNOW THE DIFFERENCE BETWEEN VICTORY OR DEFEAT.
YOUR *PURPOSE* HAS BEEN LOST TO THE CENTURIES PASSED.
IT'S TIME TO REMIND YOU WHY YOU TRAINED--WHY YOU FIGHT.
YOU MUST ***REDISCOVER*** THE GLORY OF YOUR CAUSE.
YOU WILL BE INTRODUCED TO WHOM YOU MUST BOW.

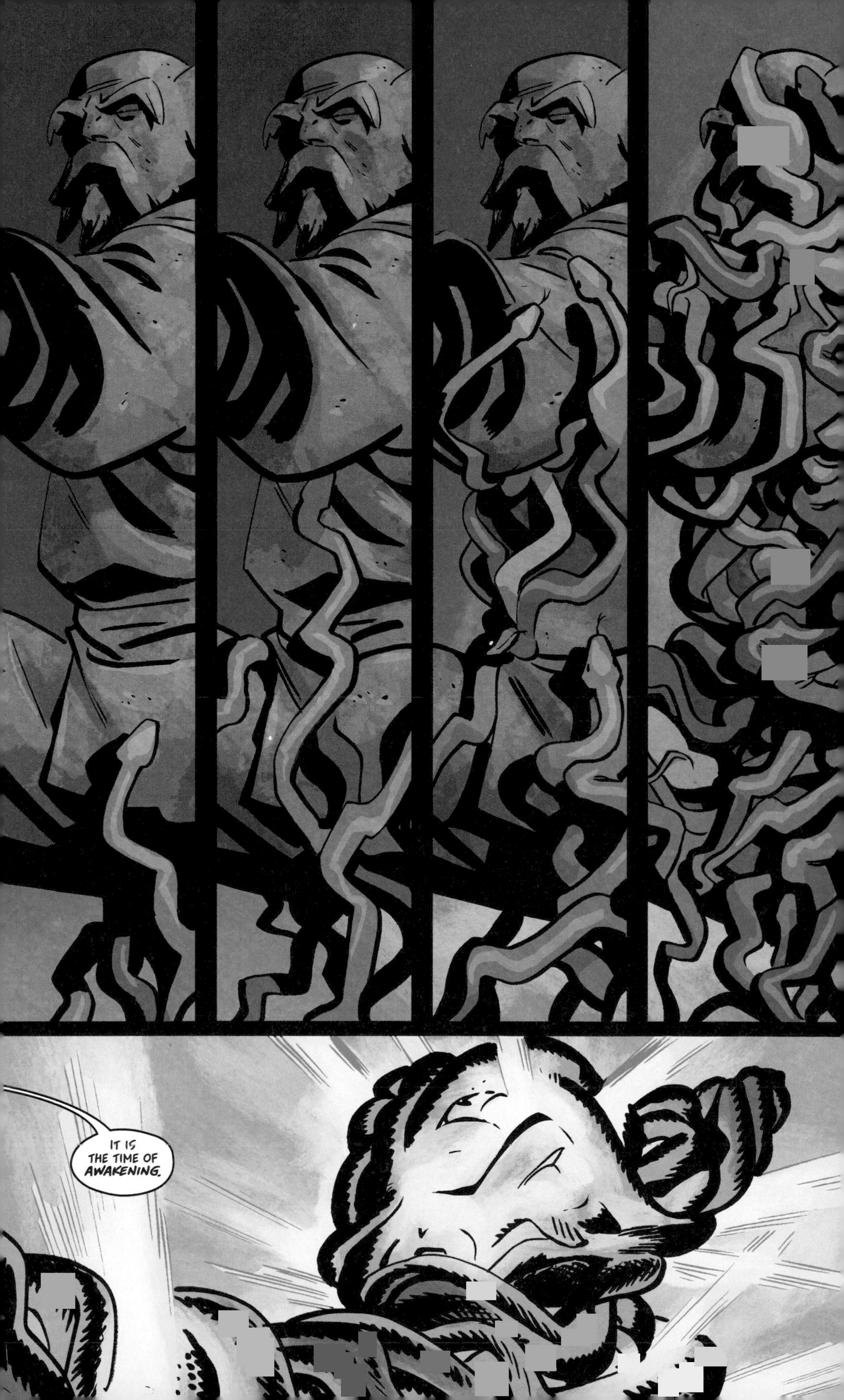
IT IS THE TIME OF AWAKENING.

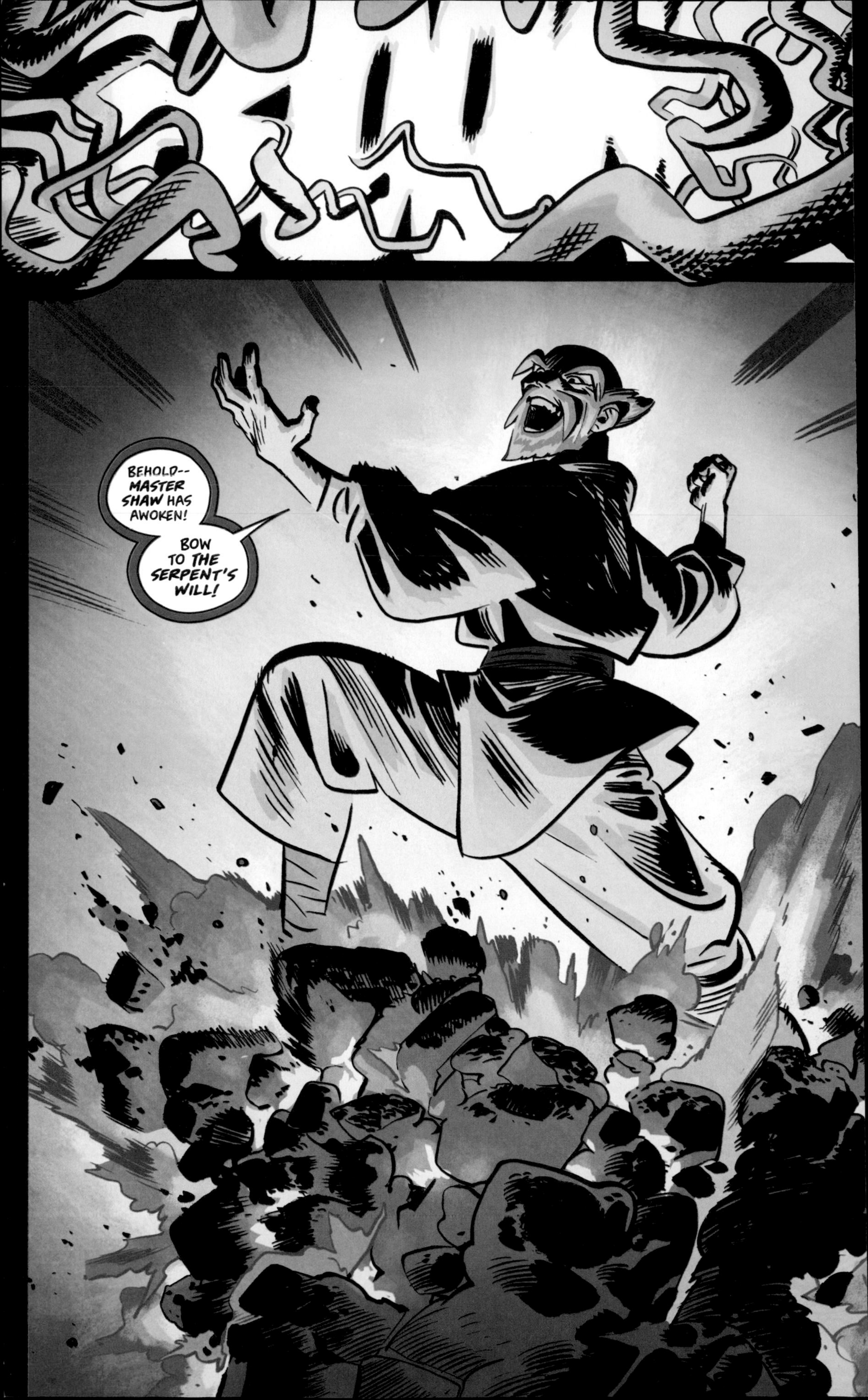
BEHOLD--
MASTER SHAW HAS AWOKEN!
BOW TO THE SERPENT'S WILL!

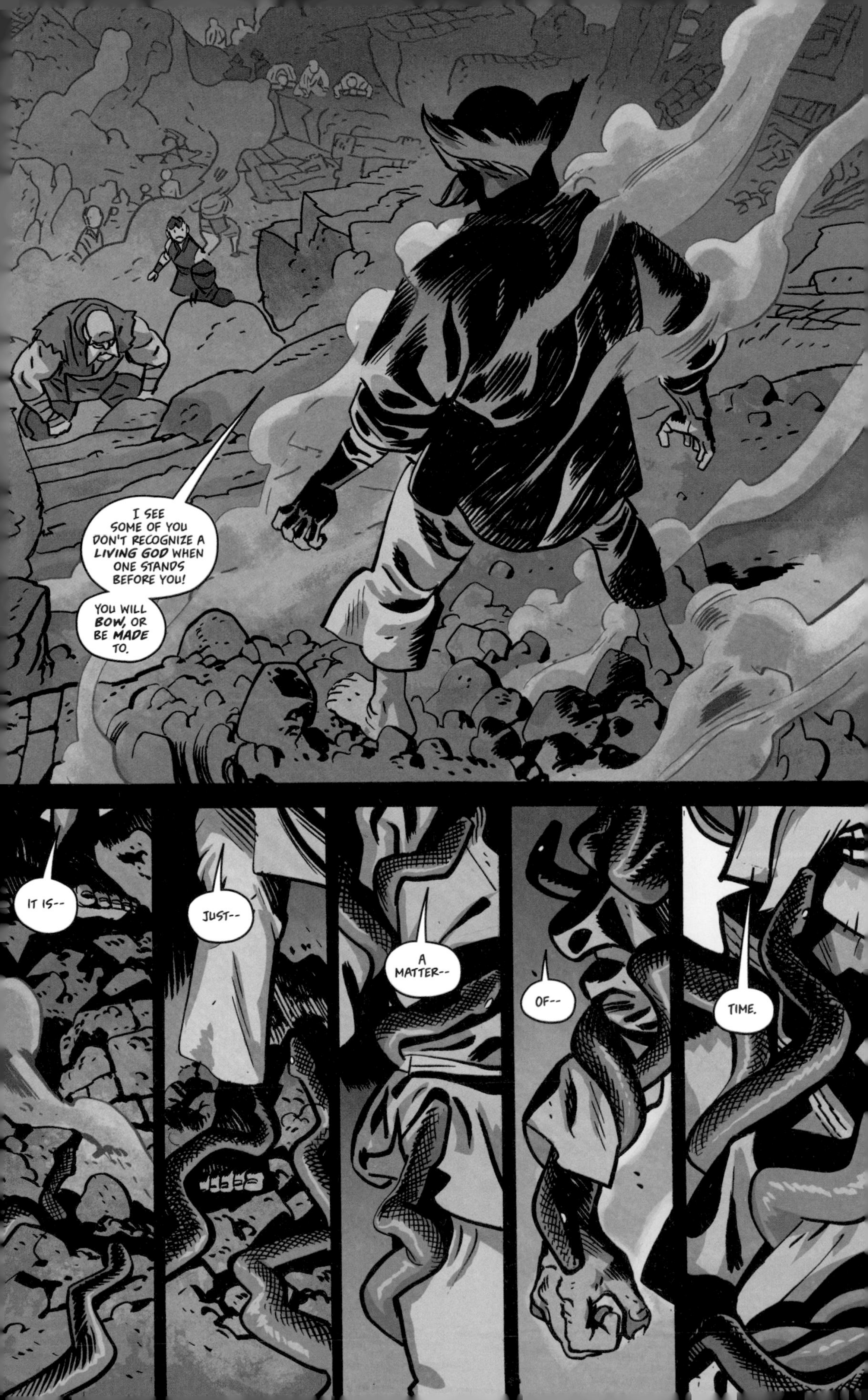
I SEE SOME OF YOU DON'T RECOGNIZE A *LIVING GOD* WHEN ONE STANDS BEFORE YOU!
YOU WILL *BOW,* OR BE *MADE* TO.
IT IS--
JUST--
A MATTER--
OF--
TIME.

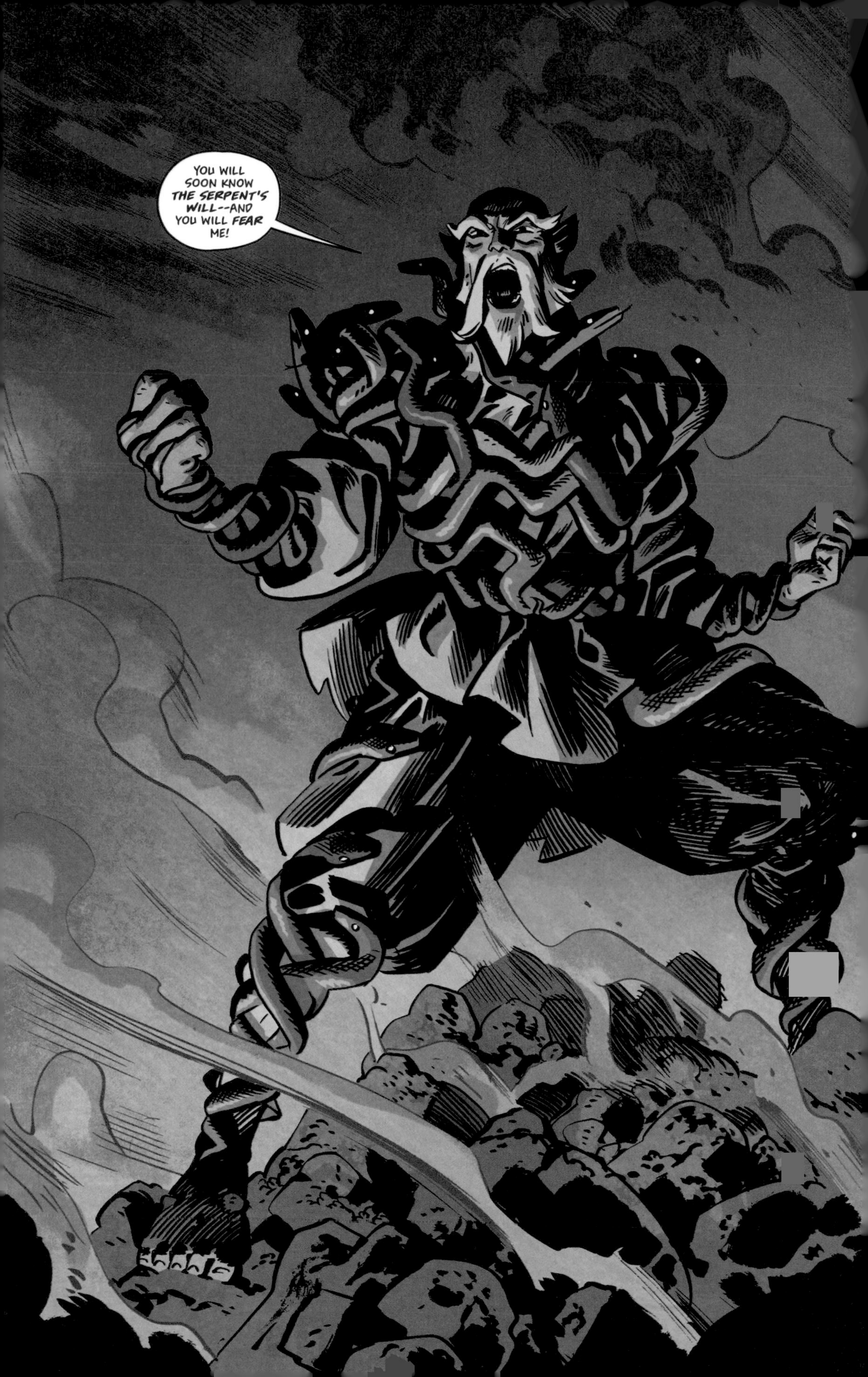
YOU WILL SOON KNOW THE SERPENT'S WILL--AND YOU WILL FEAR ME!

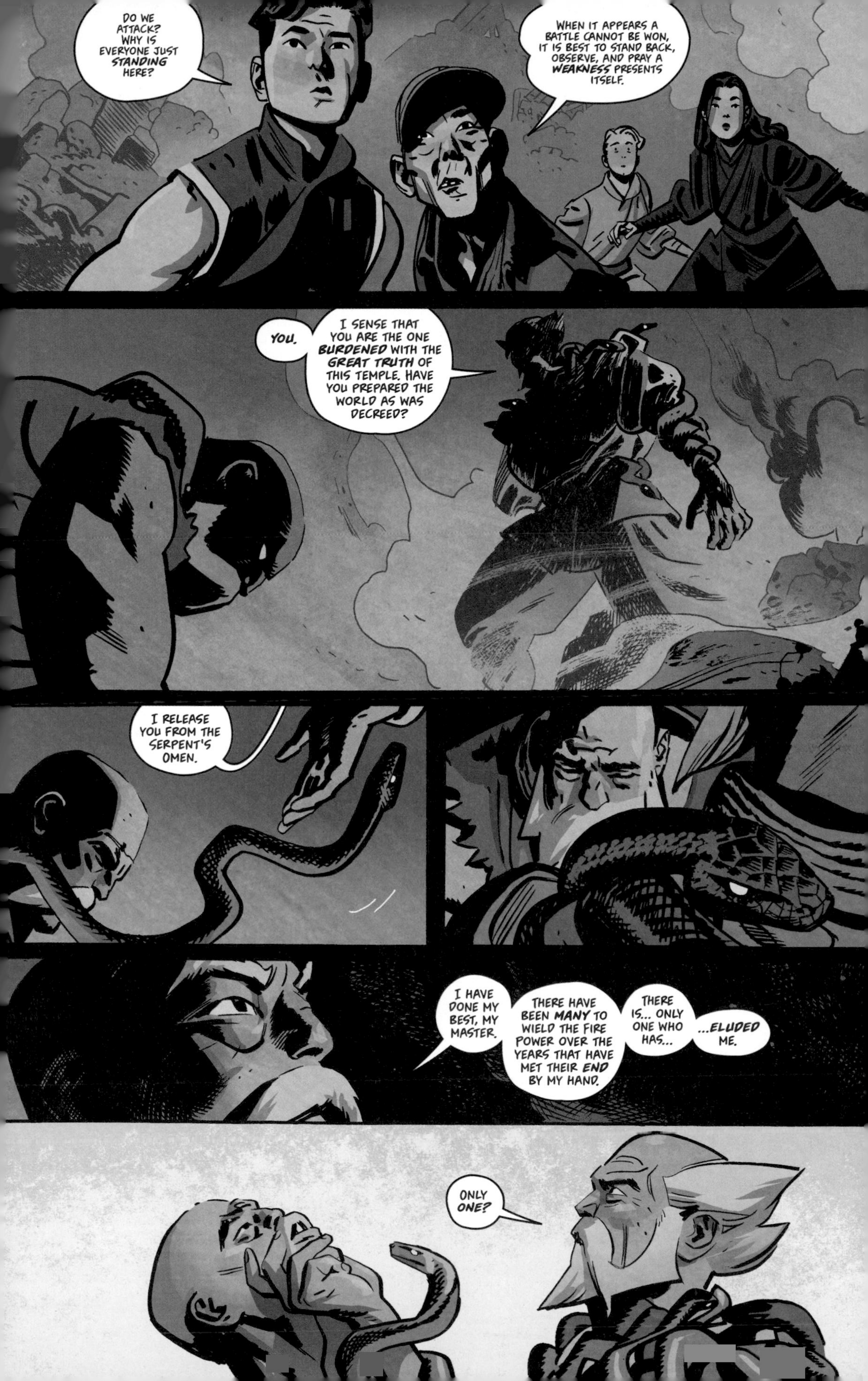
DO WE ATTACK? WHY IS EVERYONE JUST STANDING HERE?
WHEN IT APPEARS A BATTLE CANNOT BE WON, IT IS BEST TO STAND BACK, OBSERVE, AND PRAY A WEAKNESS PRESENTS ITSELF.
YOU.
I SENSE THAT YOU ARE THE ONE BURDENED WITH THE GREAT TRUTH OF THIS TEMPLE. HAVE YOU PREPARED THE WORLD AS WAS DECREED?
I RELEASE YOU FROM THE SERPENT'S OMEN.
I HAVE DONE MY BEST, MY MASTER.
THERE HAVE BEEN MANY TO WIELD THE FIRE POWER OVER THE YEARS THAT HAVE MET THEIR END BY MY HAND.
THERE IS... ONLY ONE WHO HAS...
...ELUDED ME.
ONLY ONE?

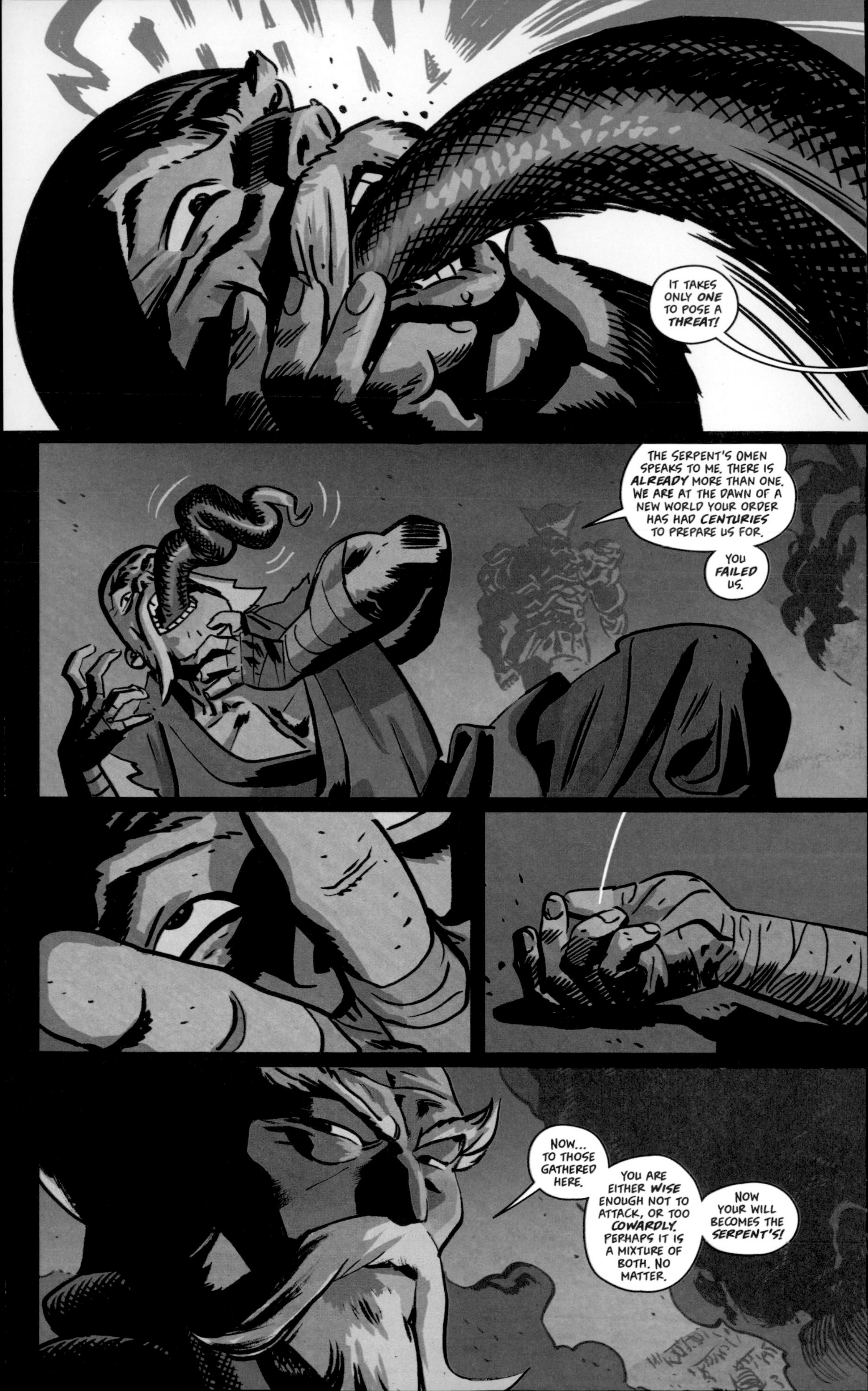
IT TAKES ONLY ONE TO POSE A THREAT!
THE SERPENT'S OMEN SPEAKS TO ME. THERE IS ALREADY MORE THAN ONE. WE ARE AT THE DAWN OF A NEW WORLD YOUR ORDER HAS HAD CENTURIES TO PREPARE US FOR.
YOU FAILED US.
NOW... TO THOSE GATHERED HERE.
YOU ARE EITHER WISE ENOUGH NOT TO ATTACK, OR TOO COWARDLY. PERHAPS IT IS A MIXTURE OF BOTH. NO MATTER.
NOW YOUR WILL BECOMES THE SERPENT'S!

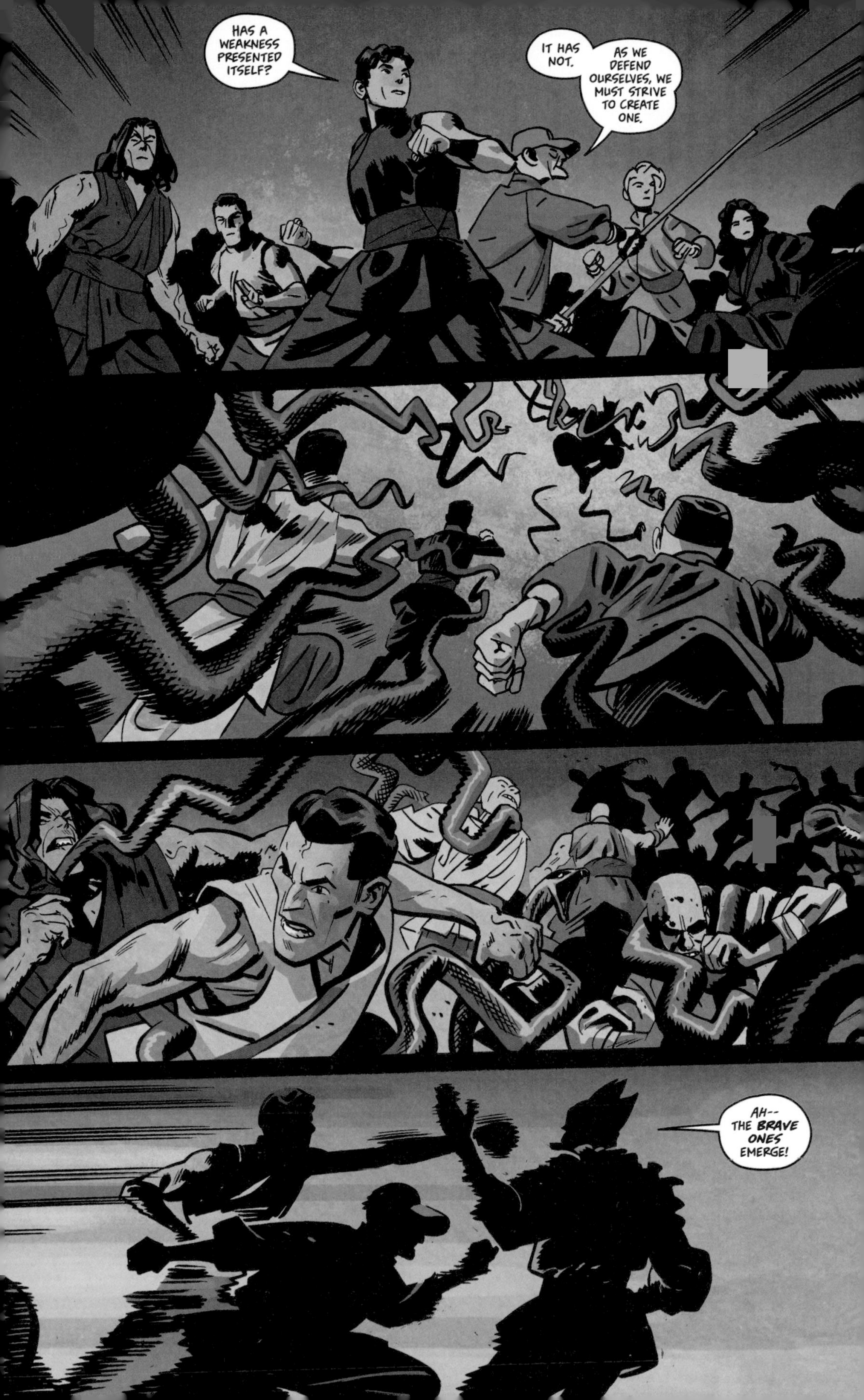
HAS A WEAKNESS PRESENTED ITSELF?
IT HAS NOT.
AS WE DEFEND OURSELVES, WE MUST STRIVE TO CREATE ONE.
AH-- THE **BRAVE ONES** EMERGE!

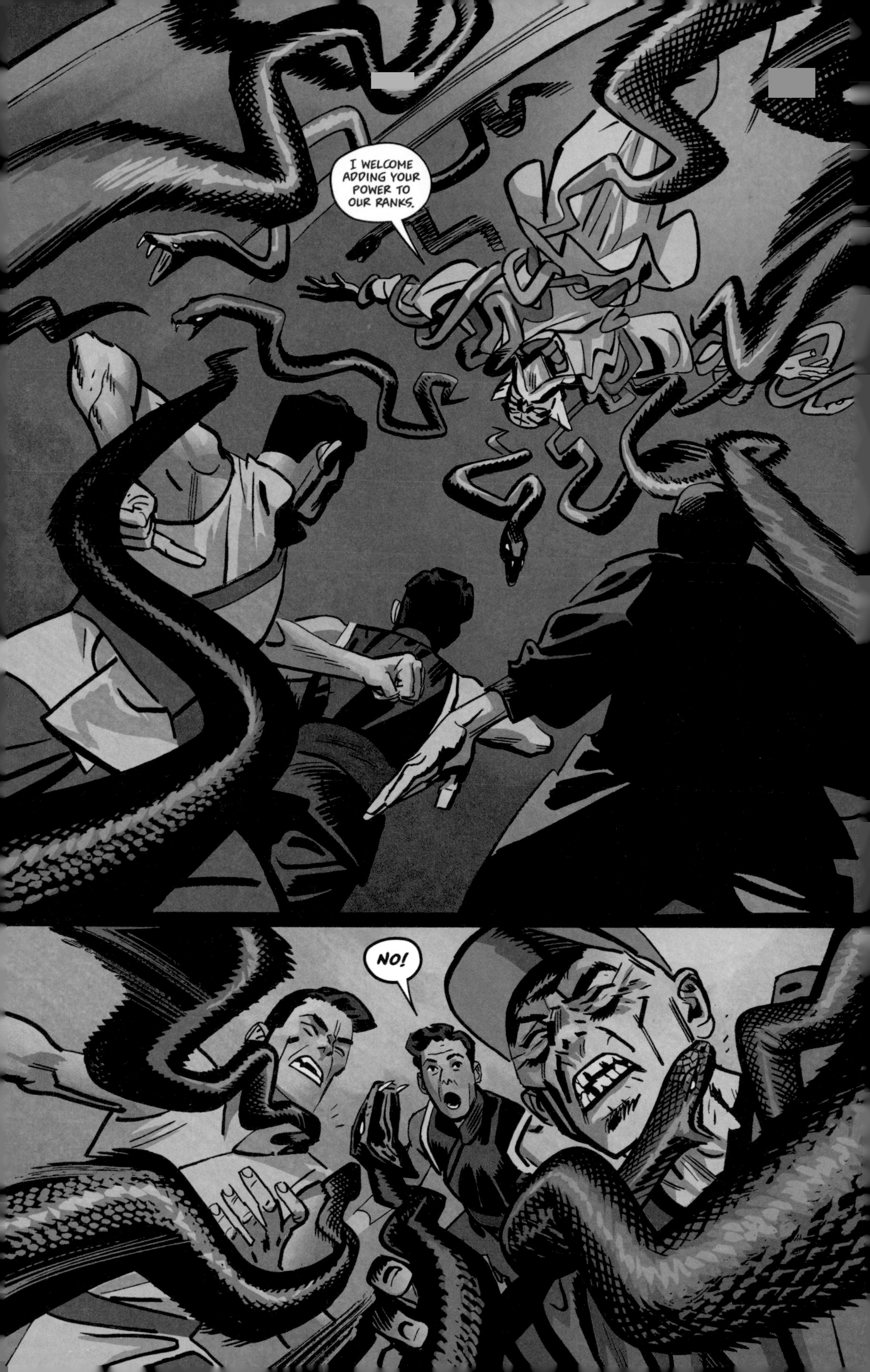
I WELCOME ADDING YOUR POWER TO OUR RANKS.
NO!

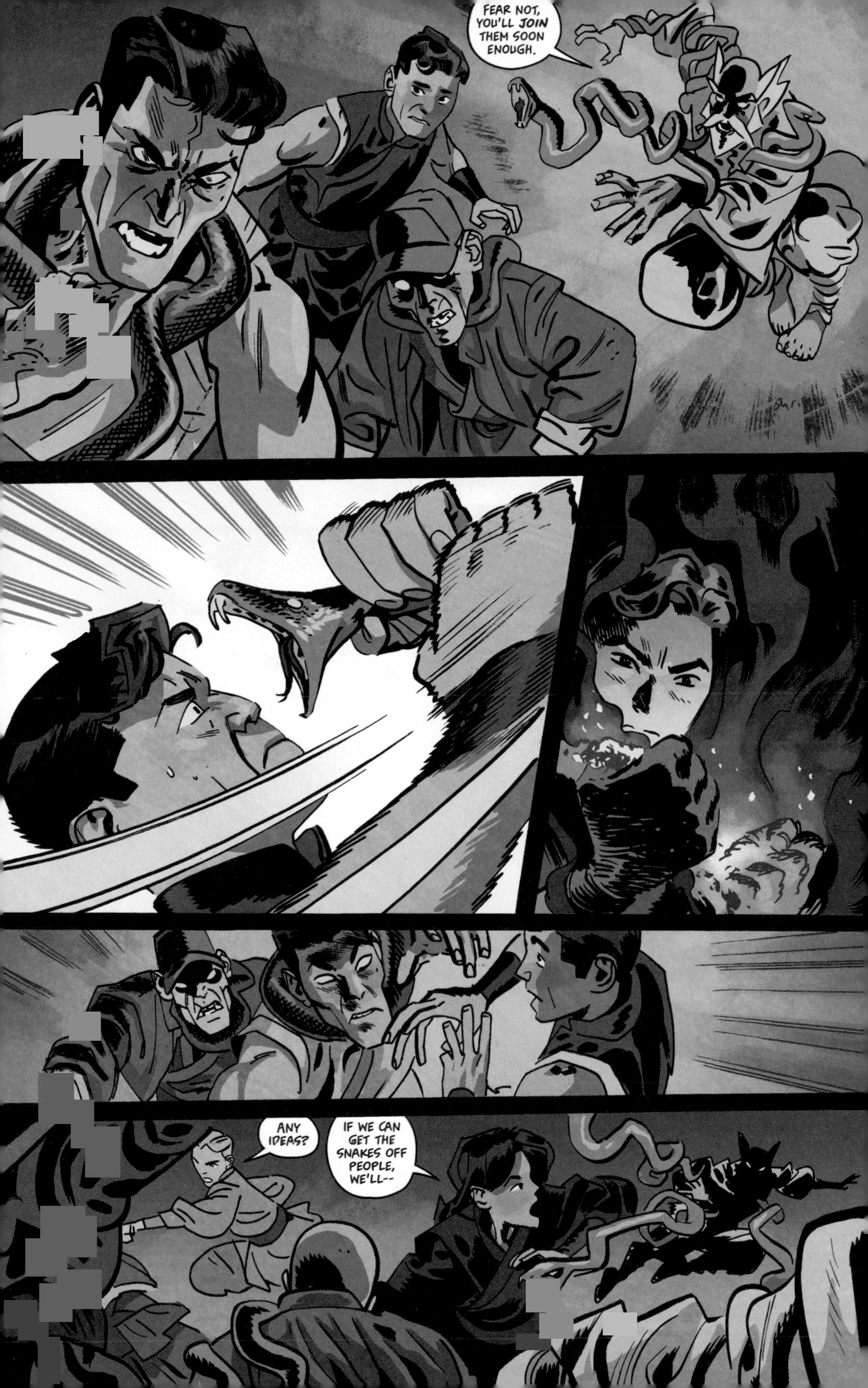
FEAR NOT, YOU'LL JOIN THEM SOON ENOUGH.
ANY IDEAS?
IF WE CAN GET THE SNAKES OFF PEOPLE, WE'LL--

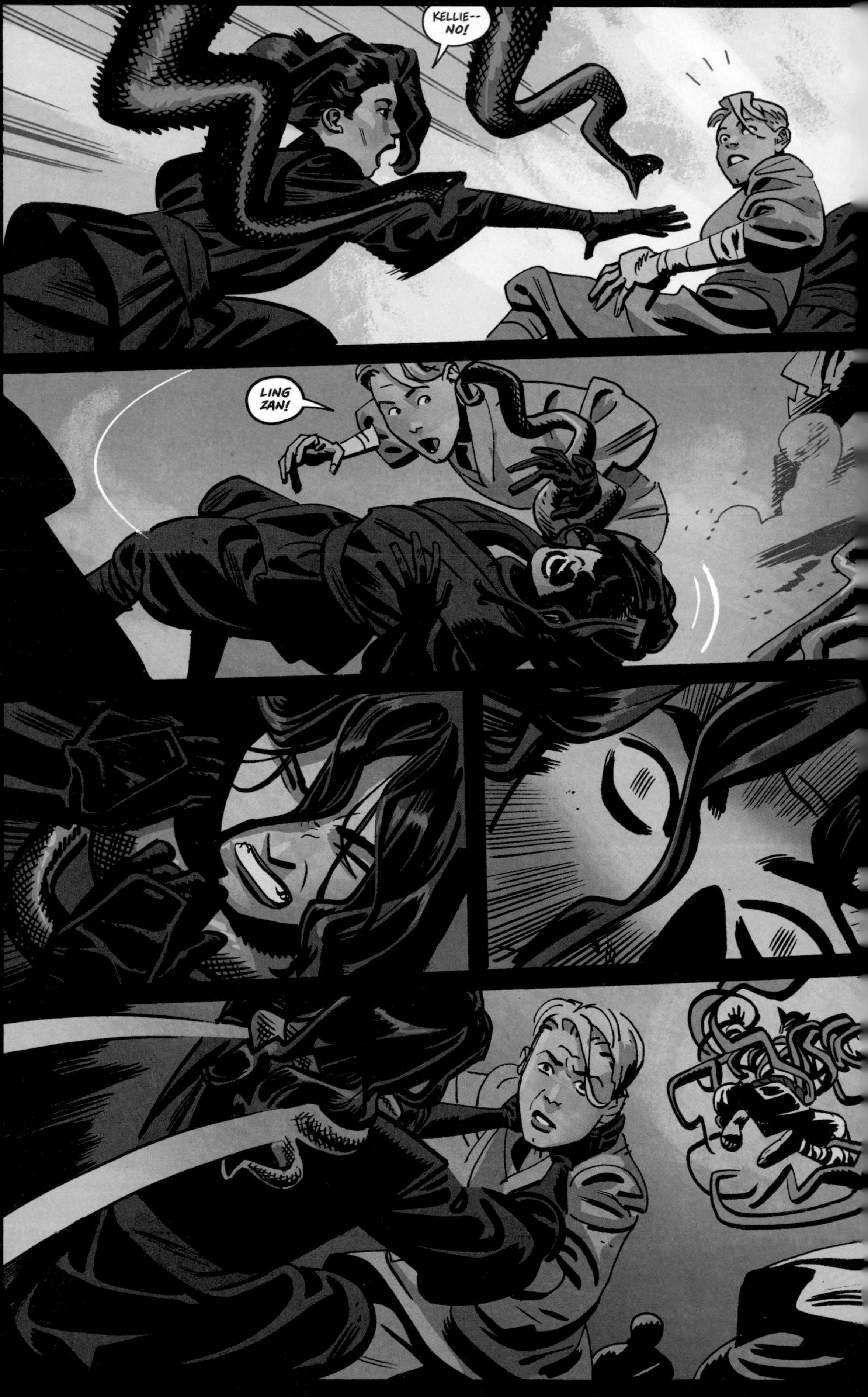
KELLIE--
NO!
LING
ZAN!

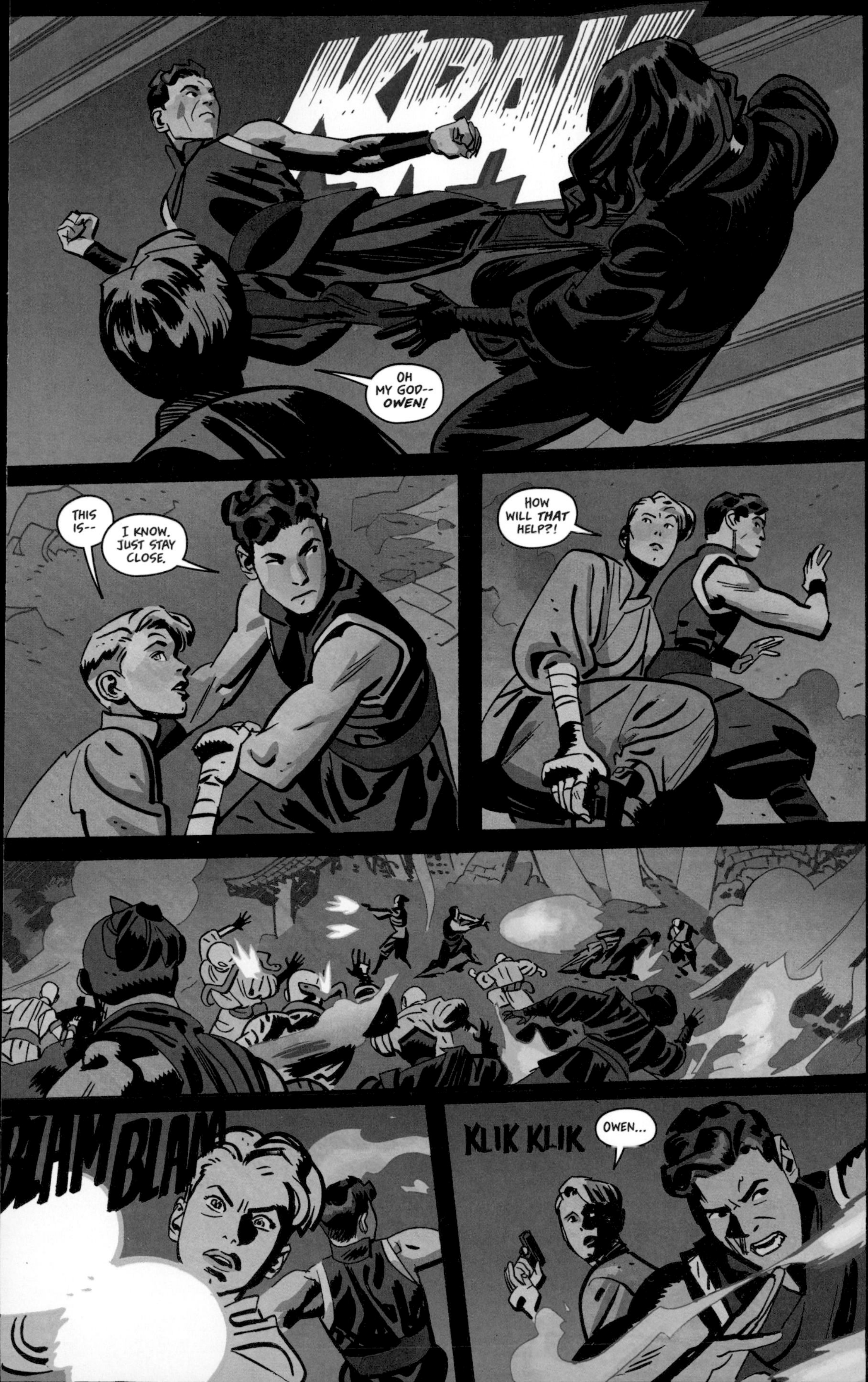
KRAK
OH MY GOD-- OWEN!
THIS IS--
I KNOW. JUST STAY CLOSE.
HOW WILL THAT HELP?!
BLAM BLAM
KLIK KLIK
OWEN...

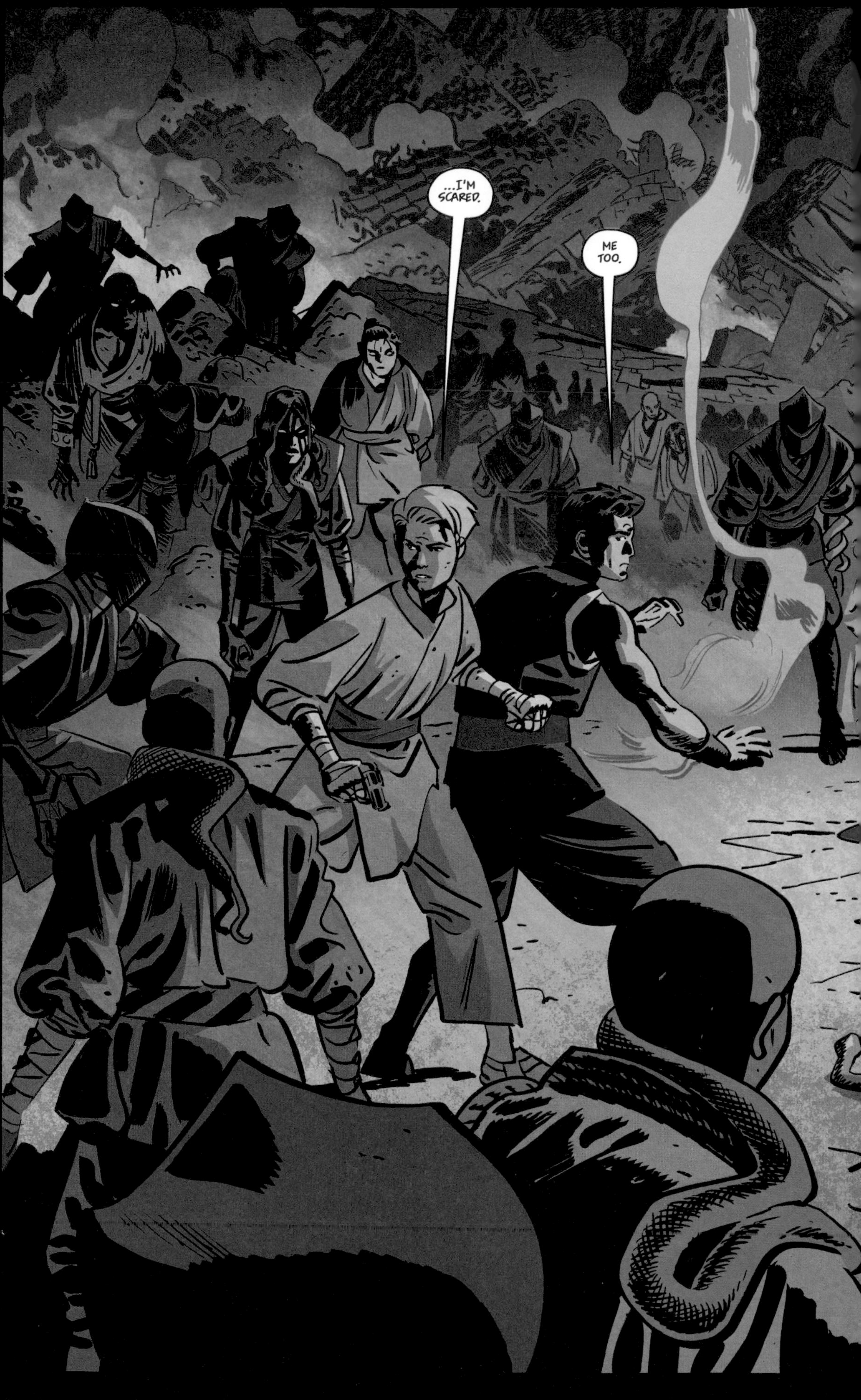
...I'M SCARED.
ME TOO.

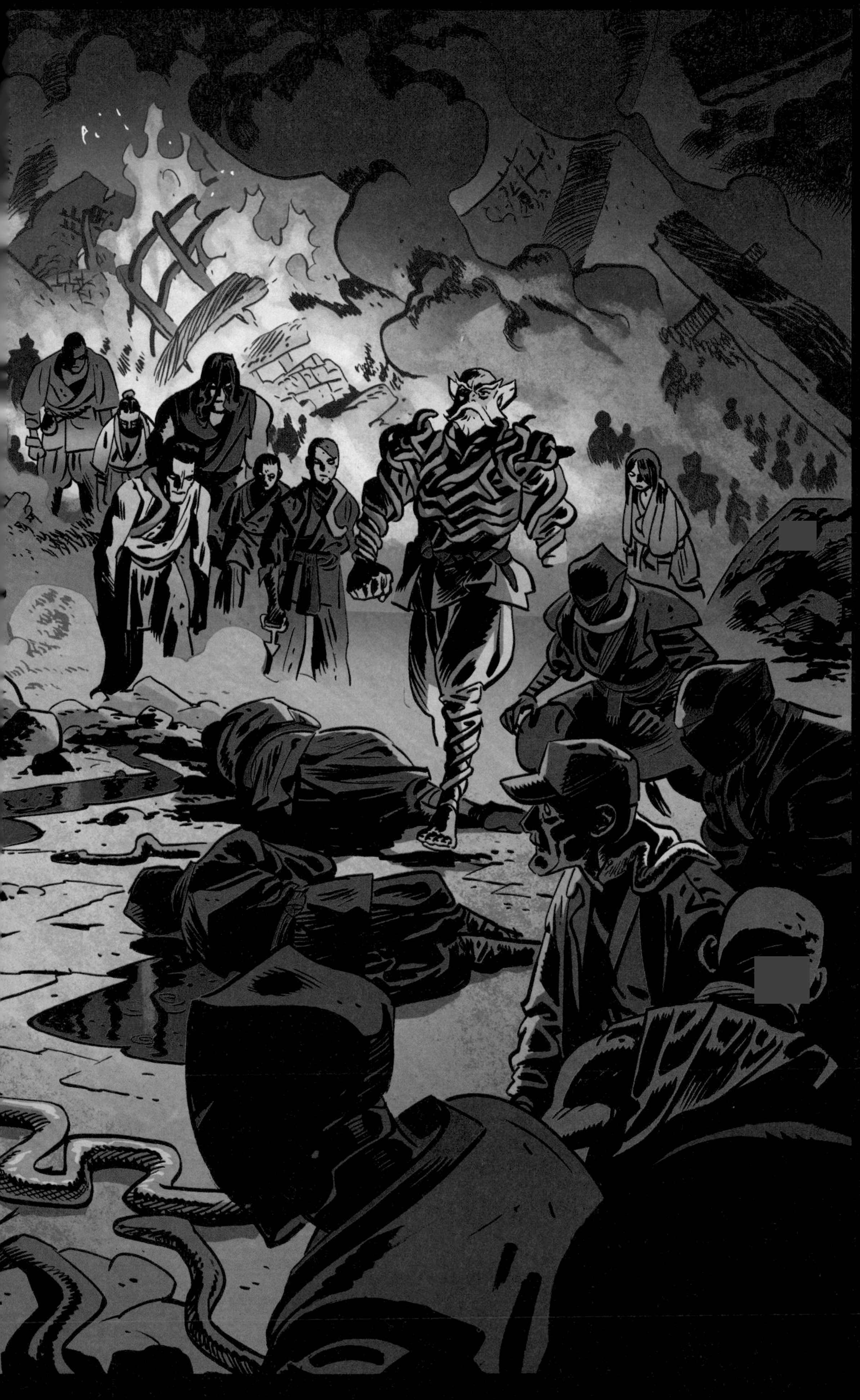

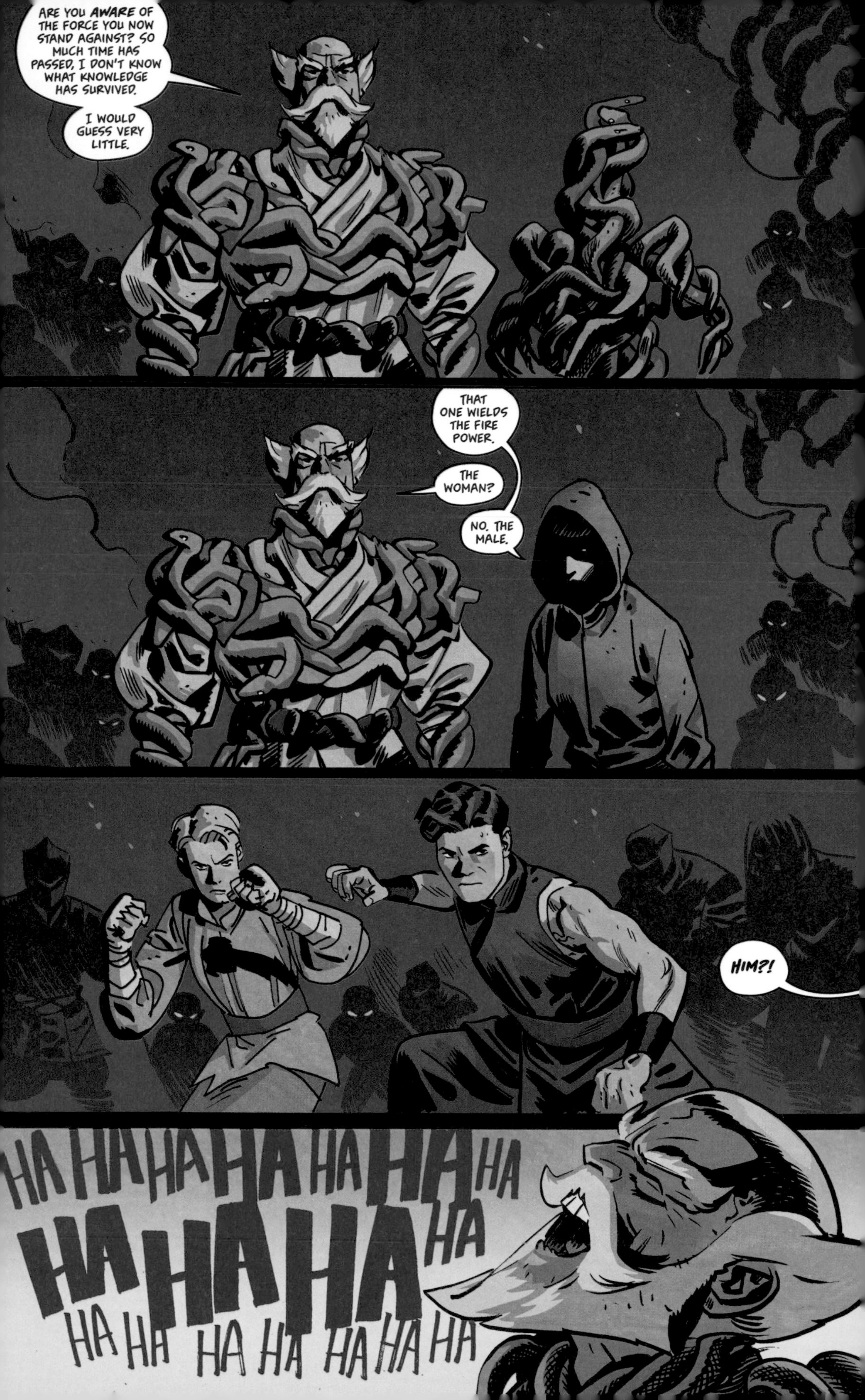
ARE YOU AWARE OF THE FORCE YOU NOW STAND AGAINST? SO MUCH TIME HAS PASSED, I DON'T KNOW WHAT KNOWLEDGE HAS SURVIVED.
I WOULD GUESS VERY LITTLE.
THAT ONE WIELDS THE FIRE POWER.
THE WOMAN?
NO. THE MALE.
HIM?!
HA HA HA HA HA HA HA HA HA HA HA HA HA HA HA HA HA HA HA HA HA HA HA HA HA HA

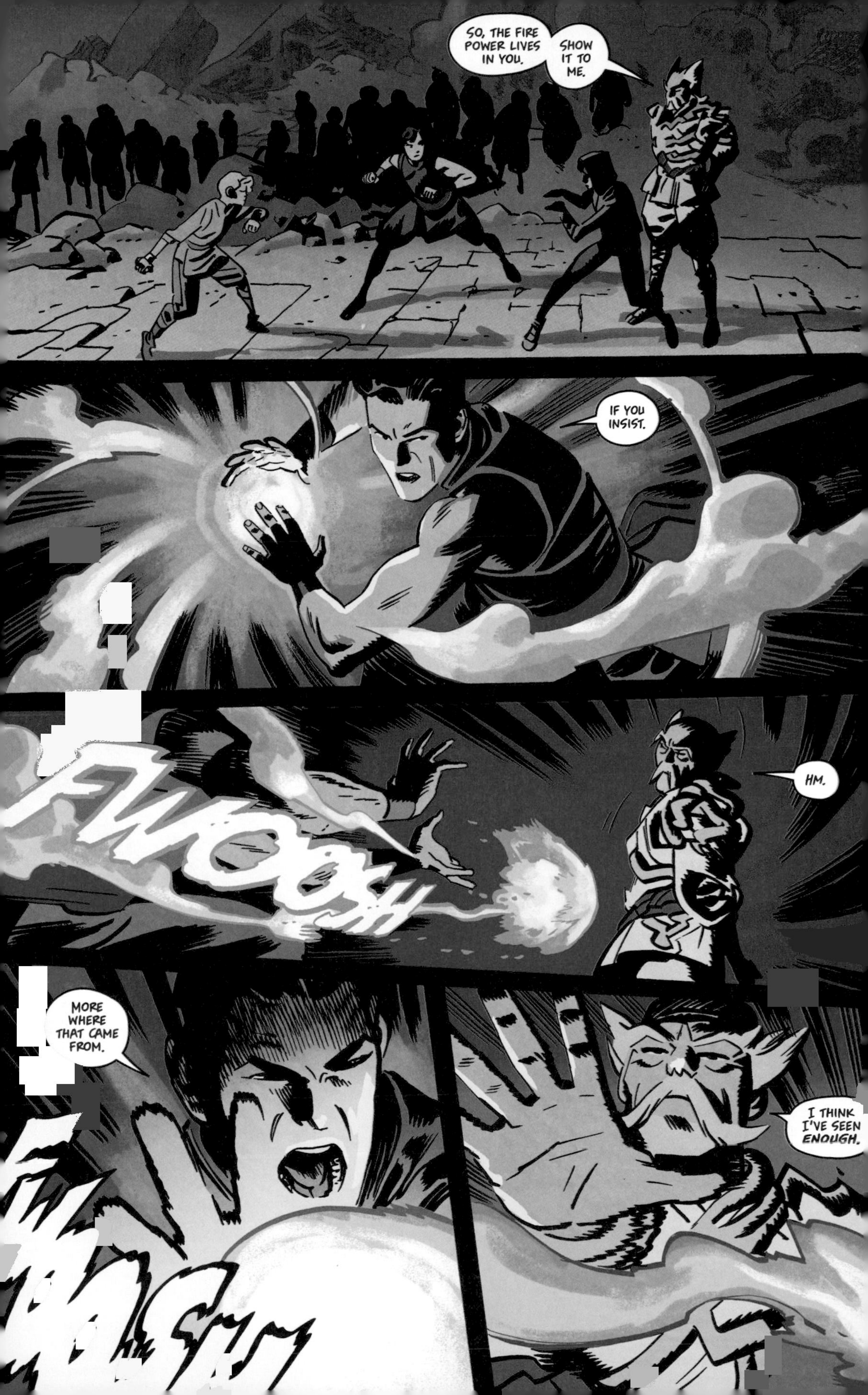
SO, THE FIRE POWER LIVES IN YOU.
SHOW IT TO ME.
IF YOU INSIST.
HM.
MORE WHERE THAT CAME FROM.
I THINK I'VE SEEN *ENOUGH.*

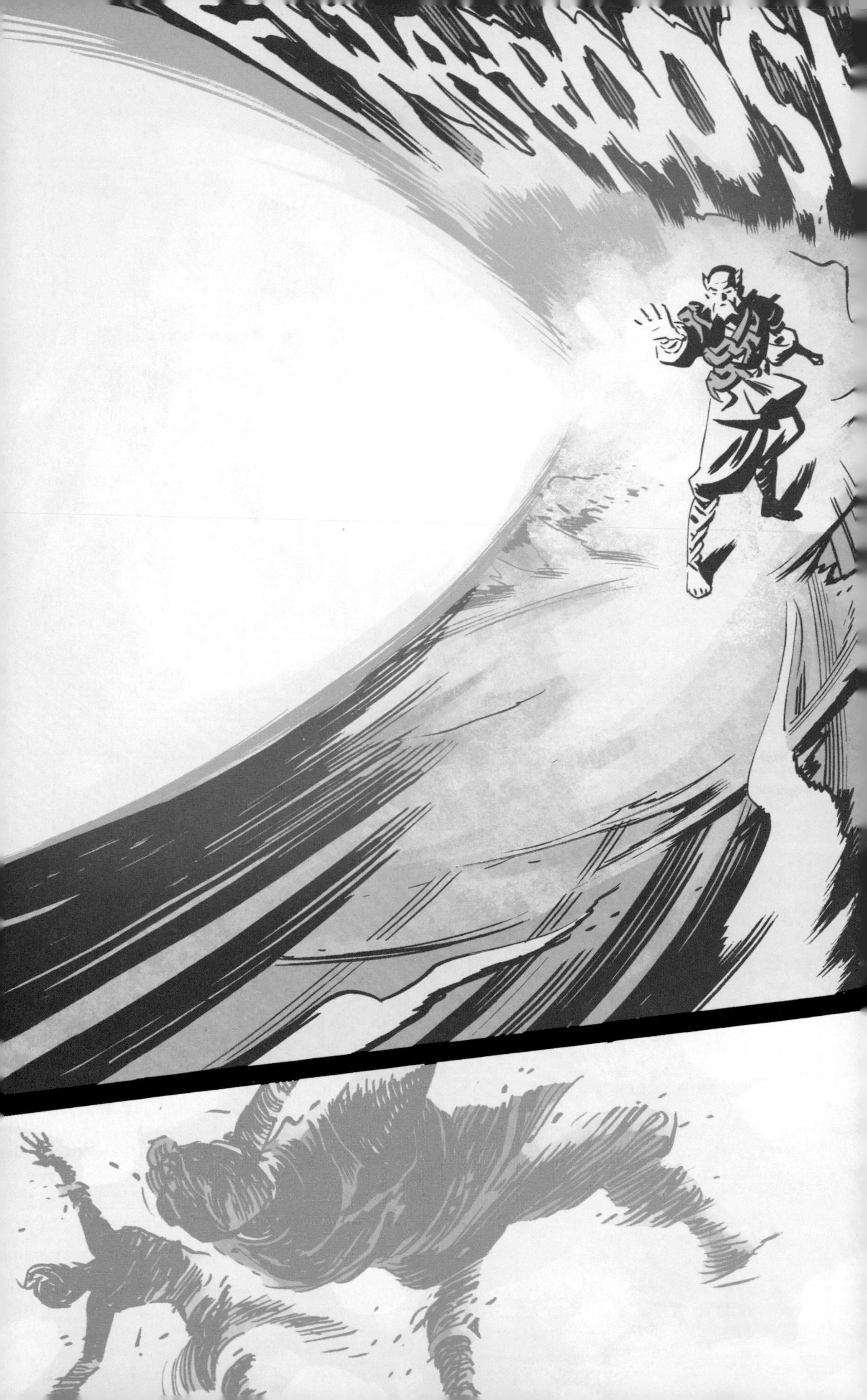

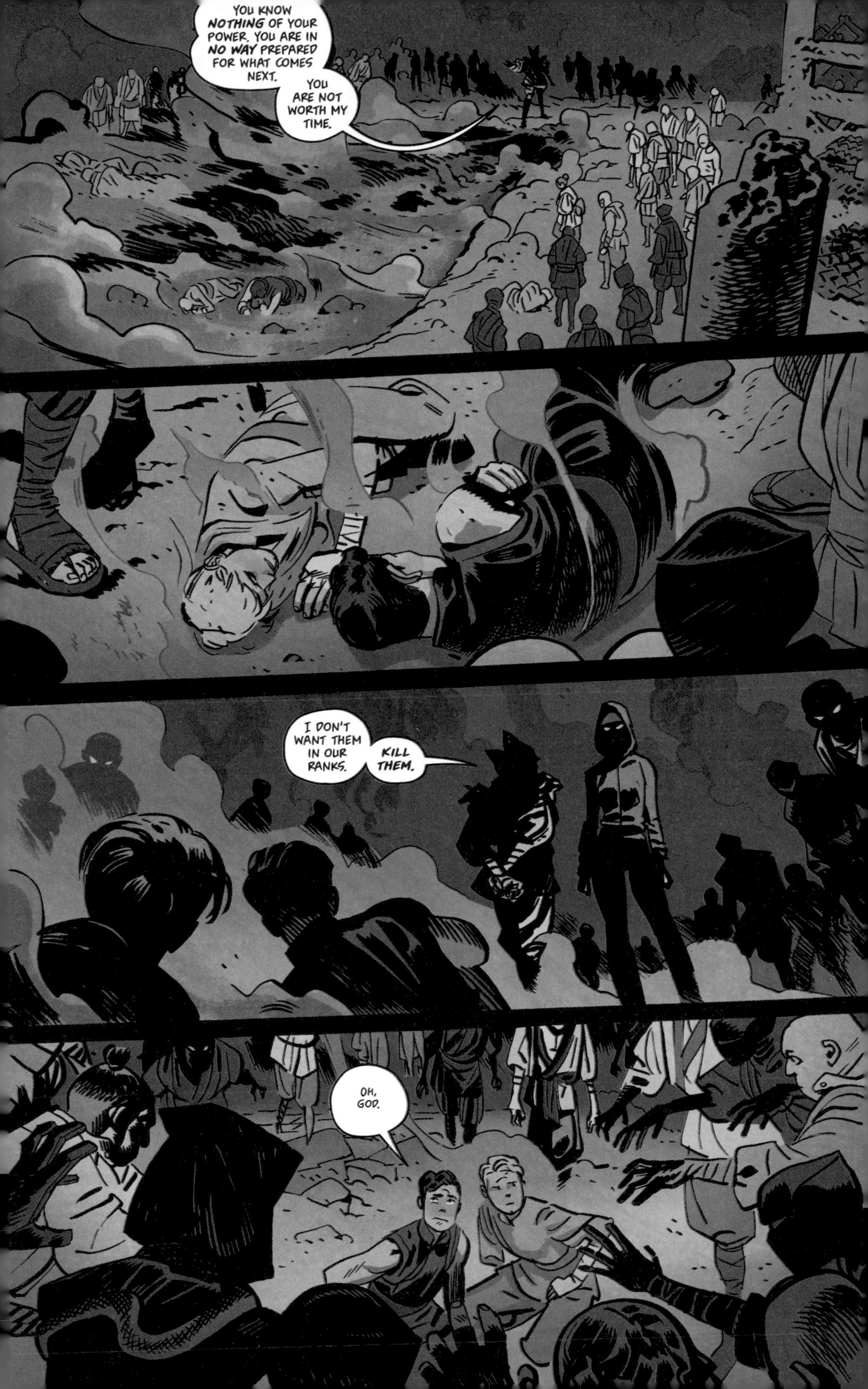
YOU KNOW NOTHING OF YOUR POWER. YOU ARE IN NO WAY PREPARED FOR WHAT COMES NEXT.
YOU ARE NOT WORTH MY TIME.
I DON'T WANT THEM IN OUR RANKS.
KILL THEM.
OH, GOD.

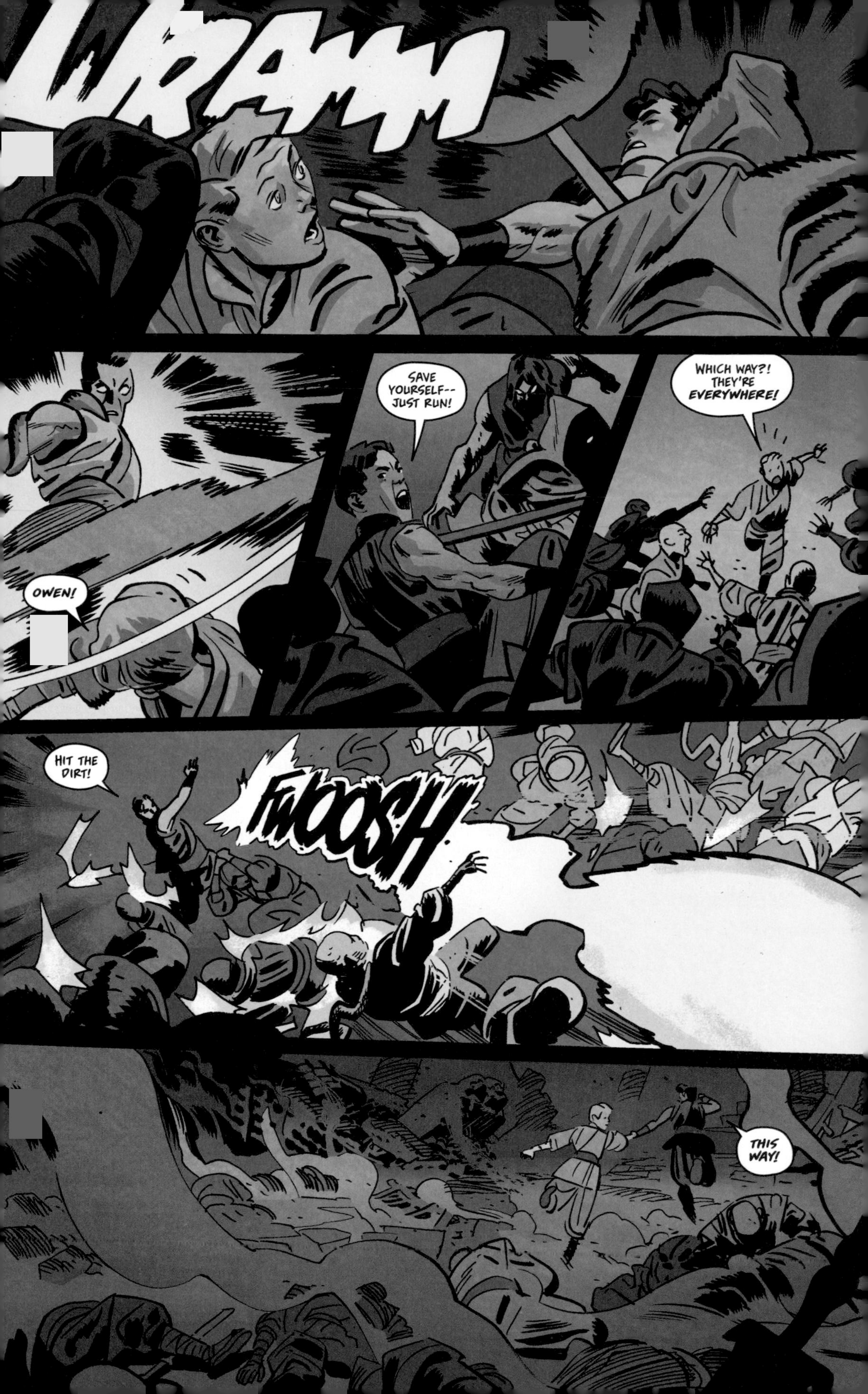
KRAMM
OWEN!
SAVE YOURSELF-- JUST RUN!
WHICH WAY?! THEY'RE EVERYWHERE!
HIT THE DIRT!
FWOOSH
THIS WAY!

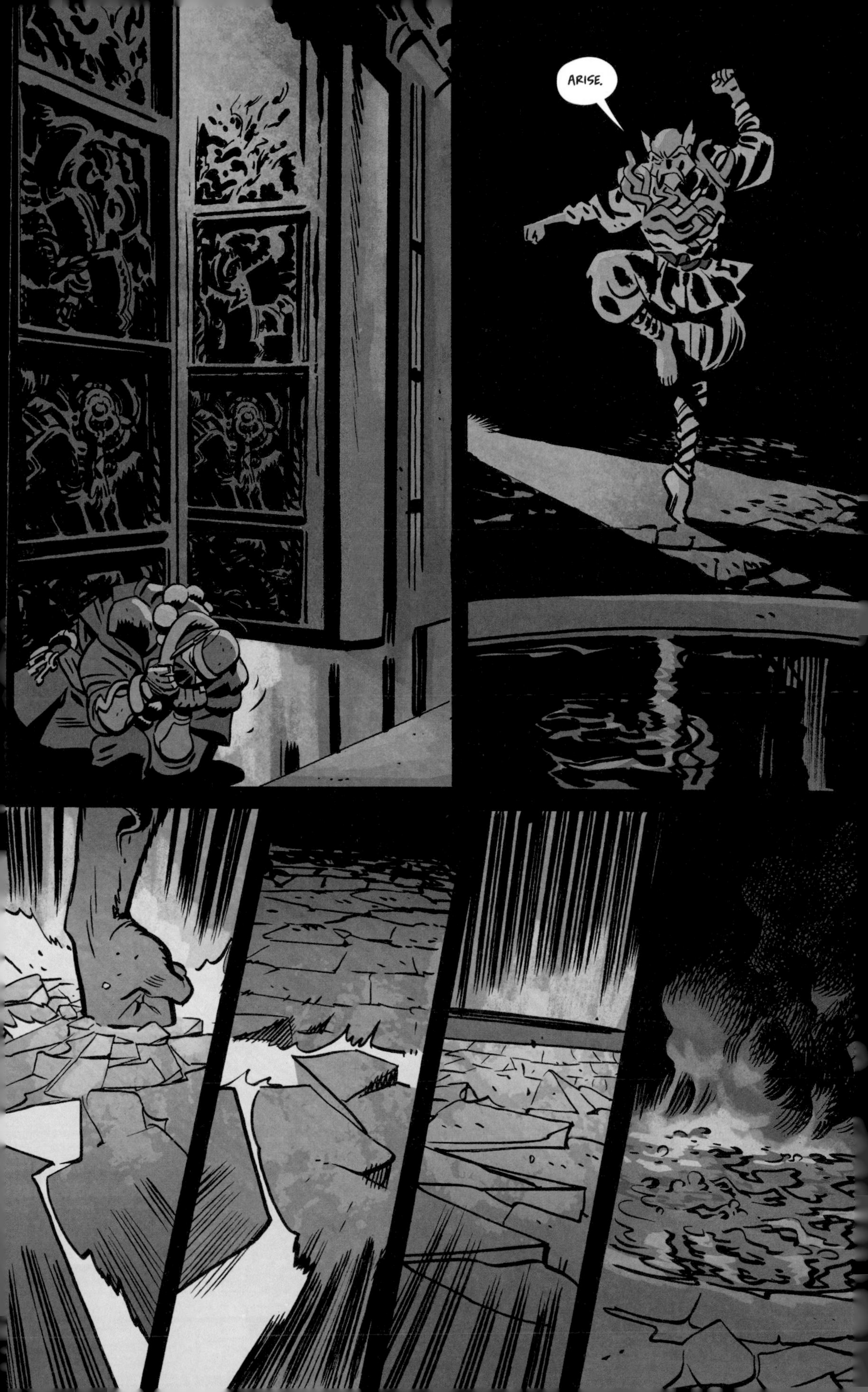
ARISE.

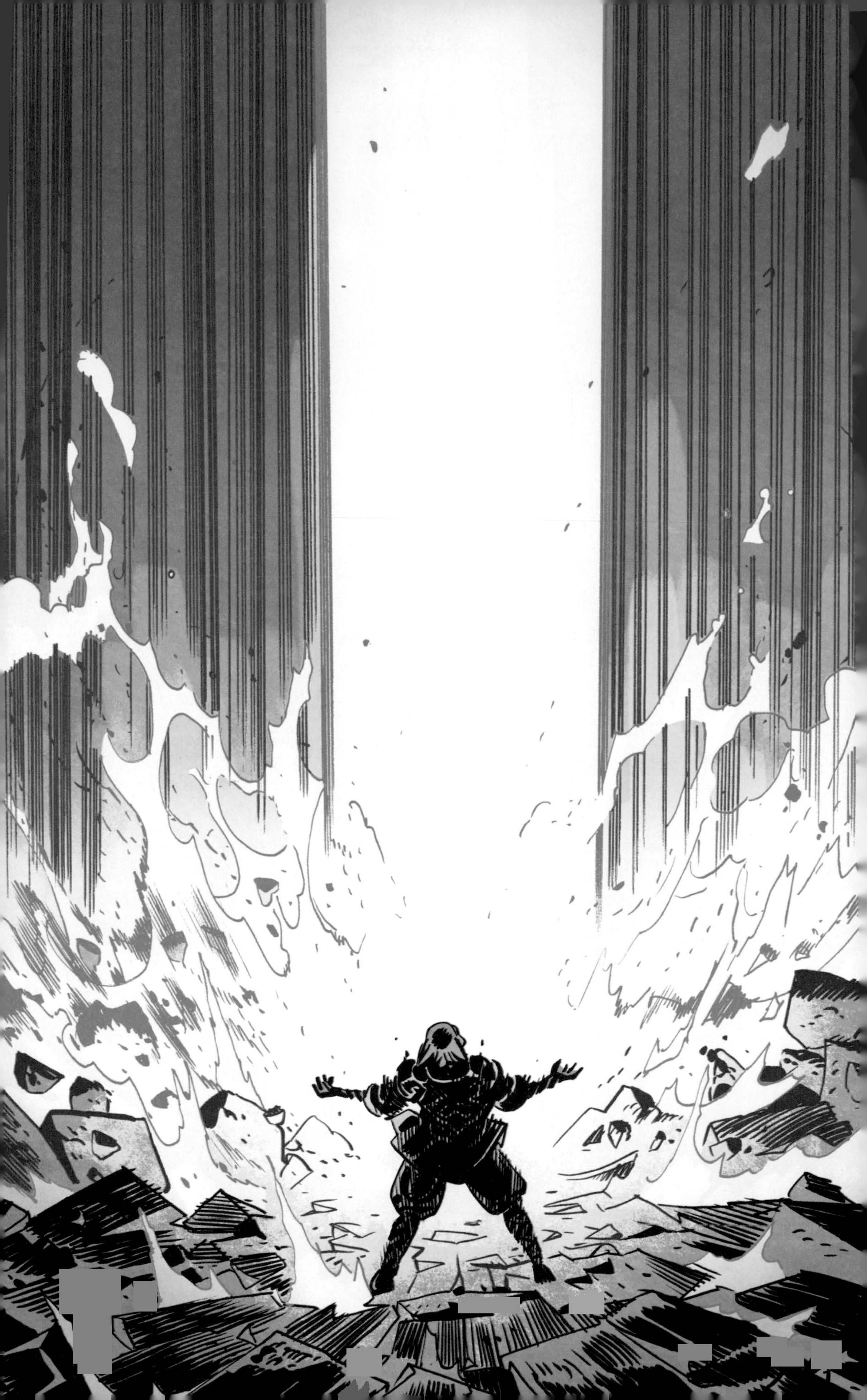

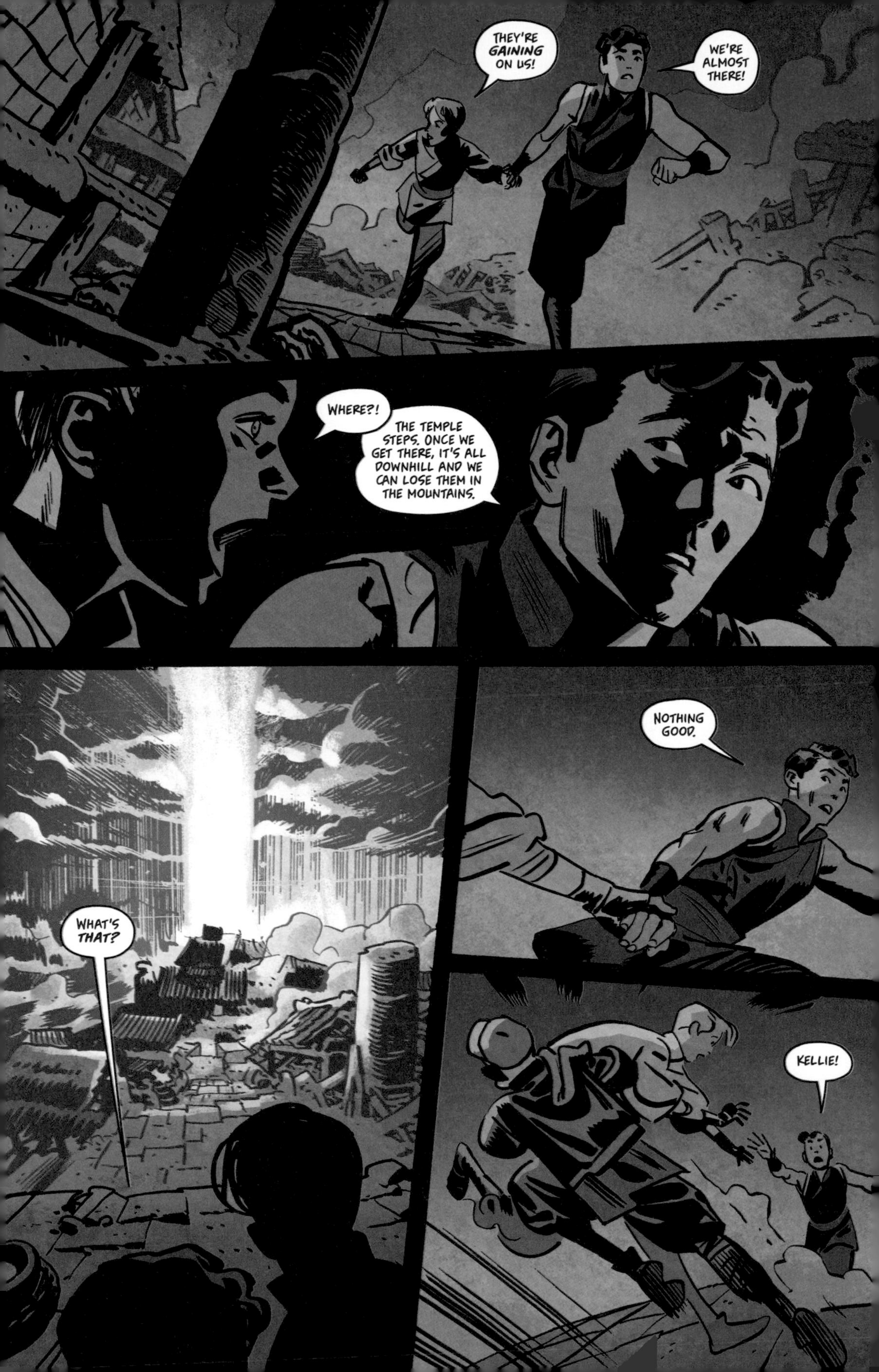
THEY'RE GAINING ON US!
WE'RE ALMOST THERE!
WHERE?!
THE TEMPLE STEPS. ONCE WE GET THERE, IT'S ALL DOWNHILL AND WE CAN LOSE THEM IN THE MOUNTAINS.
WHAT'S THAT?
NOTHING GOOD.
KELLIE!

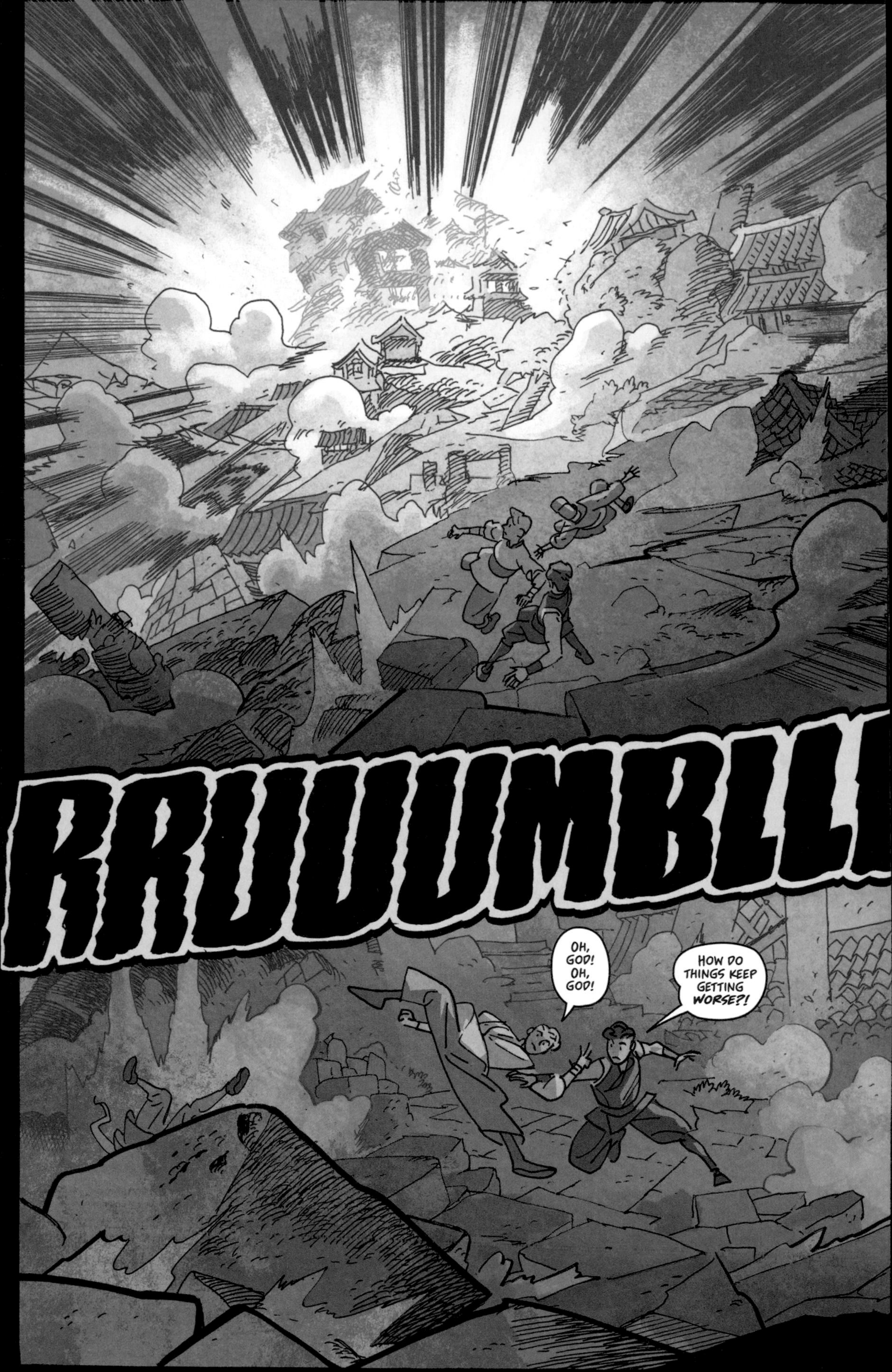
RRUUUMBLL
OH, GOD! OH, GOD!
HOW DO THINGS KEEP GETTING WORSE?!

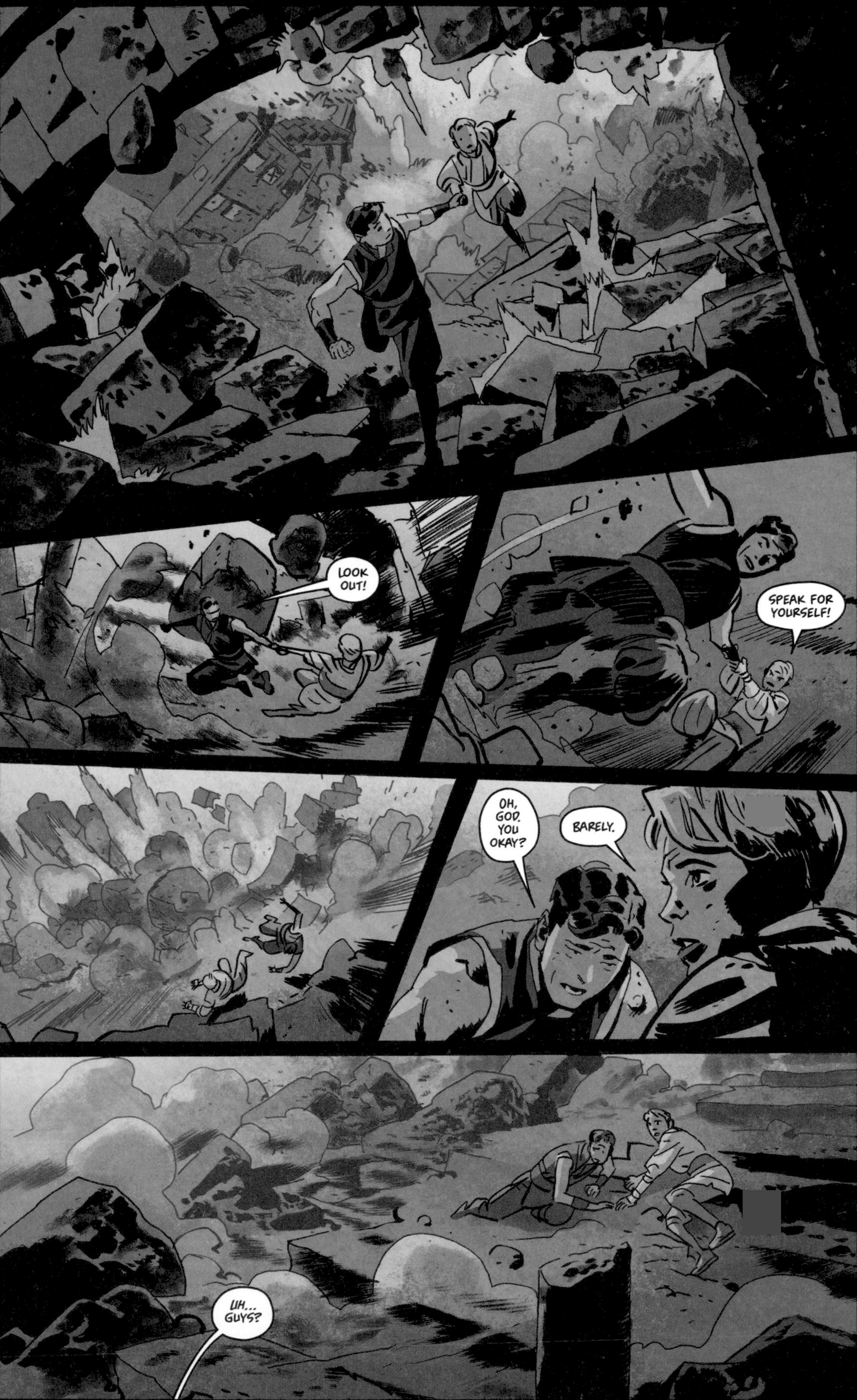
LOOK OUT!
SPEAK FOR YOURSELF!
OH, GOD. YOU OKAY?
BARELY.
UH... GUYS?

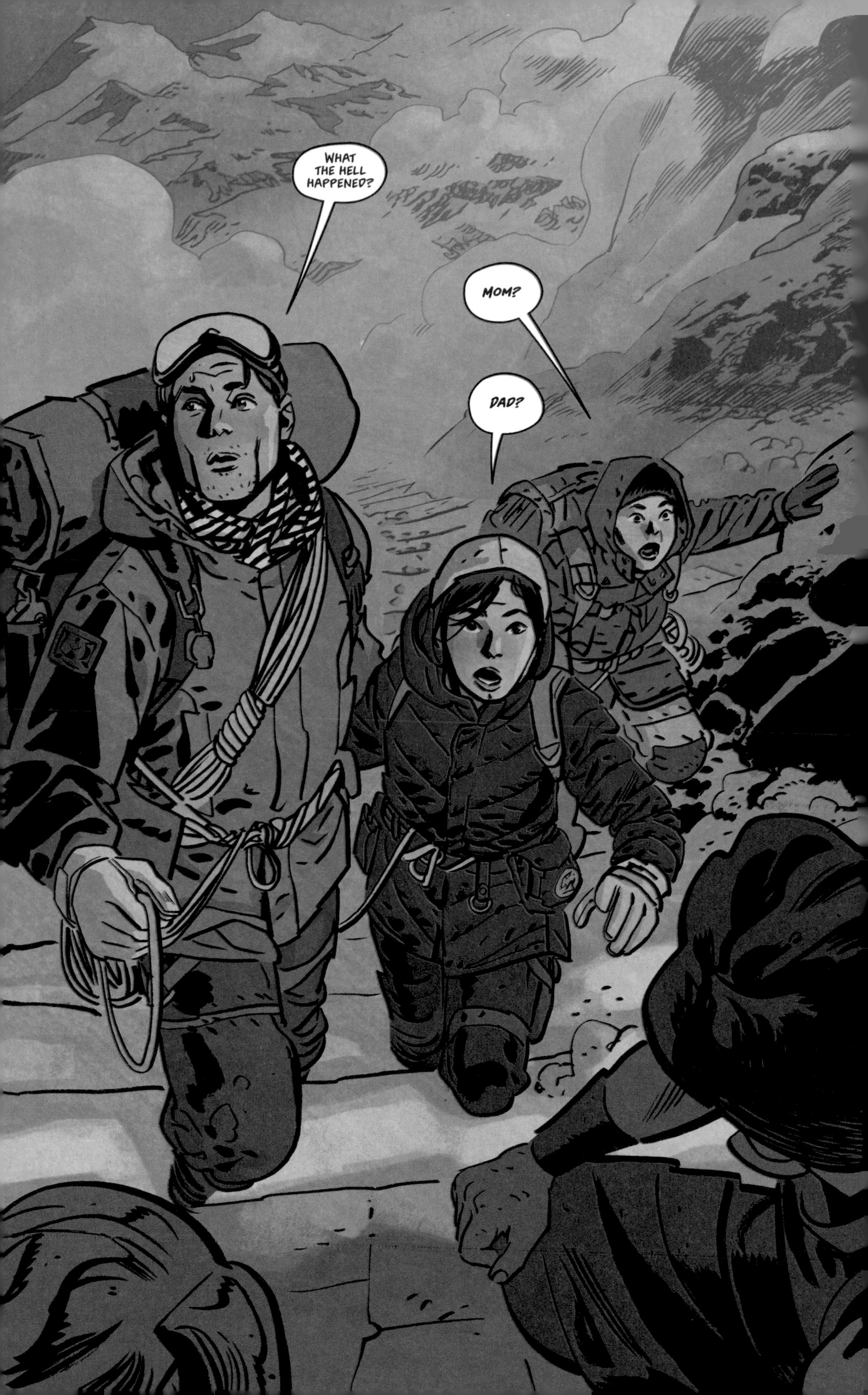
WHAT THE HELL HAPPENED?
MOM?
DAD?

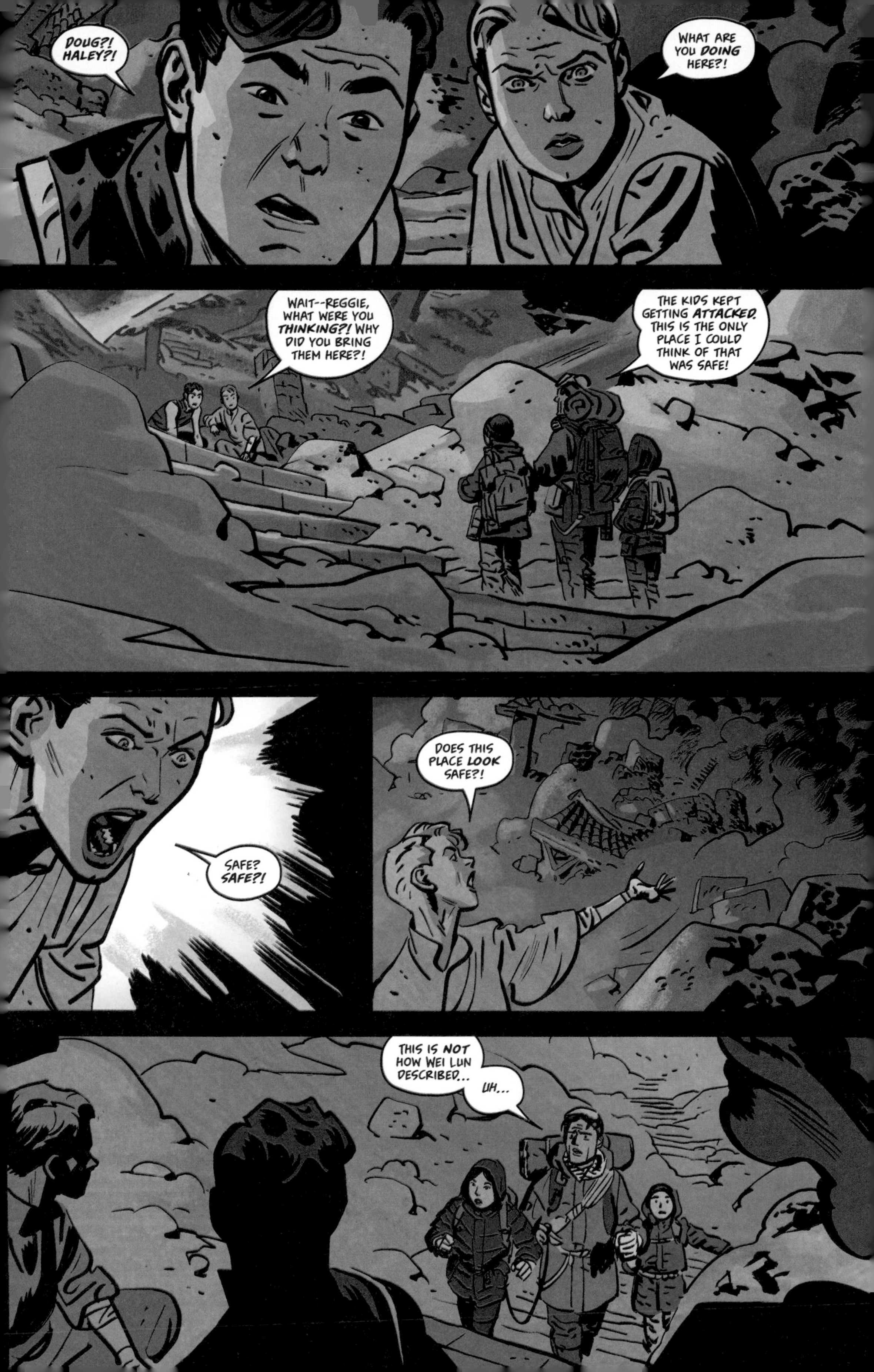
DOUG?! HALEY?!
WHAT ARE YOU DOING HERE?!
WAIT--REGGIE, WHAT WERE YOU THINKING?! WHY DID YOU BRING THEM HERE?!
THE KIDS KEPT GETTING ATTACKED. THIS IS THE ONLY PLACE I COULD THINK OF THAT WAS SAFE!
SAFE? SAFE?!
DOES THIS PLACE LOOK SAFE?!
THIS IS NOT HOW WEI LUN DESCRIBED...
UH...

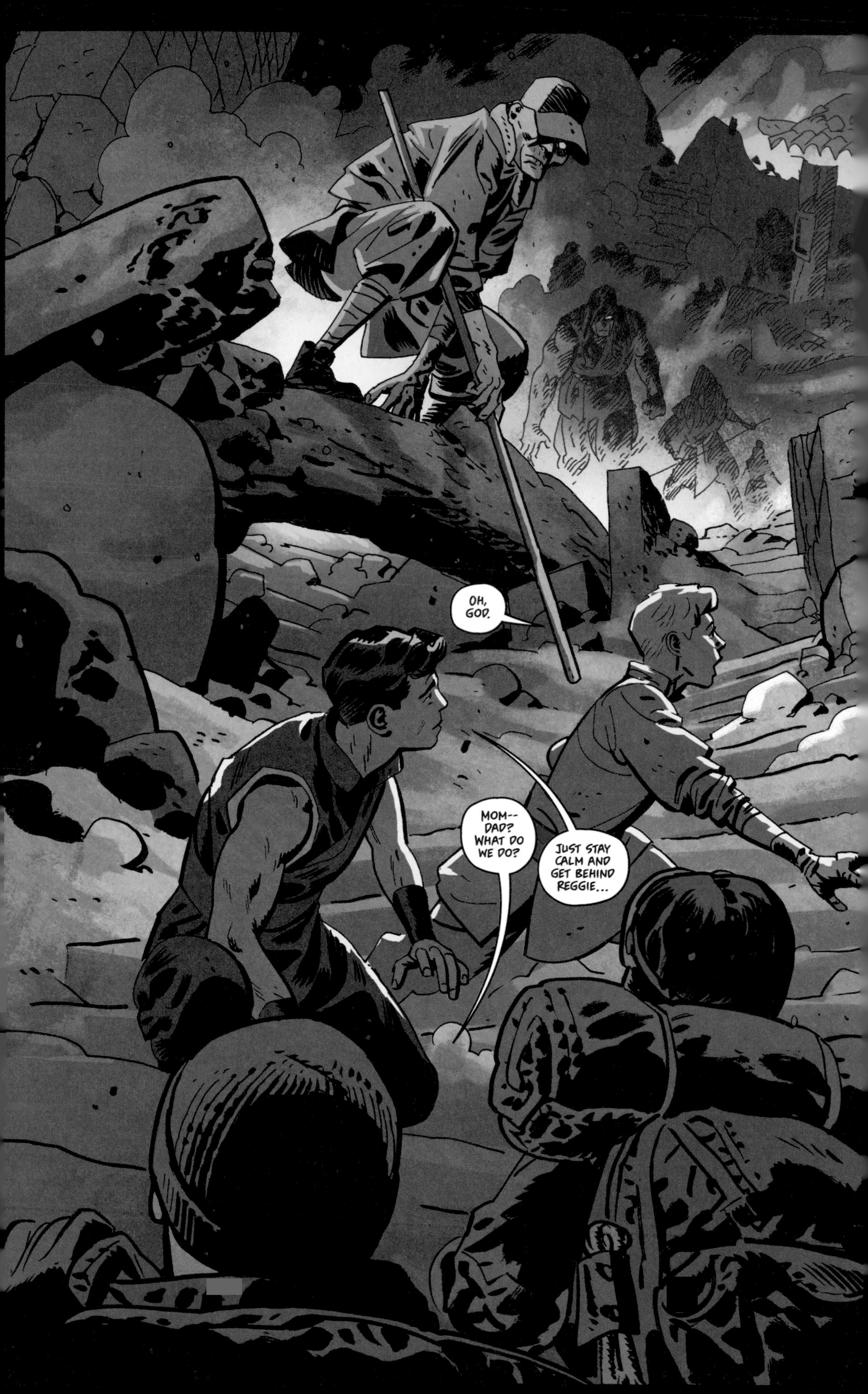
OH, GOD.
MOM--DAD? WHAT DO WE DO?
JUST STAY CALM AND GET BEHIND REGGIE...

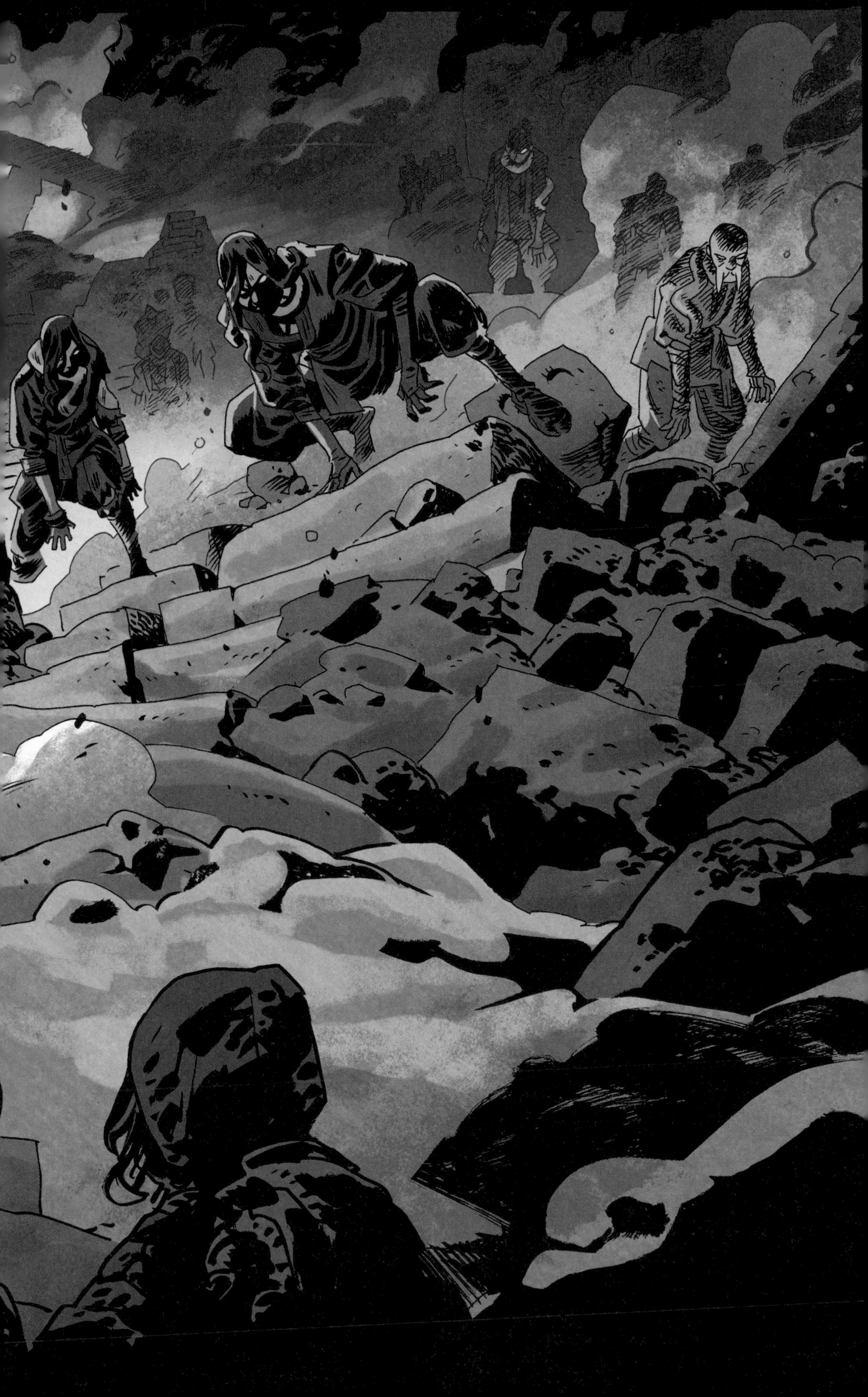

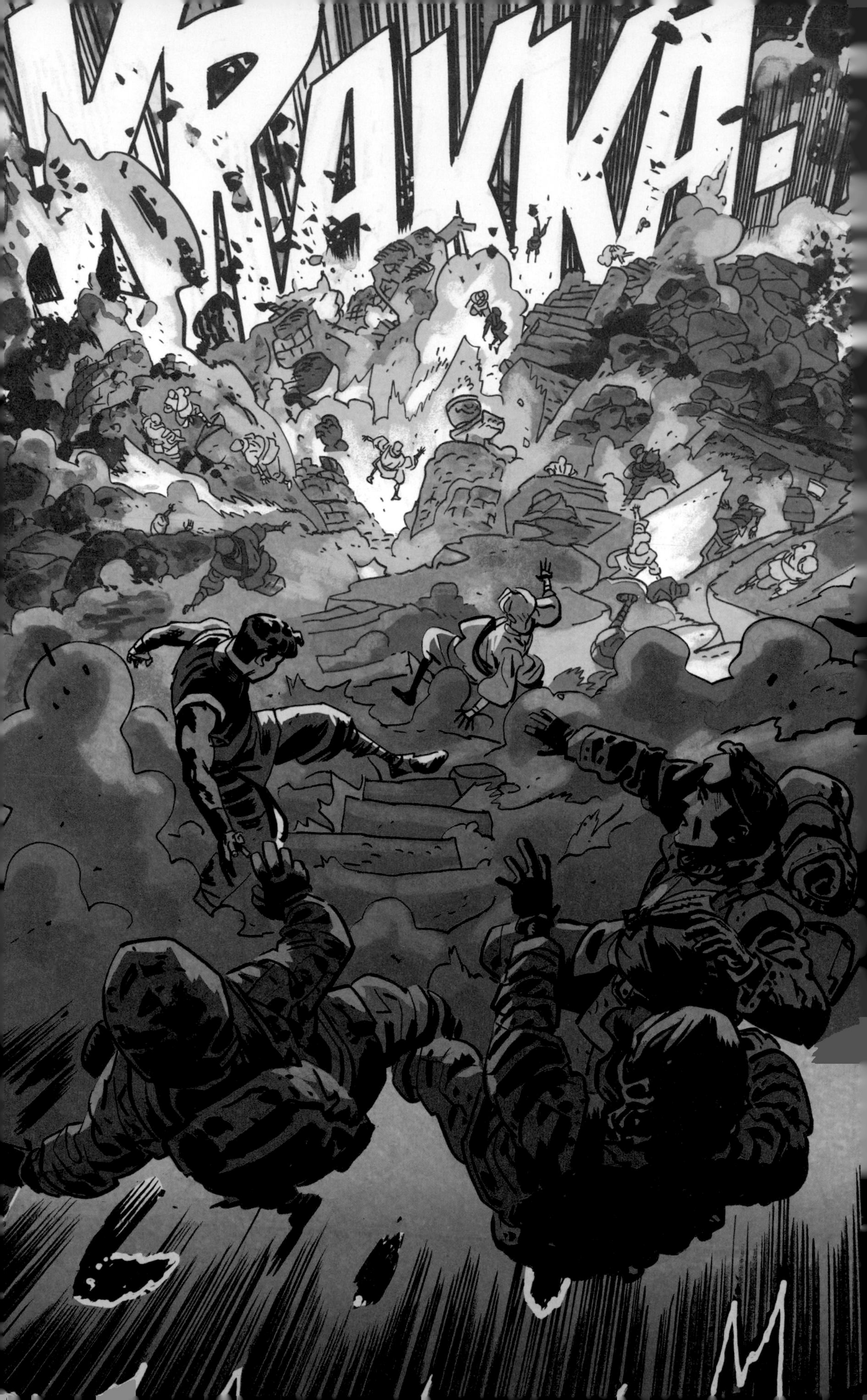
KRAKA

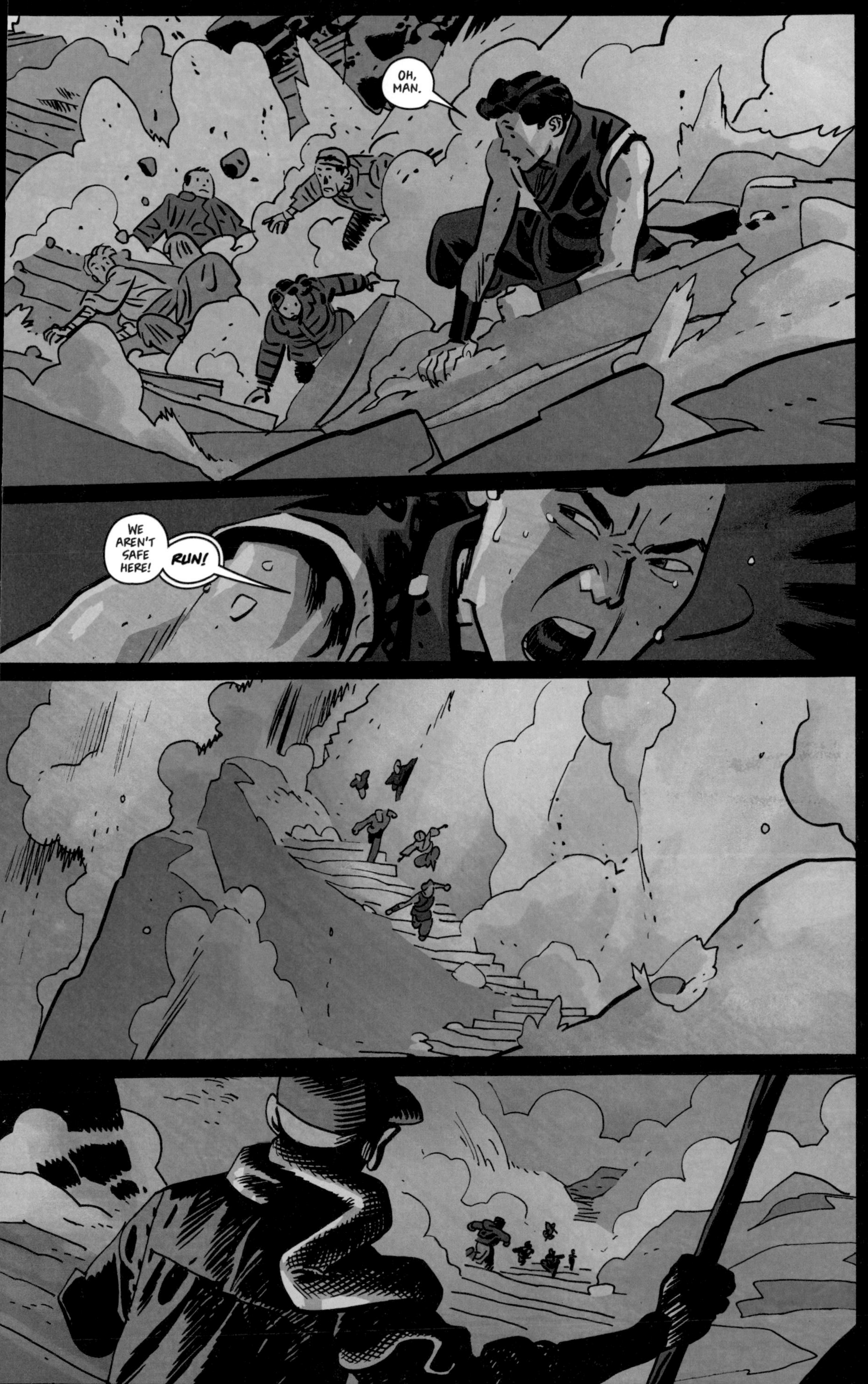
OH, MAN.
WE AREN'T SAFE HERE!
RUN!

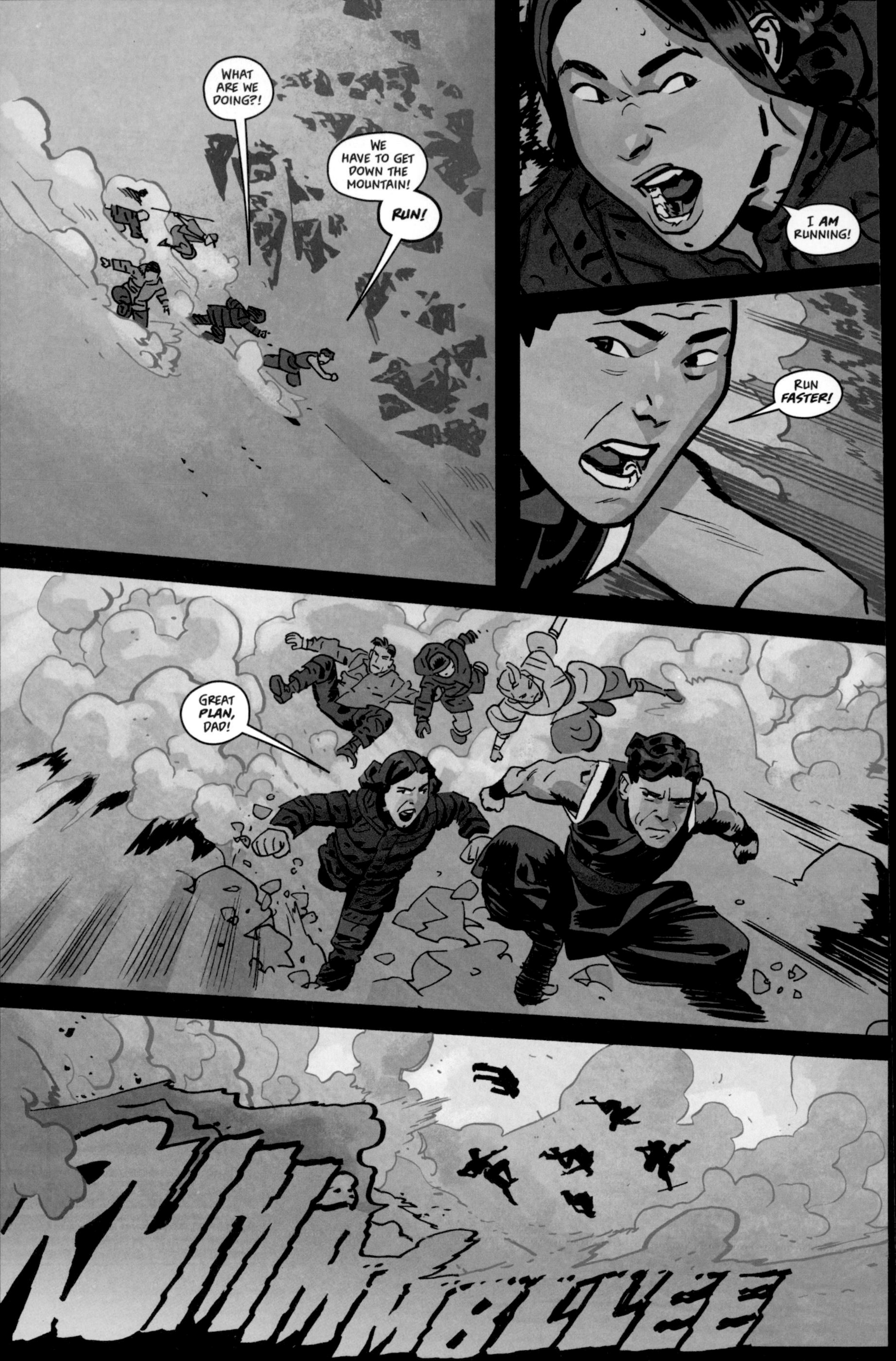
WHAT ARE WE DOING?!
WE HAVE TO GET DOWN THE MOUNTAIN!
RUN!
I AM RUNNING!
RUN FASTER!
GREAT PLAN, DAD!

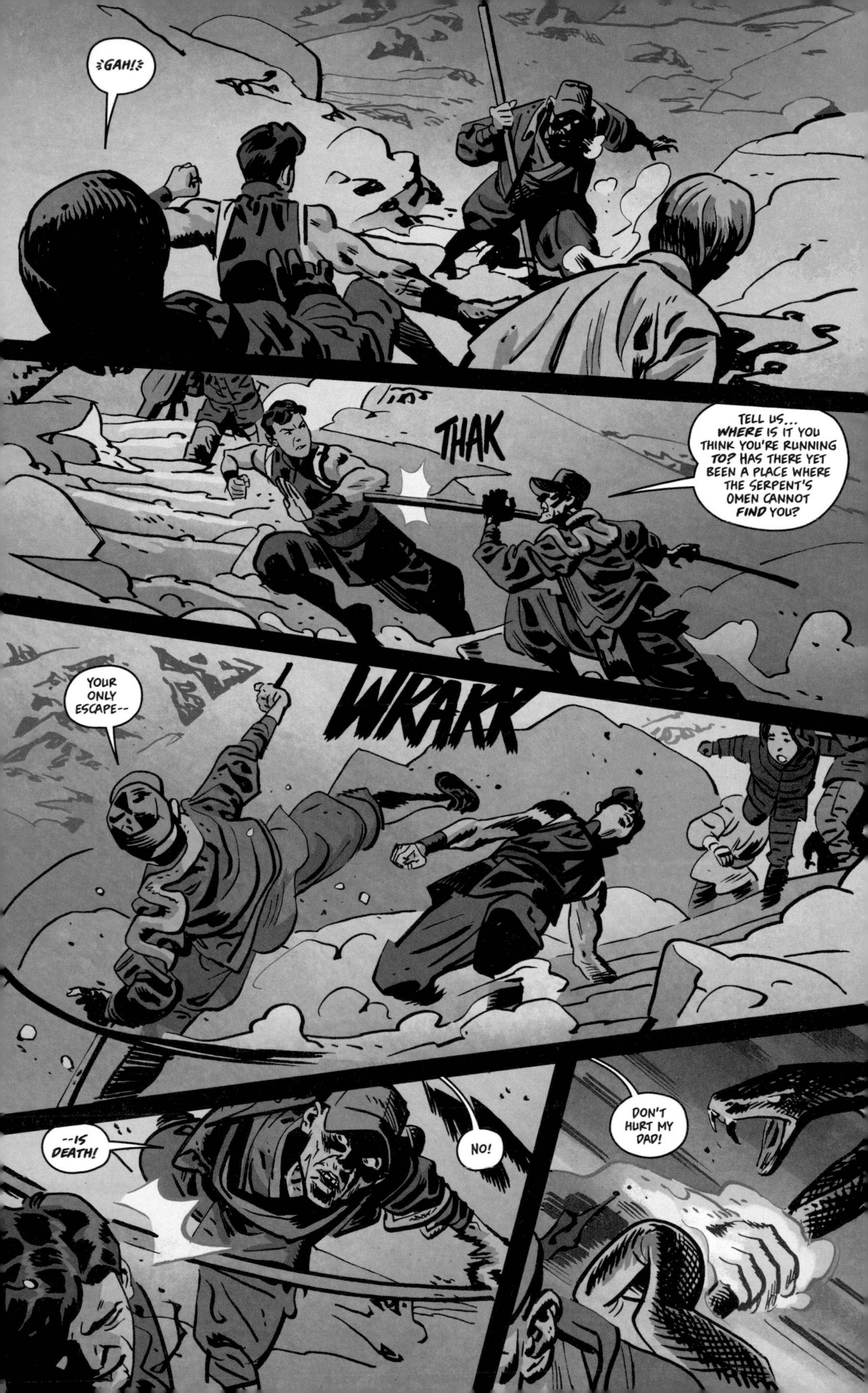
GAH!
THAK
TELL US... WHERE IS IT YOU THINK YOU'RE RUNNING TO? HAS THERE YET BEEN A PLACE WHERE THE SERPENT'S OMEN CANNOT FIND YOU?
WRAKK
YOUR ONLY ESCAPE--
--IS DEATH!
NO!
DON'T HURT MY DAD!

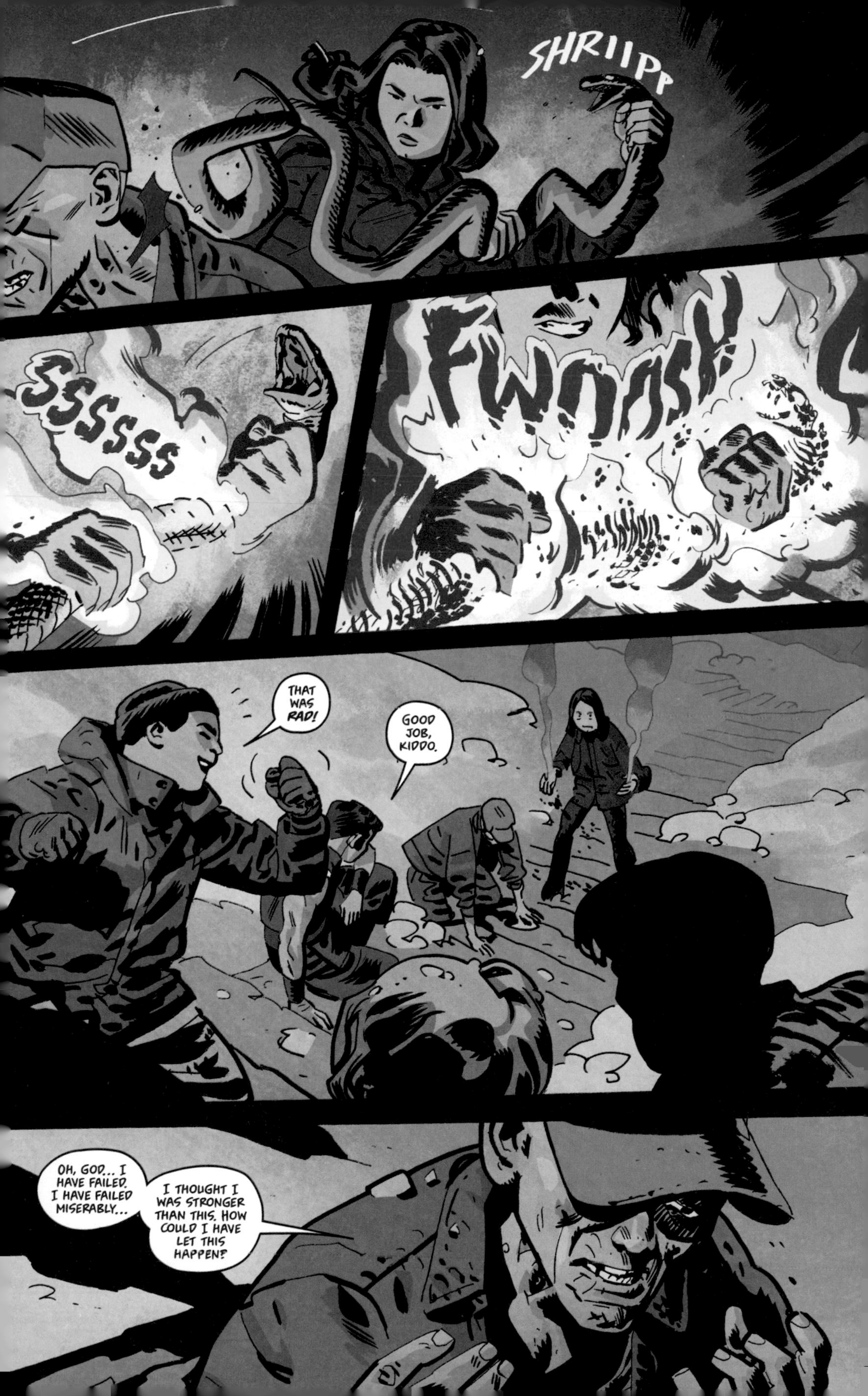
SHRIIPP
SSSSSS
FWOOSH
THAT WAS RAD!
GOOD JOB, KIDDO.
OH, GOD... I HAVE FAILED. I HAVE FAILED MISERABLY...
I THOUGHT I WAS STRONGER THAN THIS. HOW COULD I HAVE LET THIS HAPPEN?

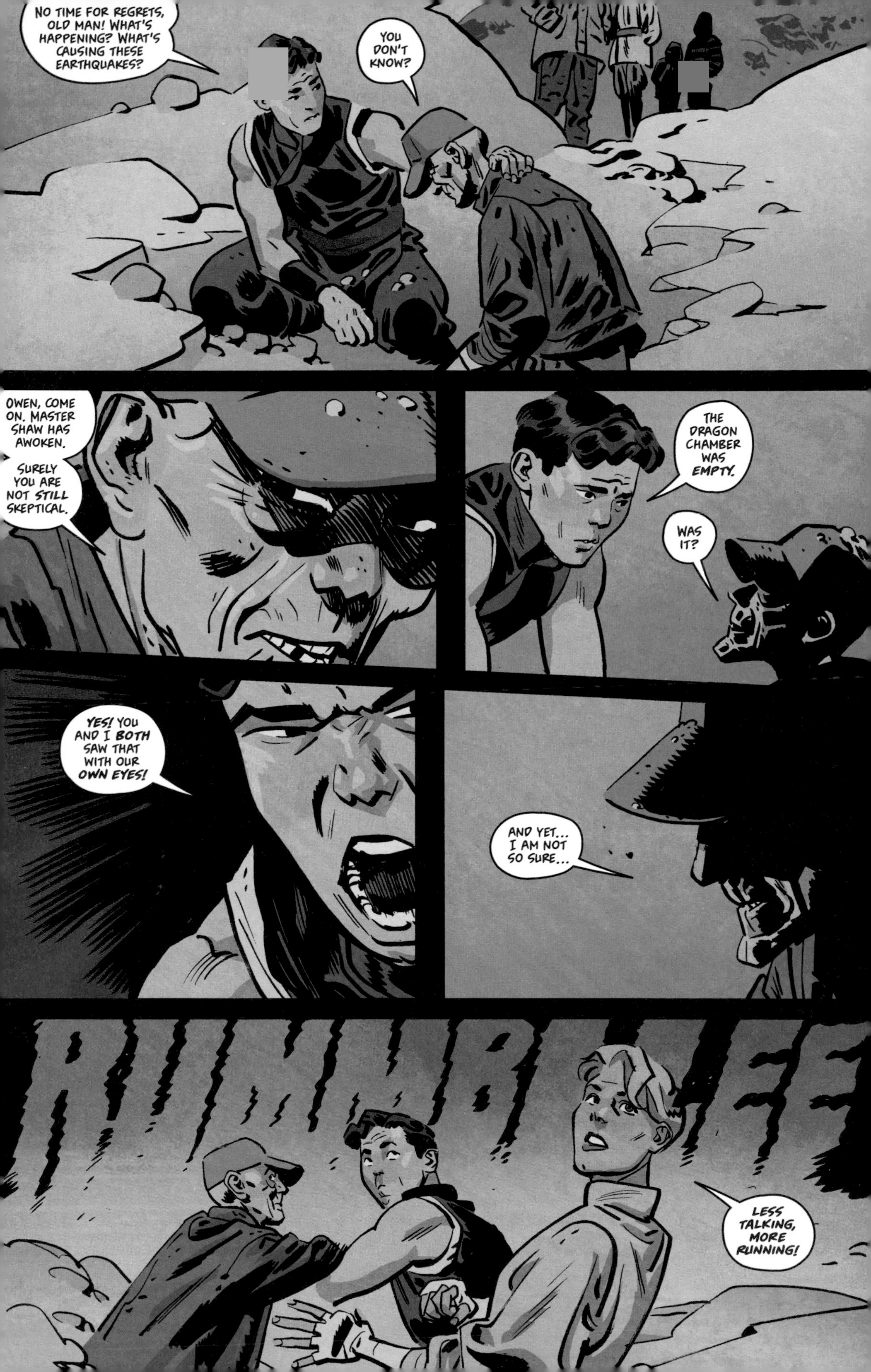
NO TIME FOR REGRETS, OLD MAN! WHAT'S HAPPENING? WHAT'S CAUSING THESE EARTHQUAKES?
YOU DON'T KNOW?
OWEN, COME ON. MASTER SHAW HAS AWOKEN.
SURELY YOU ARE NOT STILL SKEPTICAL.
THE DRAGON CHAMBER WAS EMPTY.
WAS IT?
YES! YOU AND I BOTH SAW THAT WITH OUR OWN EYES!
AND YET... I AM NOT SO SURE...
LESS TALKING, MORE RUNNING!

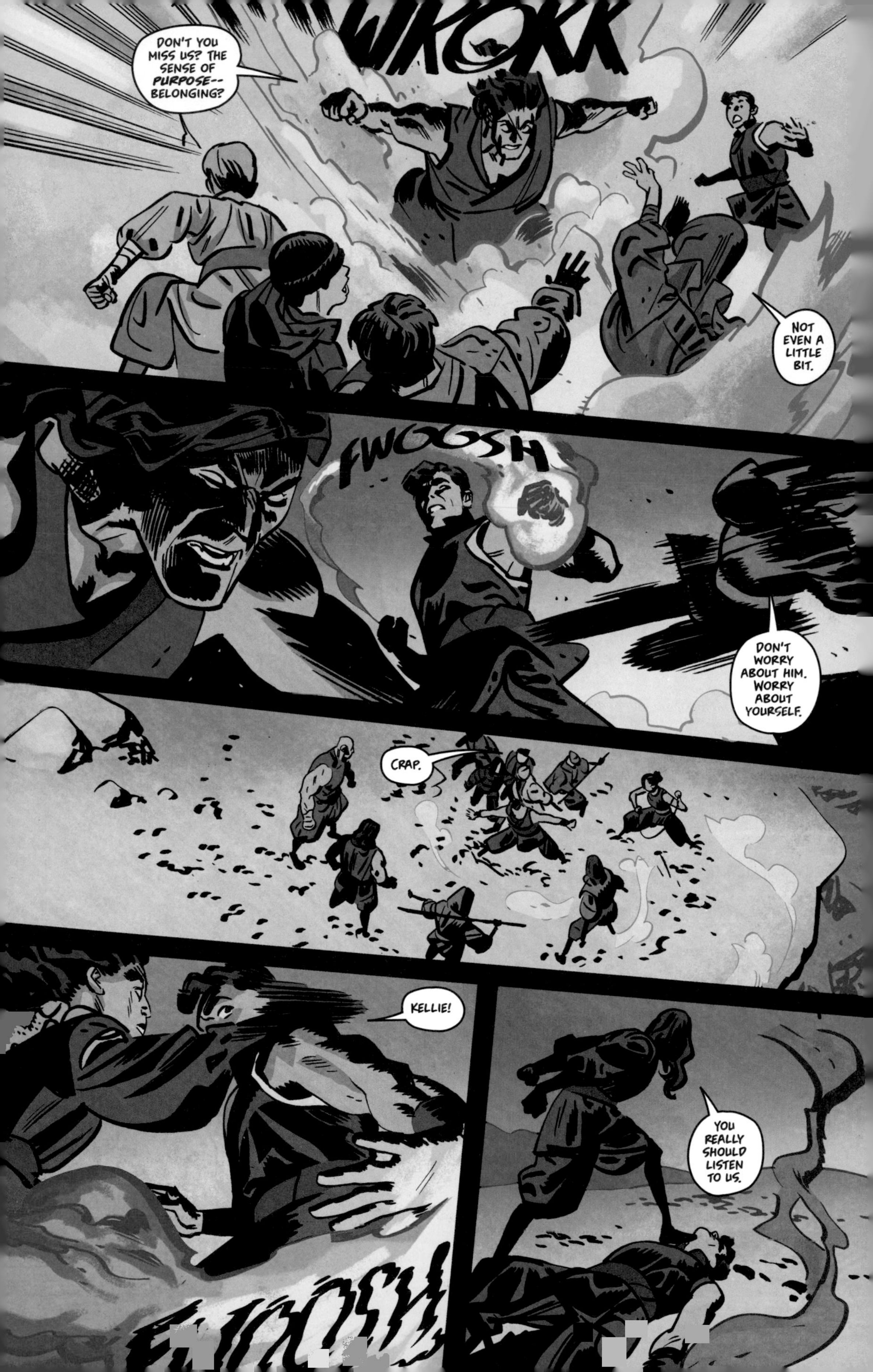
WKOKK
DON'T YOU MISS US? THE SENSE OF PURPOSE-- BELONGING?
NOT EVEN A LITTLE BIT.
FWOOSH
DON'T WORRY ABOUT HIM. WORRY ABOUT YOURSELF.
CRAP.
KELLIE!
YOU REALLY SHOULD LISTEN TO US.

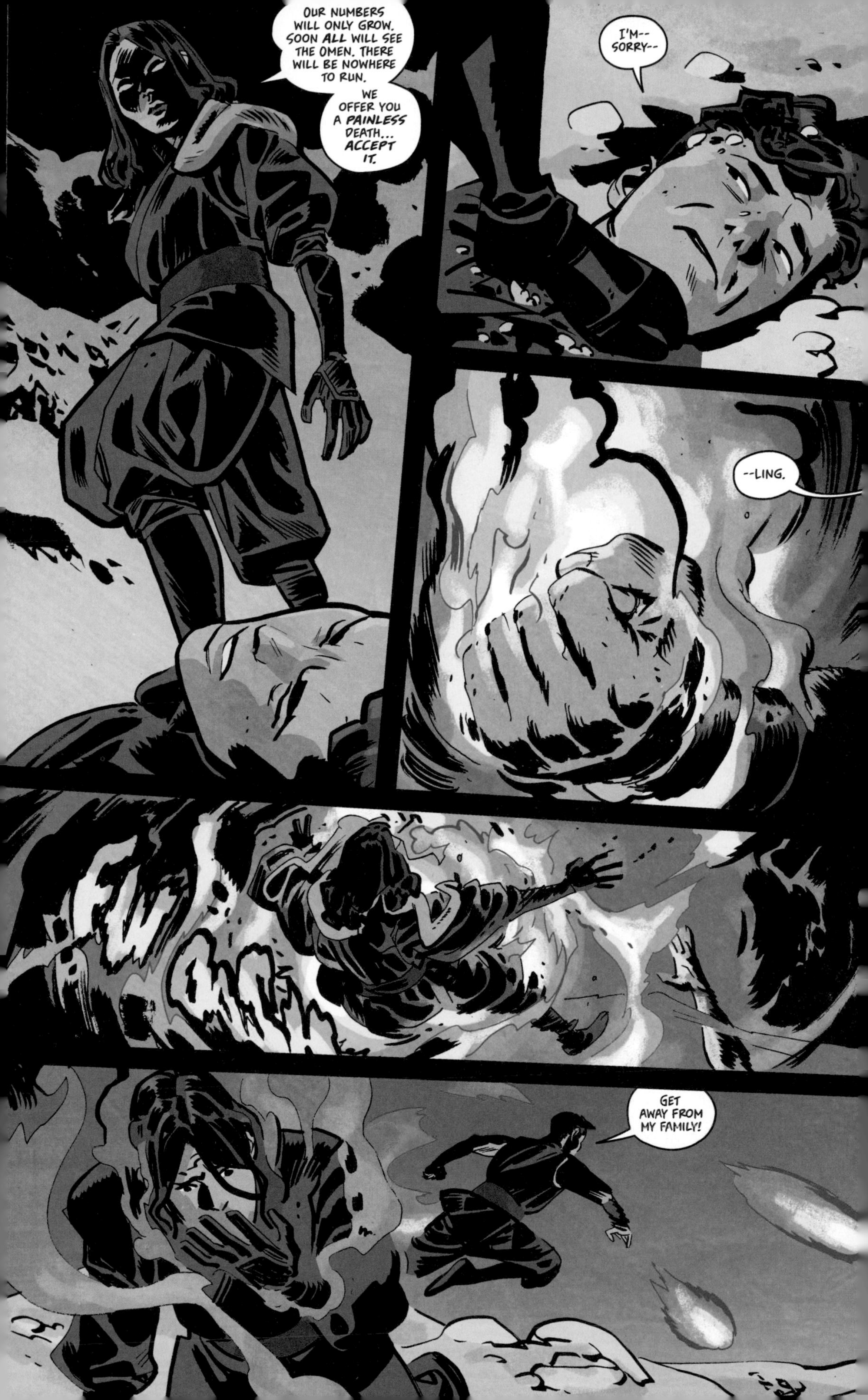
OUR NUMBERS WILL ONLY GROW. SOON ALL WILL SEE THE OMEN. THERE WILL BE NOWHERE TO RUN.
WE OFFER YOU A PAINLESS DEATH... ACCEPT IT.
I'M-- SORRY--
--LING.
GET AWAY FROM MY FAMILY!

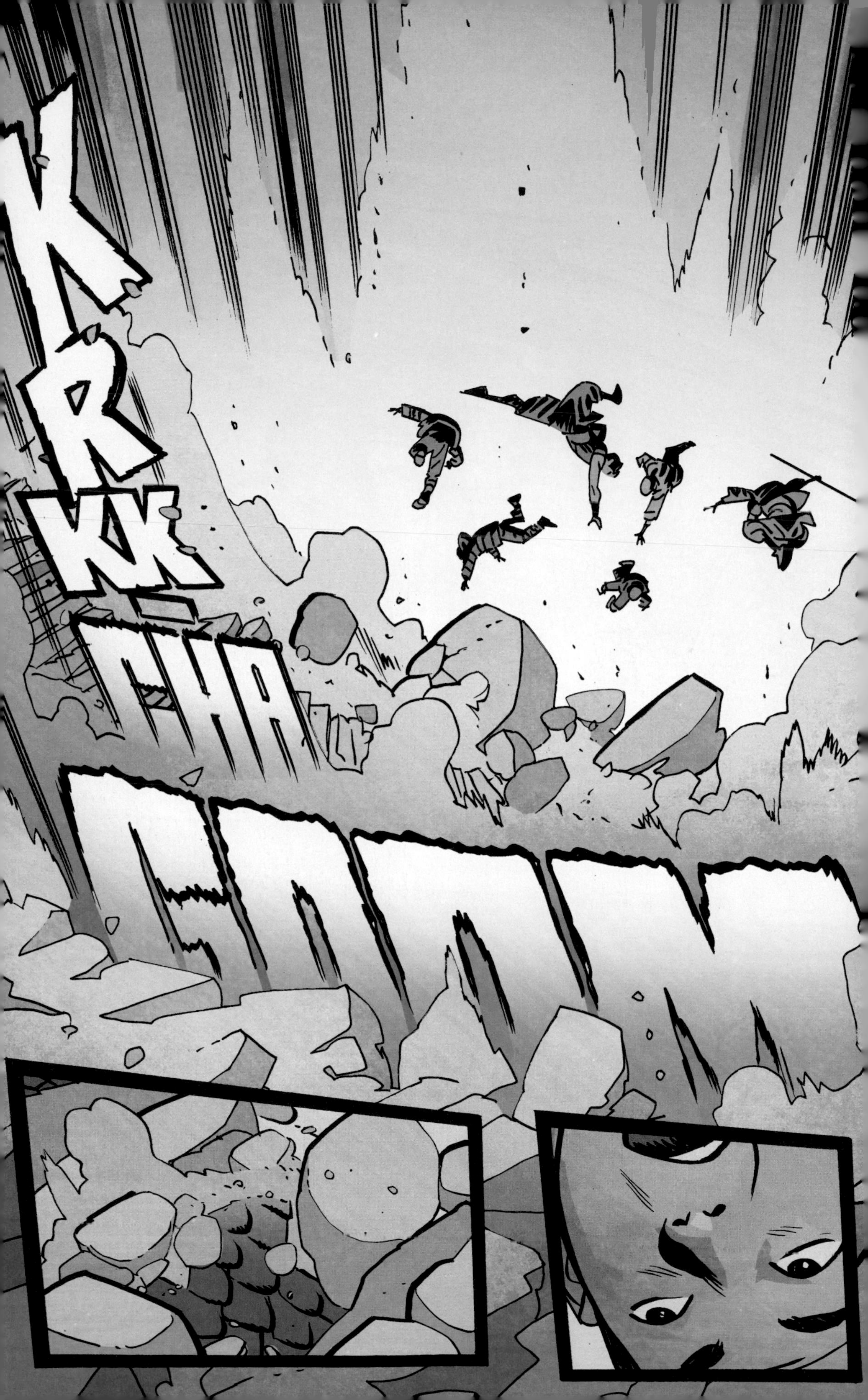
KRKK
CHA
BOOM

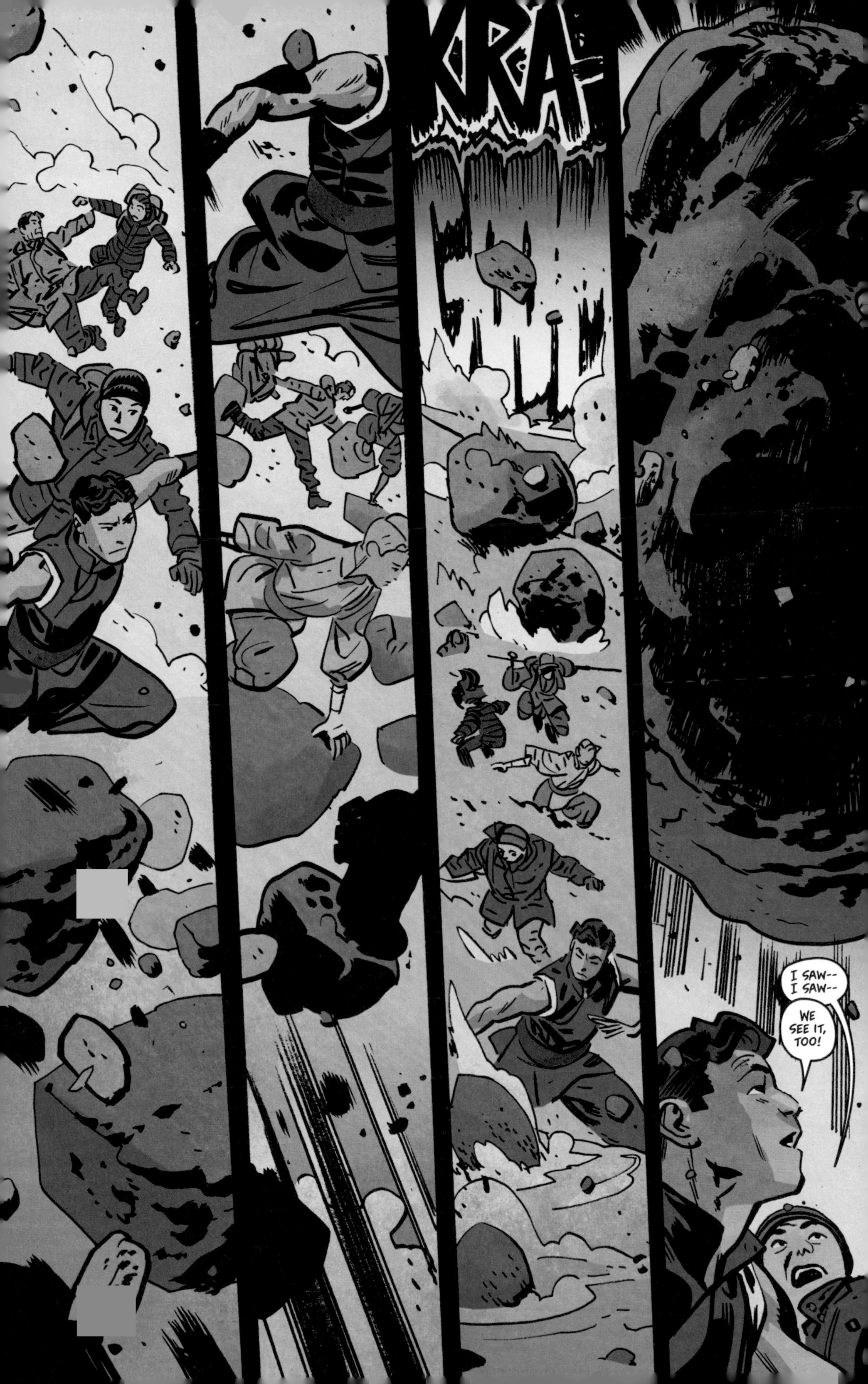
KRA
I SAW-- I SAW--
WE SEE IT, TOO!

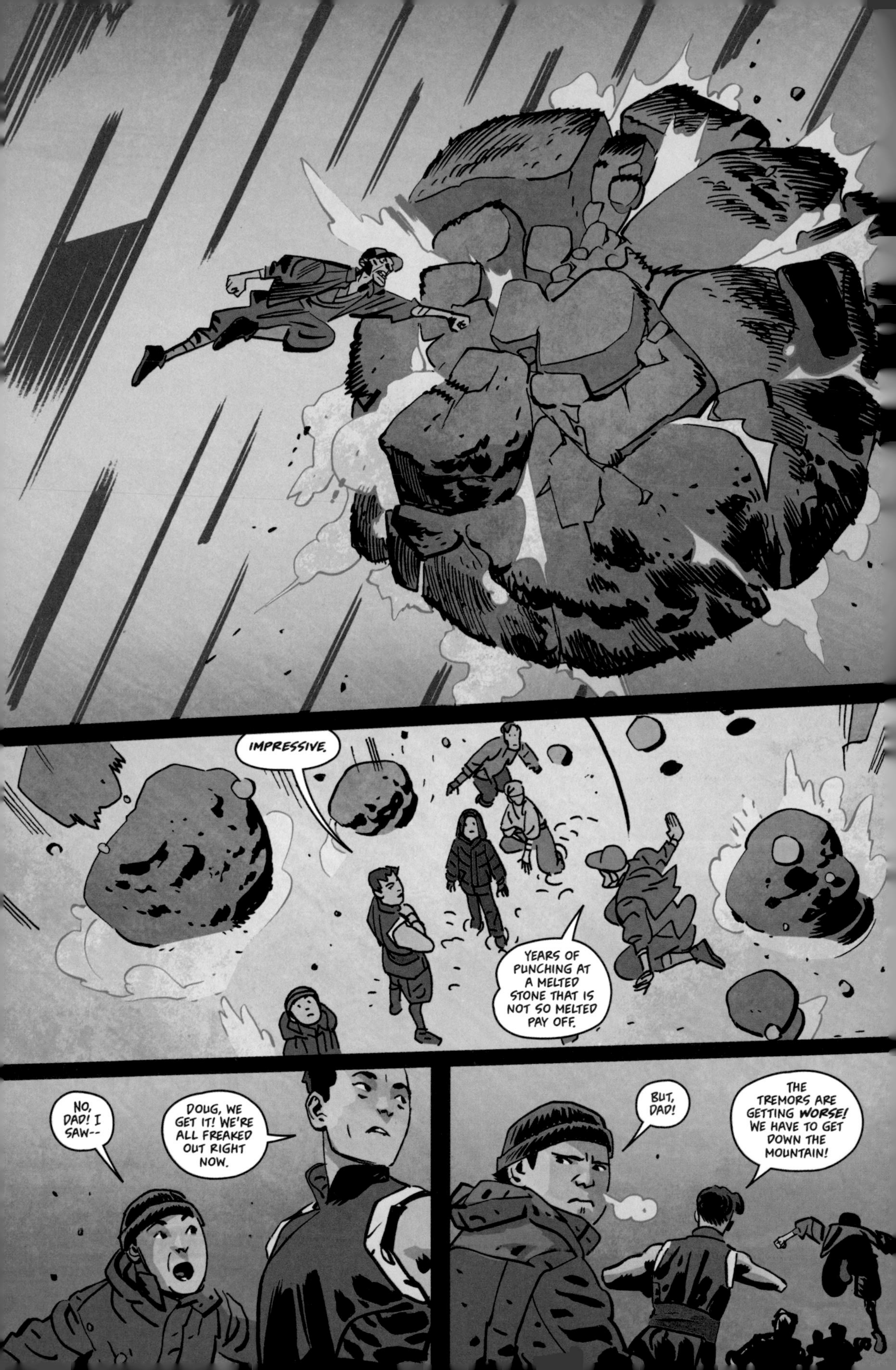
IMPRESSIVE.
YEARS OF PUNCHING AT A MELTED STONE THAT IS NOT SO MELTED PAY OFF.
NO, DAD! I SAW--
DOUG, WE GET IT! WE'RE ALL FREAKED OUT RIGHT NOW.
BUT, DAD!
THE TREMORS ARE GETTING WORSE! WE HAVE TO GET DOWN THE MOUNTAIN!

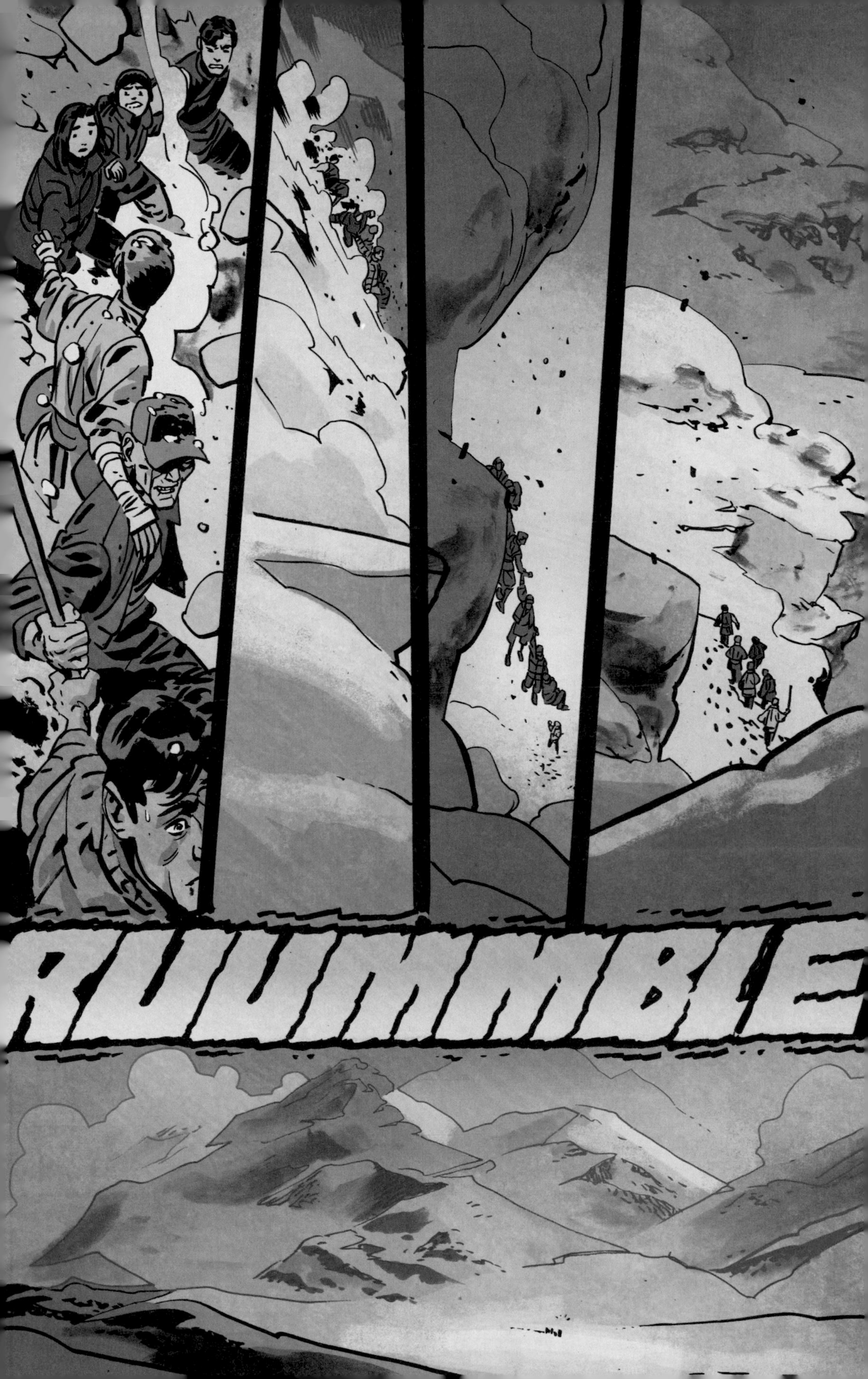
RUMMBLE

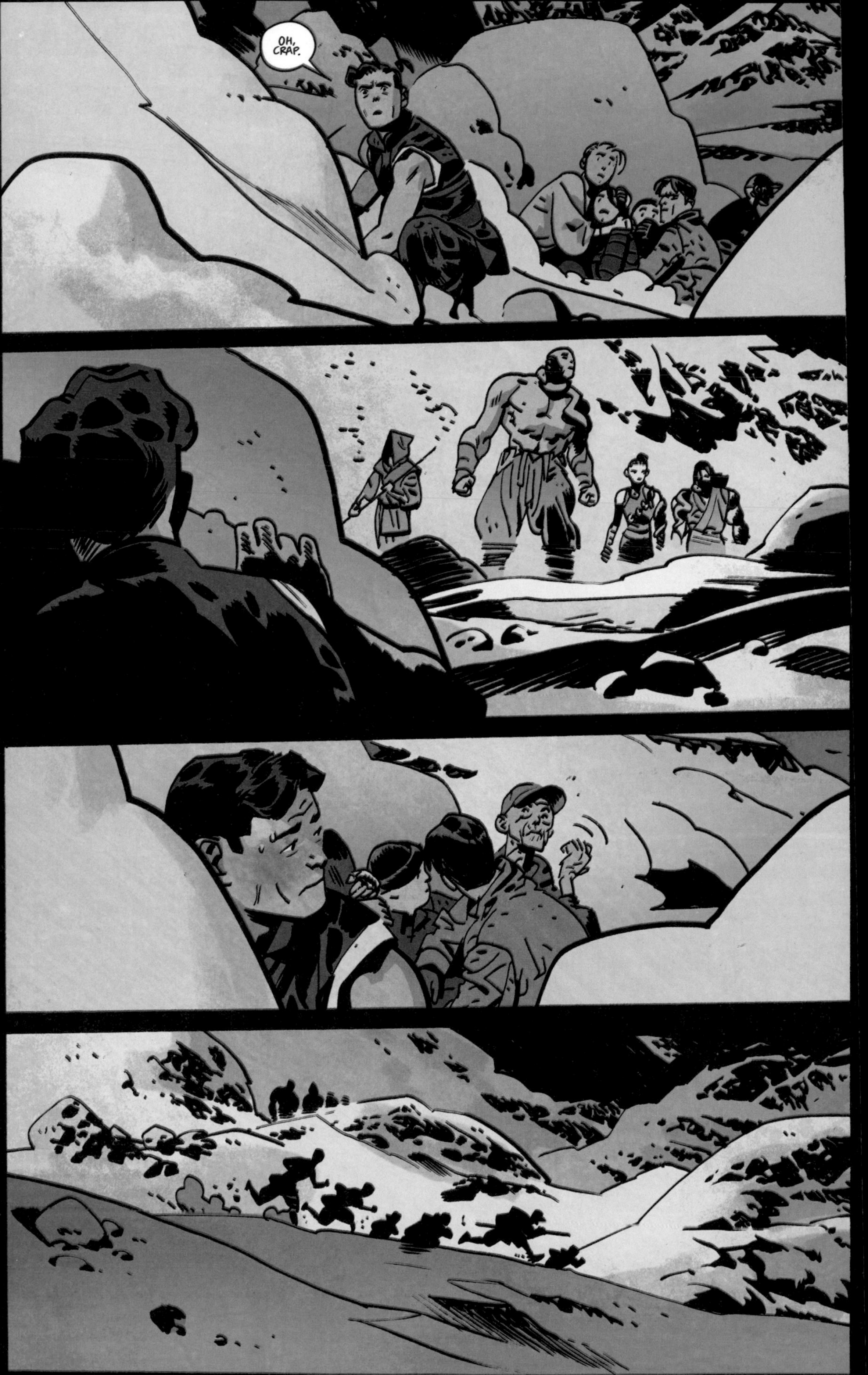
OH, CRAP.

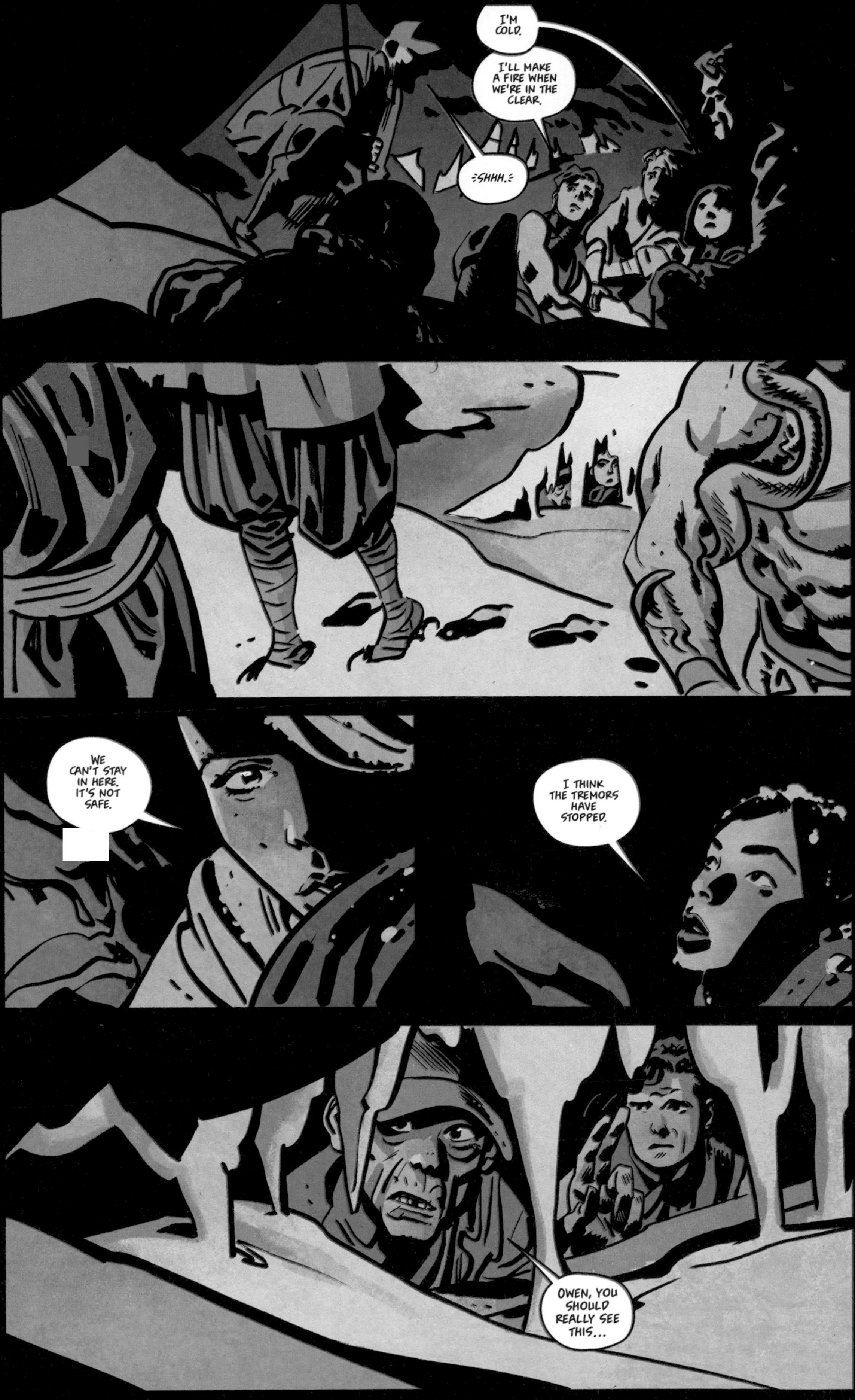
I'M COLD.
I'LL MAKE A FIRE WHEN WE'RE IN THE CLEAR.
SHHH.
WE CAN'T STAY IN HERE. IT'S NOT SAFE.
I THINK THE TREMORS HAVE STOPPED.
OWEN, YOU SHOULD REALLY SEE THIS...

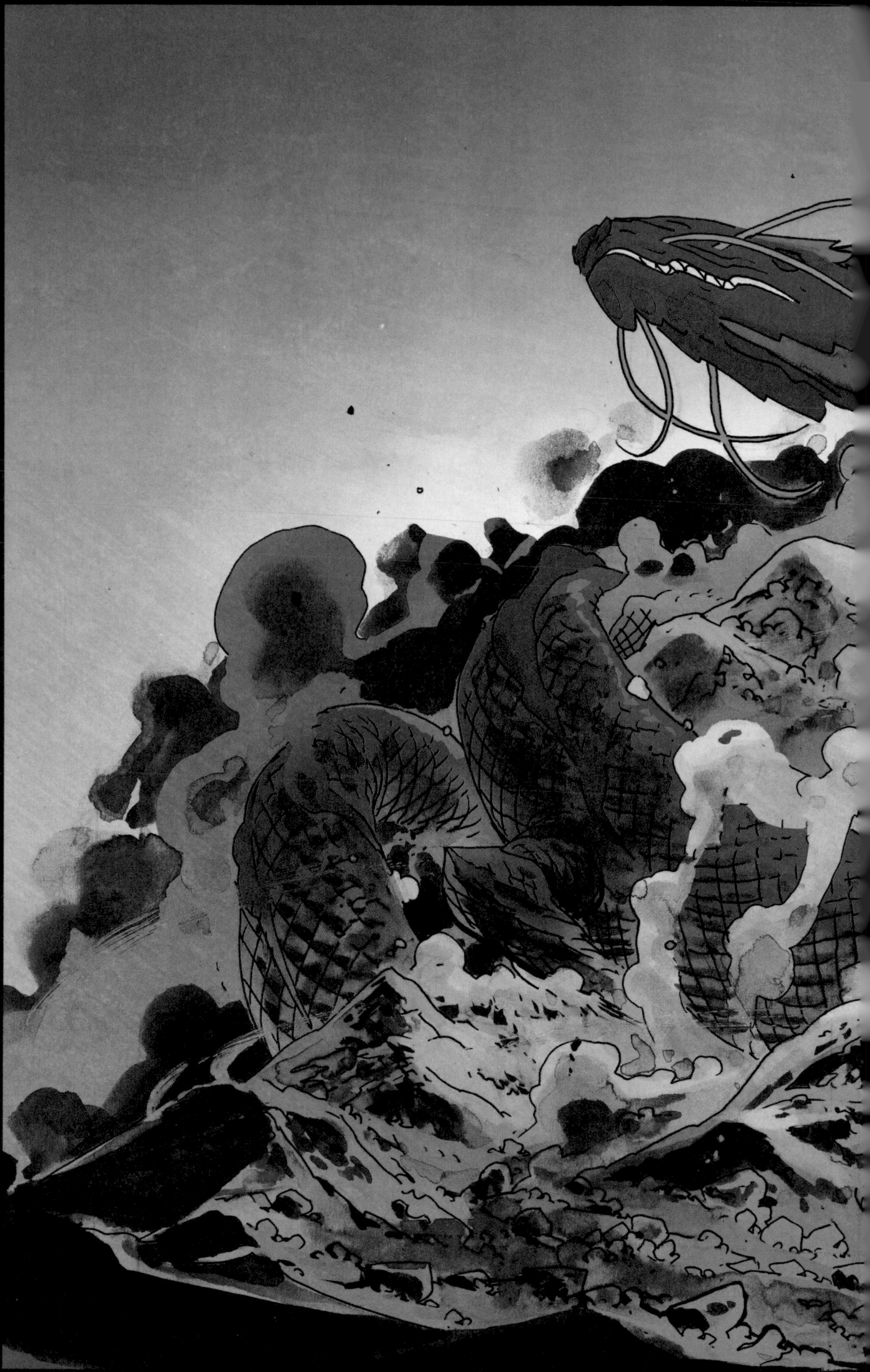

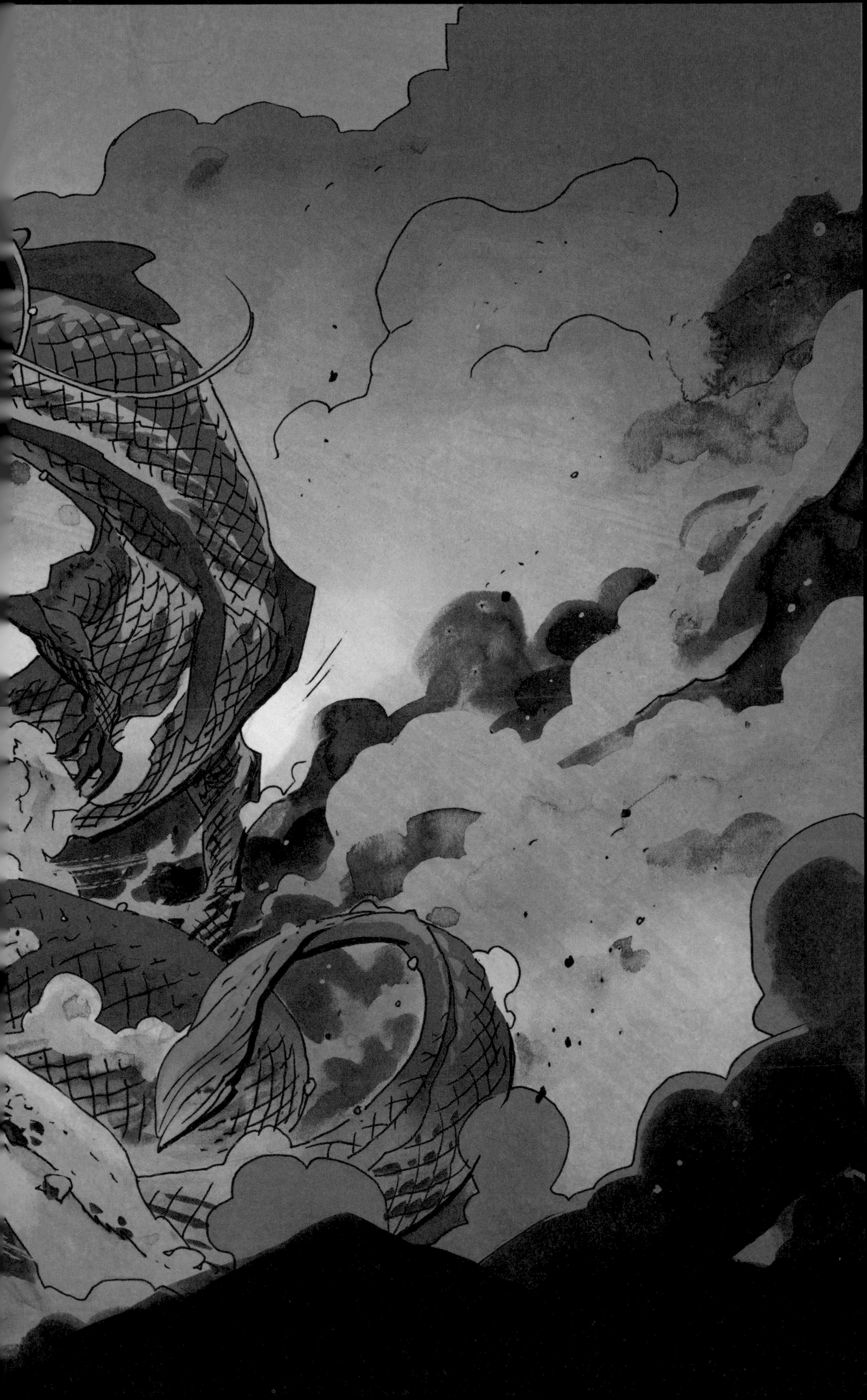

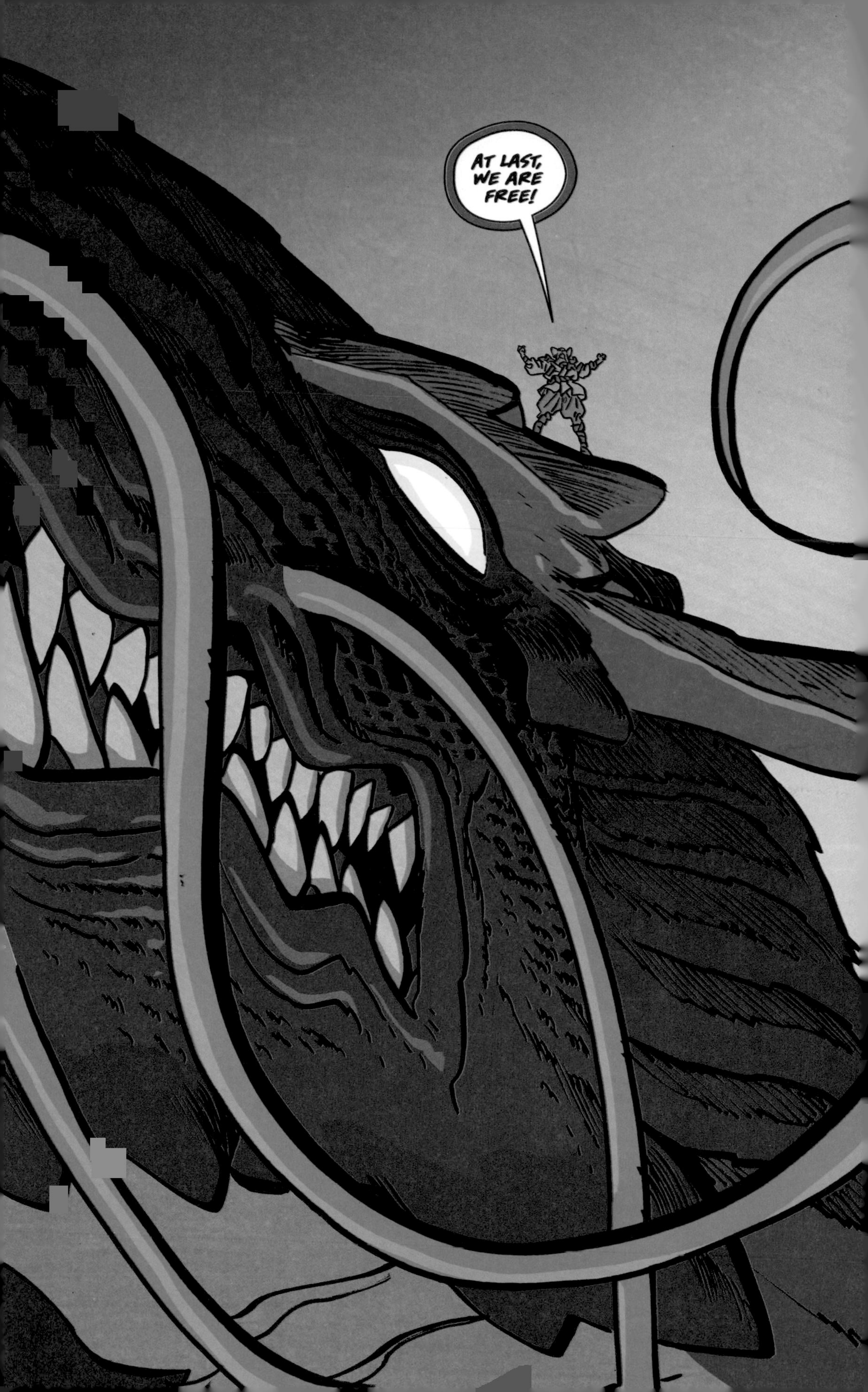
AT LAST, WE ARE FREE!

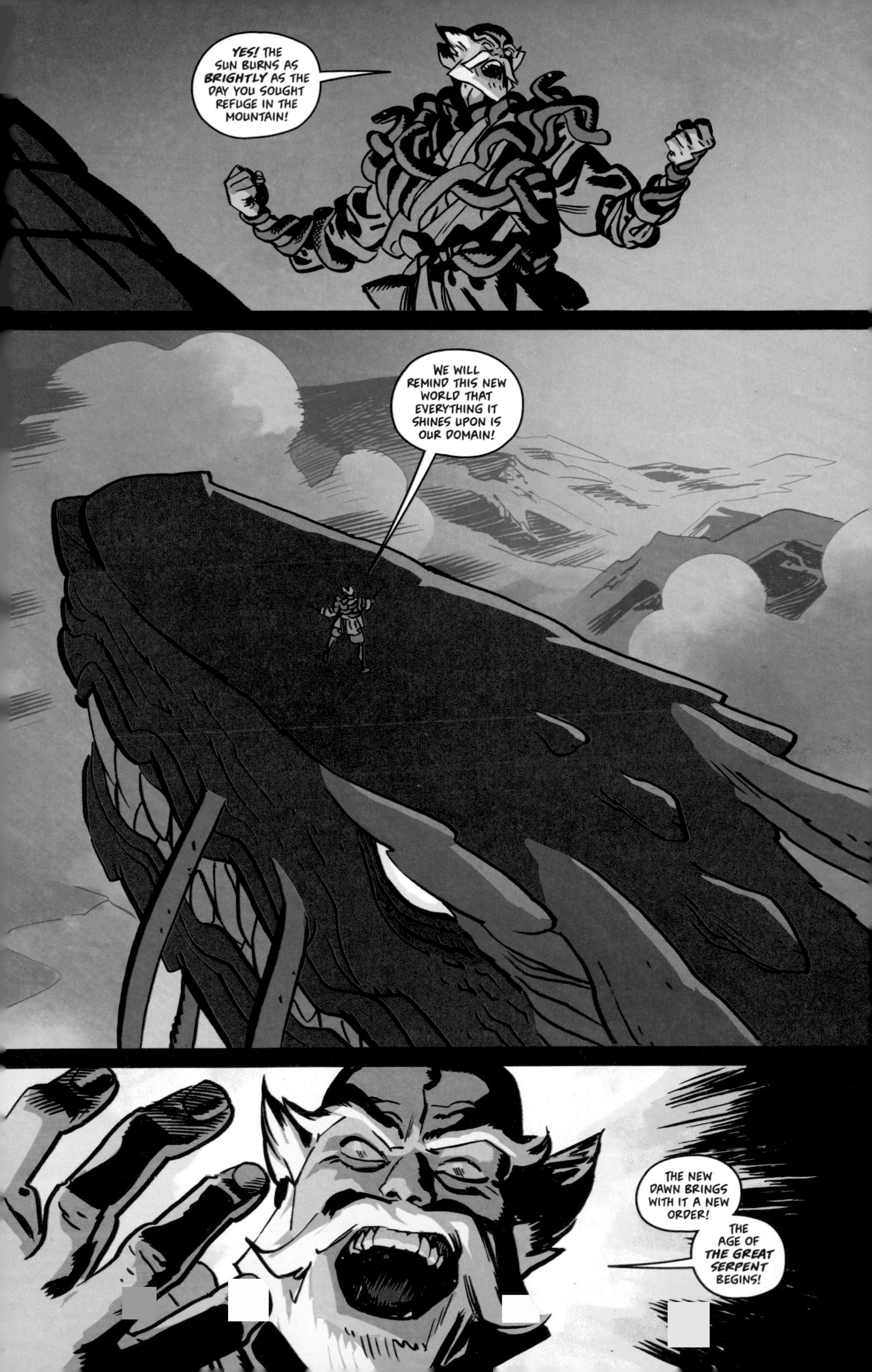
YES! THE SUN BURNS AS BRIGHTLY AS THE DAY YOU SOUGHT REFUGE IN THE MOUNTAIN!
WE WILL REMIND THIS NEW WORLD THAT EVERYTHING IT SHINES UPON IS OUR DOMAIN!
THE NEW DAWN BRINGS WITH IT A NEW ORDER!
THE AGE OF THE GREAT SERPENT BEGINS!

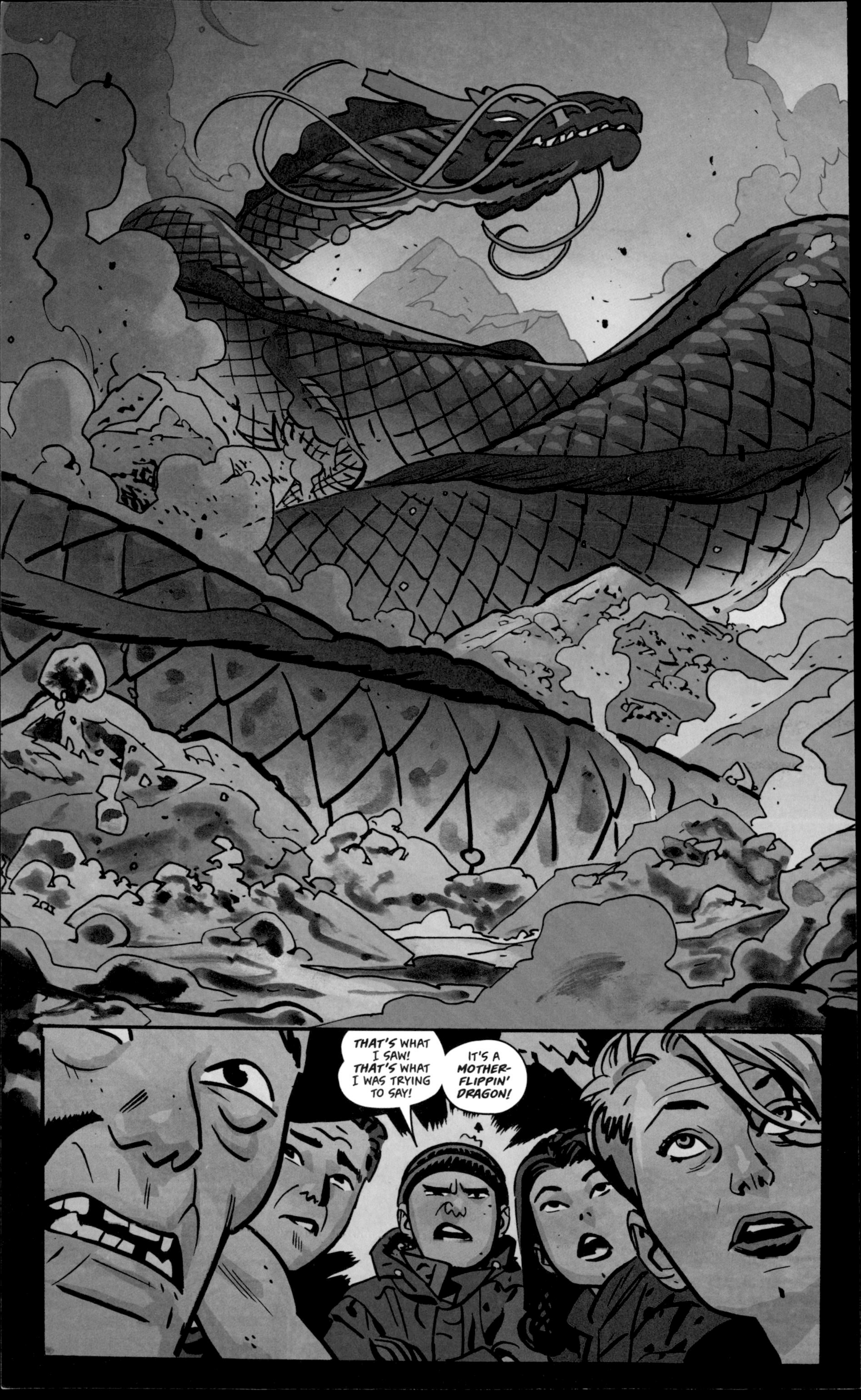
THAT'S WHAT I SAW! THAT'S WHAT I WAS TRYING TO SAY!
IT'S A MOTHER-FLIPPIN' DRAGON!

TO BE CONTINUED

FOR MORE TALES FROM **ROBERT KIRKMAN** AND *SKYBOUND*

ROBERT**KIRKMAN** CHARLIE**ADLARD** STEFANO**GAUDIANO** CLIFF**RATHBURN**

THE WALKING DEAD

VOLUME 32
REST IN PEACE

EXCELLENCE™ and ULTRAMEGA™ © 2022 Skybound, LLC. OBLIVION SONG™ © 2022 Robert Kirkman, LLC and Lorenzo de Felici. INVINCIBLE™ © 2022 Robert Kirkman, LLC., and Cory Walker. THE WALKING DEAD™ © 2022 Robert Kirkman, LLC. Image Comics® and its logos are registered trademarks of Image Comics, Inc. Skybound® and its logos are registered trademarks of Skybound, LLC. All rights reserved.